Missionary Monks

Missionary Monks

An Introduction to the History and Theology of Missionary Monasticism

Edward L. Smither

FOREWORD BY
Thomas O'Loughlin

CASCADE *Books* • Eugene, Oregon

MISSIONARY MONKS
An Introduction to the History and Theology of Missionary Monasticism

Copyright © 2016 Edward L. Smither. All rights reserved. Except for brief quotations in critical publications or reviews, no part of this book may be reproduced in any manner without prior written permission from the publisher. Write: Permissions, Wipf and Stock Publishers, 199 W. 8th Ave., Suite 3, Eugene, OR 97401.

Cascade Books
An Imprint of Wipf and Stock Publishers
199 W. 8th Ave., Suite 3
Eugene, OR 97401

www.wipfandstock.com

PAPERBACK ISBN: 978-1-4982-2416-1
HARDCOVER ISBN: 978-1-4982-2418-5
EBOOK ISBN: 978-1-4982-2417-8

Cataloguing-in-Publication data:

Names: Smither, Edward L. | O'Loughlin, Thomas (foreword)

Title: Missionary monks : an introduction to the history and theology of missionary monasticism / Edward L. Smither, with a foreword by Thomas O. Loughlin.

Description: Eugene, OR: Cascade Books, 2016 | Includes bibliographical references and index.

Identifiers: ISBN 978-1-4982-2416-1 (paperback) | ISBN 978-1-4982-2418-5 (hardcover) | ISBN 978-1-4982-2417-8 (ebook)

Subjects: LCSH: Monasticism and religious orders—History | Monastic and religious life—History | Missions—History | Religious Missions—history

Classification: BV2100 S665 2016 2016 (print) | BV2100 (ebook)

Manufactured in the U.S.A.   11/11/16

Contents

Foreword by Thomas O'Loughlin | vii
Acknowledgements | ix

	Introduction	1
Chapter 1	Early Christian Mission	4
Chapter 2	Rise of Monasticism	14
Chapter 3	Basil of Caesarea	27
Chapter 4	Martin of Tours	42
Chapter 5	Patrick of Ireland	51
Chapter 6	Celtic Monks	64
Chapter 7	Gregory the Great and Augustine of Canterbury	82
Chapter 8	Willibrord and Boniface	93
Chapter 9	Anskar	107
Chapter 10	Cyril and Methodius	119
Chapter 11	Church of the East	138
Chapter 12	The Mendicants	148
Chapter 13	The Jesuits	166
Epilogue	Toward a Monastic Theology of Mission	180

Bibliography | 183
Index | 191

Foreword

CHRISTIANS ARE ALWAYS REMEMBERING, and Christians are always forgetting! That we are always remembering is obvious: all Christians read the anthology of texts we call the Bible and remember events that happened (the most recent of them) nearly two thousand years ago. And in those texts—such as one of the most recent of them: Acts—they read about things that happened even earlier: they are remembering Christians remembering the time before the Christ (Acts 2:14–36). They have made this remembering part of their worship: there is no group of Christians who do not have some readings from the Scriptures at their assemblies. Some Christians take a real pride in their remembering and set great store by "tradition": and proudly boast that what they are doing now is what was done in the past. Indeed, the way they justify what they are doing now—no matter how crazy it might appear to outsiders—is that "this is the way we have always done it!" Remembering becomes fused with identity, and authorization and fidelity and continuity. Remembering gives them a sense of security and comfort: it assures them they are on the right track and they just have to keep recalling what they did long ago—in an almost mythical time—and repeat it, and all will be well. This is such a well-known phenomenon in religious thinking that Mircea Eliade borrowed a phrase from the Christian liturgy to describe it: it is remembering what happened *in illo tempore*—a time when wonders happened, faith was not complex, and the structures of belief seem almost as visible as trees, stones, and hills. But remembering can also be the great straightjacket: it becomes the means to quash new ideas, to prevent adaptation to new circumstances, and the make creativity seem like a betrayal of the past. Remembering is a very complex activity for Christians—and it cannot be compared with just playing a recording or searching the "memory" of a computer—it is a basic way by which we discover and declare who we are.

But we also forget—and we do not just forget details, but even what was once very important. Christians forgot that they had a new vision of peace and fraternity where each was a brother and sister and, unlike their memory of Cain, they would be concerned with each other's welfare. But it was easy to forget that that meant that slavery had no place—and in less than a generation after Jesus told them that God was their Father and they were all brothers, they had forgotten this and slavery was acceptable "within limits." They were to wash each other's feet and live as servants of one another—but that just got too much for them: so they ritualized it, limited it, and spiritualized it. Forgetting is the best way to avoid that which is awkward; and the great thing about forgetting is that once you have forgotten you do not even realize that you have forgotten. Forgetting wipes away its own track—so that is does not lurk in the back of your mind to annoy you. Forgetting is such a dangerous way of deviating from the call to discipleship announced by Jesus, that some of the early Christians saw the role of the Holy Spirit as that which would help you to remember what you had forgotten: "But the Counselor, the Holy Spirit, whom the Father will send in my name, he will teach you all things, and bring to your remembrance all that I have said to you" (John 14:26).

This task of remembering and recalling what is forgotten is the task of historical theology—and this book is a splendid example of it in practice. It looks at the lives and writings of a series of monks, who lived in worlds very different to ours, but responded to the same call to mission that we hear today. Knowing what mission meant to them helps us to clarify what is means to us, what it should mean to us, and also to evaluate our priorities: are we too much this way . . . or too much that way . . . or are there aspects that we have lost sight of completely? We do not engage in the formal practice of remembering and recalling what we have forgotten to create an ideal for imitation—that would be silly and confining. Rather, we do it because in asking our questions of people in a different time and culture to our own we hold up a mirror in which we see ourselves afresh. Ed Smither's book is a very good mirror.

Thomas O'Loughlin,

Professor of Historical Theology, University of Nottingham

Acknowledgments

I am grateful for the support and encouragement of a number of people who helped make this project possible. Specifically, I would like to thank:

- Tom O'Loughlin who first got me interested in monasticism while mentoring me through doctoral studies over a decade ago.
- Colleagues in the Patristics Study Group of the Evangelical Theological Society, who have allowed me space to think out loud about monasticism, mission, and ressourcement.
- Colleagues in the Evangelical Missiological Society, who have invited me to probe monasticism in mission history papers over the past few years.
- Students in mission and church history over the last ten years who have been my conversation partners as I've labored to highlight the work of missionary monks in the narrative of mission.
- David Cashin, Victor Cuartas, Ruth Buchanan, Dayton Hartman, and Jerry Ireland, who gave helpful feedback on this manuscript.
- My leadership at Columbia International University who value research and professional growth and have allowed space and time to pursue this project.
- Robin Parry and the editorial team at Cascade Books for believing in this project and laboring to help it see the light of day as a publication.

Most importantly, I'm grateful for the love and support of my family: my wife Shawn and my children Brennan, Emma, and Eve.

Introduction

A FEW YEARS AGO, I had the privilege to travel to Iona, a tiny island located in the Inner Hebrides of western Scotland. For Christian history, it is important for being the place where sixth-century Celtic monks led by the Irish abbot Columba (521–597) established a monastery, which served as a missionary base for evangelizing the Pictish people of the Scottish highlands. While preparing to go and study the mission history of the region, I asked my former doctoral supervisor about the best study resources on the island—things like libraries, study centers, and museums. Informing me that nothing quite that formal existed at Iona, he suggested that the most valuable study experience was to visit the island in December or January, stand outside and feel the cold North Atlantic air and wind, and imagine the sacrifice and service of the monks who went about their ministry in this environment. In many ways, that is what this book is about. We too want to stand in that cold place and walk in the shoes of Celtic and other missionary monks who sacrificed greatly to make the gospel known to the ends of the earth in their day. We want to grasp what it meant to pursue both a monastic and a missionary calling.

Why is a book on missionary monks relevant for Christians today, especially for students of mission history and mission practitioners? As we journey through the pages of mission history—especially from about AD 500 to 1500—it's impossible to do so without stumbling over quite a few missionary monks. In fact, I would argue that if we don't have monks in this period, then we really have little to talk about in the way of Christian mission. So grasping the story of mission requires getting to know missionary monks. Given this historical reality, it is important that we demystify and clarify the work of those with a missionary and monastic calling. This is especially important for evangelical Protestant students (my tribe), who often approach monastic studies with suspicion and some ignorance. Having taught courses on mission history for nearly a decade, I've seen that this part of mission history often troubles evangelical students and therefore requires some clarification.

On the other hand, there is renewed interest in monasticism, particularly among twenty- and thirty-year-old evangelicals in America. Jonathan Wilson-Hargrove's book *The New Monasticism* captures this movement of individuals and families living in deliberate community and doing something new by reflecting on something old—monasticism. Similarly, Shane Claiborne's Simple Way community has applied some monastic principles to urban mission and identifying with the poor and homeless in a ministry that is highly centered upon justice. Finally, books like Dennis Okholm's *Monk Habits for Everyday People* appeal to Protestant Christians with a desire to make use of the rule and values of the monastic innovator Benedict of Nursia (ca. 480–ca. 547) in a modern context.

Recent works in mission practice have also valued reflecting on the legacy of monastic spirituality in the work of mission. In Bill Taylor's *Global Missiology for the 21st Century*—an edited volume that emerged from the 1999 Iguassu (Brazil) Dialogue—three brief chapters are devoted to the Celtic, Church of the East, and Jesuit missionary monastic movements as these writers look for guidance from the past as the church looks forward in mission.[1] Similarly, in his recent work *Understanding Christian Mission*, Scott Sunquist reserved an entire chapter for a discussion on spirituality and mission.[2] Though Sunquist only briefly mentions monastic movements, these historic movements certainly have something to teach us today about the relationship of spirituality and Christian mission.

Even considering the relevance and interest in monasticism and mission, why should this book be written? First, there is still relatively little written on early Christian mission. While works like Eckhard Schnabel's *Early Christian Mission*, Michael Green's *Evangelism in the Early Church*, and my own *Mission in the Early Church* have endeavored to fill the gaps of our understanding of mission in this period, there is still much to unpack and addressing the monastic contribution to mission will help us toward

---

1. Taylor, *Global Missiology for the 21st Century*, 489–502, 507–11.
2. See chapter 13 ("Spirituality and Mission") in Sunquist, *Understanding Christian Mission*.

INTRODUCTION

that end. Second, while there are helpful books available that generally introduce Christian monasticism in the early and medieval church—such as Harmless' *Desert Christians*, Dunn's *The Emergence of Monasticism*, and Peters' *The Story of Monasticism*—these works do not really discuss the missionary element of monasticism. Finally, while individual books exist that explore monastic missionary orders or certain missionaries, there is no book that offers a general overview of the history of monastic missions in a single volume.

My intent in this work is to guide the reader through an introduction to the history of missionary monks and movements beginning in the fourth century and spanning to the middle of the seventeenth century. I want to tell the story of missionary monks—to meet them, learn about their contexts of service, consider their approaches to mission, discuss their challenges and victories, and grasp how they thought and theologized about mission. After narrating their stories, I will invite the reader to reflect on what can be learned from their experiences, including which of their strategies might be appropriated today in mission.

Following some initial chapters in which I survey mission in the early and medieval church and narrate the rise of monasticism as well as missionary monasticism, I craft a narrative of missionary monks and monastic mission movements, telling their stories, allowing them speak on their own terms and in their own contexts, and presenting their approaches to mission. I conclude with a short epilogue offering thoughts toward a monastic theology of mission with some reflections on what missionaries might recover today from missionary monks. In short, we will stand on the cold shores of Iona (and other places), consider what mission meant to these pioneering monks, and reflect on what their legacy means for us.

CHAPTER 1

Early Christian Mission

BISHOP STEPHEN NEILL (1900–1984), an Anglican missionary to India as well as a historian and theologian of mission, once wrote, "If everything is mission, nothing is mission."[1] While Neill was responding to twentieth-century liberal theology that was diminishing the supernatural and eternal qualities of the gospel, his admonishing statement is still relevant today. There seems to be disagreement among committed evangelicals over the meaning of mission. In this brief chapter, I will first spell out how I am using the word and then describe the major marks of mission in the early church through the end of the first millennium.

What is Mission?

Following William Larkin, I define mission as "The divine activity of sending intermediaries . . . to speak or to do God's will so that God's purposes for judgment or redemption are furthered."[2] While redemption is certainly the hope of the missionary proclaiming God's ways, judgment is also a real outcome for those who reject the gospel. Emphasizing the scope of mission, Ott, Strauss, and Tennent add that "Mission is a sign of the kingdom and an invitation to the nations to enter the kingdom and share the hope of the kingdom promised in Christ's return."[3]

---

1. Neill, *Salvation Tomorrow*, 17.
2. Larkin, "Mission," 534.
3. Ott, et al., *Encountering Theology of Mission*, 105.

Mission, which simply means "sending," is founded upon the *missio Dei* (mission of God). That is, the initiative for mission begins with a missionary God. This reality is perhaps best captured after the fall when the living God himself moves toward the fallen couple and asks Adam, "where are you?" (Gen 3:8ff), and then provides sacrificial covering for their shame. This pattern of sending continues throughout the Old and New Testaments as God sends his servants and messengers—prophets, the Messiah, and the church—to announce his saving ways to the nations.[4] Moreau, Corwin, and McGee correctly assert that "God is the one who initiates and sustains mission."[5]

In light of this, the church participates in God's mission by making disciples of all nations through evangelism, teaching, church planting, and other related ministries including things like Bible translation, community development, and ministries of justice and compassion. While mission is demonstrated in both word (proclaiming the death, burial, and resurrection of Jesus) and deed (caring for real, human needs), the greatest human needs are spiritual—namely being reconciled to God in Christ—and priority ought to be given there. Yet, mission cannot be reduced to the sequential formula of "preach now, care later," for sometimes ministries of compassion may precede evangelism in daily concrete situations. On this tension between word and deed, Mike Barnett has wisely written:

> I prefer not to think of proclamation as the first thing in a sequence followed by deeds. I understand proclamation as our main and ultimate thing. Thus, it is our priority. Do we first proclaim and then serve? Maybe, maybe not. It depends on the situation, the relationships, the leadership of God's Spirit in the life of the witness and the sought one. But regardless of how and when we serve, we have not fulfilled the Great Commission unless we proclaim.[6]

In short, if we do not embrace the central task of proclaiming the death, burial, and resurrection of Jesus in mission, then we can no longer claim that our mission is distinctively Christian.

To summarize this understanding of mission, I also affirm the following six characteristics articulated by Larkin. First, there is a sender. Mission is based on the sender's authority and purpose and, for our purposes, it is

---

4. On mission in the Old Testament, see McDaniel, "Mission in the Old Testament," 11–20.

5. Moreau, et al., *Introducing World Missions*, 17.

6. Barnett, "The Missing Key to the Future of Evangelical Mission," 227.

the Father's accomplishment and application of salvation. Next, there is a commission or an act of sending. This includes the response of God's people to go to a particular place or people. Third, and related, there are the sent ones—God's agents in mission who demonstrate obedience to the sender. Fourth, there is the task of mission, which as we have noted, involves both word and deed. Subsequently, there are the outcomes of mission, which includes the advancement of the kingdom of God. Finally, there is a theological framework for mission—the church viewing its mission activity in light of God's salvation history.[7]

One may reasonably ask—at what point did mission become mission in the history of the church? Is it not anachronistic to refer to mission in the early or medieval church? David Bosch correctly notes that in the patristic period "the Latin word *missio* was an expression employed in the doctrine of the Trinity, to denote the sending of the Son by the Father, and of the Holy Spirit by the Father and the Son."[8] However, Dana Robert asserts: "The idea of 'mission' is carried through the New Testament by 206 references to the term 'sending.' The main Greek verb 'to send' is *apostollein*. Thus *apostles* were literally those sent to spread the 'Good News' of Jesus' life and message."[9] So mission has been central to the identity of the Christian movement since its inception—Christianity is a missionary faith. Referring to mission-related vocabulary, Bosch adds: "For fifteen centuries the church used other terms to refer to what we subsequently call 'mission': phrases such as 'propagation of the faith,' 'preaching of the gospel,' 'apostolic proclamation,' 'promulgation of the gospel,' 'augmenting the faith,' 'expanding the church,' 'planting the church,' 'propagation of the reign of Christ,' and 'illuminating the nations.'"[10] In short, throughout Christian history, we continually observe missionary motives and endeavors even when the word "mission" is not always used.[11]

---

7. Larkin and Williams, *Mission in the New Testament*, 3–4.

8. Bosch, *Transforming Mission*, 228.

9. Robert, *Christian Mission*, 11.

10. Bosch, *Transforming Mission*, 228.

11. Smither, "Did the Rise of Constantine Mean the End of Christian Mission?" 130–45.

Context of Early Christian Mission

Though it is beyond the scope of this chapter to narrate thoroughly the geographical spread of the church in the first millennium, it is evident that Christianity experienced broad and significant growth.[12] By the early fourth century when Constantine came to power, it is estimated that Christians comprised 10 percent of the population of the Roman Empire.[13] This is quite remarkable when we consider that for most of the first four centuries, Christians did not have the freedom to construct buildings, gather publically, or experience a tolerated existence in Rome. Some parts of the Empire—particularly North Africa—experienced especially accelerated growth.[14] By the end of the sixth century, Christian communities flourished in the Roman Empire, from the British Isles in the West to Asia Minor in the East.

The history of the church within the Roman Empire is, of course, only part of the story, as the faith expanded eastward during this period as well.[15] Beginning in Edessa and Syria, the gospel spread through Central Asia and, by the seventh century, had even reached China through the witness of Church of the East believers. Even before the Emperor Constantine had converted, the Armenian monarch Trdat was baptized in 301 and declared his kingdom to be a Christian nation. The church was also expanding into Persia and India at this time. Towards the end of the first millennium, the gospel took hold in Scandinavia, Eastern Europe, as well as Russia.

The spread of Christianity is even more remarkable when we consider the political and religious contexts that the church encountered. As noted, prior to Constantine's reign in the Roman Empire, Christians were not tolerated and at times faced discrimination and even periods of persecution.[16] Though the peace and favor that Constantine gave to the church was certainly appreciated by many Christians and celebrated by others, the

---

12. For a brief summary of global Christian expansion in this period, see Smither, *Mission in the Early Church*, 8–16. For a more thorough presentation, see Latourette, *History of the Expansion of Christianity* and Irvin and Sunquist, *History of the World Christian Movement*.

13. Stark, *Rise of Christianity*, 6.

14. Neill, *History of Christian Missions*, 27; also Decret, *Early Christianity in North Africa*.

15. For more on the eastward expansion of the church, see Irvin and Sunquist, *History of the World Christian Movement*; Moffett, *History of Christianity in Asia*; Jenkins, *Lost History of Christianity*; and Cragg, *The Arab Christian*.

16. Smither, *Mission in the Early Church*, 16–20.

emergence of a Christian emperor and Rome's eventual acceptance of the faith as an imperial religion posed problems for the church. What should the church's relationship be to the state? What does conversion to Christianity mean in a developing context of Christendom?

While the church in the Roman Empire was dealing with these issues in the fourth century, neighboring churches in Persia did not have the same rights and were facing continued persecution. Later, following the early seventh-century rise of Islam, Christians in the East quickly came under Muslim dominance with many in the church even converting to Islam as a result. Irvin and Sunquist write, "Within a century of the death of Muhammad [ca. 732], as many as half of the world's Christians were under Muslim political rule."[17] In sum, part of the developing identity of global Christians in the first millennium involved figuring how to relate to political authorities.

The expanding church also encountered various worldview frameworks and part of mission involved crossing frontiers of thought. In the Roman context, the church communicated the faith within the contexts of paganism and also Greek philosophy. In Persia, Christians encountered Zoroastrian thinking. Farther East, missionaries thought about the gospel in light of the concerns of Hindu, Buddhist, and Taoist adherents. Of course, the church also related to the Abrahamic religions of Judaism and Islam.

Finally, while the early and medieval church faced challenges from other religious and worldview systems, it also had to combat unsound doctrine developing within the church itself. During the second and third centuries, Gnosticism posed many challenges to Christian thought. Although modern scholars do not agree on a comprehensive definition for the philosophy,[18] generally speaking, Gnosticism viewed creation and matter in a negative light and it taught that redemption came through a secret knowledge (*gnosis*) that liberated the spirit from the body.

One of the great points of contention in early Christian thought came with articulating the doctrine of Christ. In the first three centuries, the church responded to the heresy of docetism—that Jesus was a mere phantom and only appeared (*dokeo*) to have a human body.[19] Later controversies included adoptionism (Jesus being adopted as the Son of God and taking

---

17. Irvin and Sunquist, *History of the World Christian Movement*, 271.
18. Smith, "Post-Bauer Scholarship on Gnosticism(s)."
19. Sweet, "Docetism," 24–31.

on divinity at his baptism)[20] and subordinationism (that Jesus was not fully divine in the way that the Father was). In the fourth century, Apollinarius (ca. 310–ca. 390) emphasized Jesus' divinity to such an extent that he essentially denied the Lord's human will and nature.[21] Finally, in the midst of a confusing theological battle with Cyril of Alexandria (ca. 376–444), Nestorius (ca. 386–ca. 451) seemed to teach that there were two Christs—a divine Jesus and a human one. His thinking was subsequently denounced at the Council of Chalcedon of 451.[22]

Fourth-century church fathers in particular sought to understand and articulate how the Father, Son, and Holy Spirit—particularly the Father and the Son—related together in essence and action. The Alexandrian Presbyter Arius (ca. 250–336) taught that as the Father was eternal and uncreated and that the Son was created by the Father, then Jesus was necessarily subordinate to the Father. The issue was addressed at the Council of Nicaea in 325 where a creed resulted and Arius was deposed. However, the Arian controversy raged on for most of the fourth century.[23]

Also in the fourth and fifth centuries, the church wrestled with the doctrines of grace—including free will, the effects of the fall, and original sin—through the Pelagian controversy. Pelagius' (ca. 354–ca. 420/440) assertions that humanity did not have a sinful nature and that perfection was possible and even obligatory were answered thoroughly by Augustine and some colleagues in a number of books, letters, and church councils.[24]

Given this brief survey of the expansion of Christianity in the first thousand years, one might ask—who were the missionaries? According to the author of the *Didache* (late first and early second century), Origen (ca. 185–254), and Eusebius of Caesarea (ca. 260–341), evidence exists for unnamed, itinerant evangelists who traveled and crossed cultures to proclaim the gospel during the first three centuries.[25] Origen wrote: "Some of them, accordingly, have made it their business to itinerate not only through cities,

---

20. Muers, "Adoptionism," 50–58.

21. Kelly, *Early Christian Doctrines*, 289–301.

22. Irvin and Sunquist, *History of the World Christian Movement*, 281; also Ward, "Africa," 194–96.

23. Kelly, *Early Christian Doctrines*, 223–79.

24. Ibid., 357–74.

25. *Didache* 11–13; Origen, *Against Celsus* 3.9; and Eusebius, *Church History* 3.37.1–3.

but even villages and country houses, that they might make converts to God."[26]

While some operated as vocational evangelists, one remarkable element of early Christianity was its anonymous missionary element. It is intriguing that the two largest church communities in the Roman Empire—those in Rome and Carthage—had anonymous origins. Adolph von Harnack affirms, "the great mission of Christianity was in reality accomplished by means of informal missionaries,"[27] while Stephen Neill adds that "every Christian was a witness ... nothing is more notable than the anonymity of these early missionaries."[28] This spirit of early Christian mission seems best captured in the anonymous *Letter to Diognetus*:

> For Christians are no different from other people in terms of their country, language, or customs. Nowhere do they inhabit cities of their own, or live life out of the ordinary. . . . They inhabit both Greek and barbarian cities according to the lot assigned to each; . . . they participate in all things as citizens. . . . They live in their respective countries, but only as resident aliens; they participate in all things as citizens, and they endure all things as foreigners. They marry like everyone else and have children, but they do not expose them once they are born. They share their meals but not their sexual partners. They are found in the flesh but do not live according to the flesh. They live on earth but participate in the life of heaven.[29]

As mission seemed to be owned by much of the church, this was also expressed in the number of "bi-vocational" missionaries in the early church—those who witnessed to Christ while occupied with other work. For instance, philosophers and teachers such as Justin Martyr (ca. 100–165) and Origen taught philosophy and directed schools while also engaging in cross-cultural witness. Likewise, a number of bishops, those set apart to lead established congregations, engaged in missionary work. In Gaul, Irenaeus (ca. 115–200) reached out as an apologist to gnostics and also learned Gaelic in order to preach in rural villages in addition to serving the church at Lyons. Similarly, Martin of Tours (ca. 316–397) was an itinerant preacher and cared for the poor on top of being a bishop. In Asia Minor,

---

26. Origen, *Against Celsus* 3.9 cited in Schnabel, *Early Christian Mission*, 2.1528.
27. Harnack, *Mission and Expansion of Christianity*, 368.
28. Neill, *History of Christian Missions*, 24.
29. *Letter to Diognetus* 5.1–6, cited in Schnabel, *Early Christian Mission*, 2.1566.

Gregory Thaumaturgus (ca. 213–270) was set apart as bishop of his native Pontus and spent many days caring for the poor and oppressed while also evangelizing intellectuals.[30] A final group of missionaries occupied with a primary vocation were monks, who will, of course, be the focus of this book.

Marks of Early Christian and Medieval Mission

What were some of the characteristics or marks of mission in the early and medieval church? First, mission was marked by suffering, especially in the period prior to Constantine's rule. While no responsible student of history would claim that Christians were unceasingly persecuted in the centuries prior to Constantine, it is difficult to deny the accounts of the churches in places like Lyons, Carthage, Alexandria, and Rome. Examination of various accounts of persecution and martyrdom, including the words and actions of those who suffered, show that, in an indirect manner, suffering did serve as a strategic means for the advancement of the gospel.[31] For instance, the public context of persecution allowed Christians the opportunity to witness verbally about their faith and to clarify and defend the gospel. In some cases, it was reported that some bystanders were converted to Christianity because of the persecution they witnessed; while in other cases, non-Christian observers sympathized with suffering Christians—an influence that seemed to lay further groundwork for the growth of the church. Persecution against Christians also resulted in apologetics, written treatises that defended and articulated Christian belief. Finally, suffering served to invigorate the church and its mission through the death of martyrs. As they were memorialized on feast days, mentioned in sermons, remembered in sacred biographies *(vitae)*, and honored through the construction of churches, Christian martyrs strengthened the witness of the church.

Next, evangelism was central to early Christian mission.[32] As shown in the *Letter to Diognetus,* many Christians witnessed as a way of life in the marketplace and in their spheres of influence. Philosophers such as Justin, Pantaenus (ca. 120–ca. 200), and Origen focused on sharing the gospel with intellectuals, while Gregory the Enlightener (ca. 240–332), Patrick of Ireland (ca. 387–461), and Columba set a pattern of engaging politi-

---

30. Smither, *Mission in the Early Church*, 32–39.

31. See my expanded discussion in Smither, *Mission in the Early Church*, 49–73.

32. Smither, *Mission in the Early Church*, 74–90.

cal leaders with the Christian message. Others focused their attention on evangelizing heretics. Augustine of Hippo (354–430) reached out to the schismatic Donatists, while John of Damascus (ca. 650–749) and Timothy of Baghdad (727–823) sought to evangelize the "heretics" of their day—Muslims.[33] Finally, some early Christian leaders—including Justin in his *Dialogue with Trypho* and Augustine in his *Confessions*—shared public, recorded testimonies of how they were converted for the benefit of a broader audience.

A third mark of mission was translating the Scripture into the local language of evangelized peoples.[34] Once churches were established, many congregations worshipped in a regional trade language and Christians, who were fluent in another language, benefited from Scripture or Christian literature through that medium. However, in a rather short period of time, the vernacular principle prevailed making Scripture available in many of the heart languages of peoples where the gospel had taken hold. In the early Christian period, this included Syriac, Latin, Coptic, Gothic, Armenian, Georgian, and Ethiopic. Irvin and Sunquist correctly assert, "translocation [of the gospel message] and [Bible] translation went hand in hand."[35]

Another quality of mission in this period involved contextualizing or clarifying the gospel in diverse contexts.[36] This was accomplished through missionaries being conversant with ideas and forms of communication, through redeeming sacred space and pre-existing festivals, by connecting with visual culture, and by understanding the culture of the marketplace. Through these approaches, the gospel began to take root among many peoples and in many areas. This demonstrated that Christianity was a faith that could be at home in a given culture while also bringing transformation to that culture.

Fifth, early Christian mission was characterized by ministry in both word and deed.[37] That is, mission was not restricted to proclamation alone; nor did mission ever become gospel-less humanitarian aid. While the gospel message remained unchanged—a message centered on the death, burial, and resurrection of Christ and supported by the rule of faith and early Christian creeds—there was some diversity in deed ministry. Various

---

33. Smither, "Augustine, Missionary to Heretics?," 269–88.
34. Smither, *Mission in the Early Church*, 91–108.
35. Irvin and Sunquist, *History of the World Christian Movement*, 54.
36. Smither, *Mission in the Early Church*, 109–26.
37. Ibid., 127–47.

ministries included caring for the poor, hungry, imprisoned, enslaved, and otherwise marginalized; but it could also be observed through works of healing and casting out evil spirits.

Finally, mission in the early church was quite church-centered.[38] Though strategies changed over time and church forms looked different, a time never came when there was a church-less Christianity. Interestingly, the church was a powerful means for mission as well as its most visible outcome. In the first century, mission was accomplished through a deliberate house-to-house approach and the *oikos* (household) structure facilitated an organic church, especially during periods of time when Christians were unable to exist as a legitimate organization. Even after peace was given to the church in the fourth century, mission flowed from the church and back to the church in the absence of any structured missions societies. That evangelism, catechesis, and baptism efforts were located in the context of the church solidified this church-focused mission. The phenomenon of church art showed that non-believers could embrace the gospel through seeing the gospel visually in basilicas built after the fourth century. While the public acceptance of Christianity and the construction of buildings probably thwarted the spontaneous multiplication of churches that the house churches facilitated, there was still a sense of mission and the church remained a central element.

Summary

This chapter has offered a baseline for comprehending mission in the early and medieval church. I began by offering a basic definition of mission from a biblical foundation. Next, I have briefly summarized the status of mission in the early church with attention to the geographical spread of Christianity, the political and religious context in which the church witnessed, the identity of early Christian missionaries, and some defining characteristics of mission in this period. This chapter has offered some background in order to locate the work of missionary monks. The following chapter will give further context by summarizing the origins and emergence of monasticism.

---

38. Ibid., 149–63.

CHAPTER 2

Rise of Monasticism

SEVERAL YEARS AGO, I was teaching a church history survey course at an evangelical seminary. When we reached the module on monasticism, I wanted the students to engage the subject a bit more personally. So I arranged for the class to get in contact with a community of Benedictine monks in England who had set up an online outreach called "Ask a monk." The monks were gracious to field our students' inquiries and many students responded by asking some honest questions: Why did you choose to become a monk? How do you spend your day? Do you ever regret your decision? Isn't a monastic lifestyle a little selfish when there is so much ministry to be done in the world?

In this chapter, our aim is somewhat similar—to understand the motivation and work of monks in history. Beginning with a basic definition of monasticism, I will narrate the movement's historic rise, its essential elements, the diversity within it, and some of its key innovators in the early church. By shedding light on these background questions, we will be better able to grasp the rise of missionary monasticism.

The Origins and Essence of Monasticism

The word "monasticism" comes from the Greek word *monasterion*, which referred either to a monk's individual cell or to the cloister where a group of monks lived. Related, the term "monk" stems from two Greek ideas—*monos* ("alone") and *monachos* ("solitary one"). The earliest reference to a *monachos* is found in an Egyptian manuscript from around the year 324.[1]

The question of the origins of Christian monasticism is not an easy one to resolve, and a number of theories have been advanced. As monasticism has played an important role in Buddhism, Hinduism, and Jainism, some have speculated that these movements influenced Christian asceticism. In the Graeco-Roman context, there was a form of ascetic discipline associated with the temples of Serapis. Further, there were some monastic elements in Judaism, particularly the Essenes who lived at Qumran and the Therapeutae of Egypt. Finally, beginning in the third century, ascetic communities could be observed within the Manichean sect.[2] Though these basic similarities are interesting to consider, Goehring argues that no real correlation can be made between these ascetic groups and Christian monasticism.[3] Harmless asserts that the origins of Christian monasticism are probably mostly Christian, as "praying in deserts, fasting, celibacy, renunciation of family and wealth" were characteristic of Jesus and Paul and these values shaped Christianity from the first century onward.[4] For Goehring, the biggest factor that influenced the rise of fourth-century Christian monasticism was the theological reflection and practice that developed as the church's status began to change in society. He writes: "The origin of the Christian monastic life is instead found in the transformation of the eschatological communion of saints brought on by the delay of the second coming of Christ and the increasing success of Christianity."[5] Martyrdom had been the "ultimate expression of Christian commitment" in the Roman context in the first three centuries; however, following the rise of Constantine and the peace and favor given to the church, "the monk replaced the martyr as a Christian hero" and "they became the earthly embodiment of the heavenly communion of saints."[6] In short, monks were the new martyrs.

Determining the birthplace of monasticism has also been a challenging task. Though many have assumed that it originated in Egypt, this is

---

1. See Goehring, "Monasticism," 769; also Harmless, *Desert Christians*, 459, 493; and Dunn, *Emergence of Monasticism*, 1.

2. Laboa, *Historical Atlas*, 10–17, 20–21; Goehring, "Monasticism," 769; and Dunn, *Emergence of Monasticism*, 11–12.

3. Goehring, "Monasticism," 769.

4. Harmless, "Monasticism," 493; cf. Laboa, *Historical Atlas*, 22–25; also Wilken, *First Thousand Years*, 99.

5. Goehring, "Monasticism," 769.

6. Ibid.; cf. Noll, *Turning Points*, 82.

largely because the earliest and most plentiful written accounts of monasticism are about Egyptian monks and communities. But the Egyptian accounts are not the only accounts. Showing the diverse and parallel origins of early Christian monasticism, Harmless writes, "Egypt was not *the* birthplace but *a* birthplace. Syria has at least an equal claim, and Palestine and Cappadocia may as well."[7]

While this chapter will highlight some of monasticism's diversity, one unifying element across monastic groups was a renunciation of the world and a deliberate attempt to mortify the flesh and its desires. Early Egyptian monasticism was characterized by a pessimistic view of the body, largely informed by neo-Platonic philosophy and Origen's theology. This drove an asceticism that was quite rigorous in which monks fasted from sleep and food and kept to the most basic diet.[8] Later, other monastic leaders such as Basil (329–379), Augustine, and Benedict advocated a more moderate ascetic approach.[9] As men and women in the monastic tradition renounced the world, they embraced voluntary poverty and celibacy. Their daily lives largely revolved around the three major disciplines of prayer, reading Scripture, and manual labor. Monks prayed individually, in groups, during liturgical assemblies, and as they went about their work. Prayer was facilitated by the discipline of regular fasting, but also through work (i.e., weaving mats) that helped the monk to stay focused while praying.[10] They also read Scripture and sang psalms individually and in groups, as well as during worship gatherings. Finally, monks engaged in manual labor to stay focused in prayer, but also to sustain themselves and their community. While these three disciplines were the foundation of monastic living, over thirty monastic rules or manuals emerged in the early Christian period that reveal much diversity in monastic theology and practice.[11]

Monastic Diversity and Innovators

Beginning in the late third century, monasticism began to take on some recognizable forms. Due to a significant body of literature celebrating the lives of monks, we are afforded a window of sorts into this development.

7. Harmless, *Desert Christians*, 434.
8. Dunn, *Emergence of Monasticism*, 6–8.
9. Ibid., 64–69, 71–72.
10. Ibid., 125.
11. Laboa, *Historical Atlas*, 116.

This body of literature included works on individuals such as Athanasius' *Life of Antony*, Jerome's *Life of Paul*, and the *Life of Pachomius*. In addition, there were general histories published, such as the *History of the Monks of Egypt*, the *Lausiac History*, and the *Sayings of the Desert Fathers* (*Apophthegmata Patrum*). The latter work, recorded between 330 and 460, consists of more than a thousand stories about Egyptian monks, including many statements directly attributed to them.[12] As these works were translated and circulated in multiple languages, especially Coptic, Greek, and Latin, they had a great influence on the early church and certainly aided the growth of monasticism.[13]

There was much diversity in the world of early Christian monasticism. Goehring describes it as the "complex continuum from the fully solitary monk to the fully communal monk."[14] On one end of the spectrum, hermitic or anchoritic monasticism emphasized the "extreme solitary life."[15] Spiritual growth and victory over the flesh happened best through *anachoresis* ("withdrawal"). This was the type of monasticism practiced by Antony (ca. 251–ca. 356) and celebrated by Athanasius in his *Life of Antony*.

On the other end of the spectrum, there was coenobitic or communal monasticism, where "monks lived together in a community under a common monastic rule."[16] While withdrawing from the world, this group believed that community with other monks was necessary for spiritual growth. Over time, the coenobitic approach became the most prominent form of Christian monasticism.

It would be too simple to limit monasticism to these two groups because there was much room in between. For instance, the fourth-century monks of Nitria (Egypt) formed semi-hermitic communities in which "a group of monks constructed their solitary cells in relatively close proximity to one another."[17] Dunn points out that "Egyptian hermitic monasticism was never an entirely solitary affair. Antony himself received visitors and

---

12. For an in-depth introduction to this literature, see Harmless, *Desert Christians*, 167–305; cf. Dunn, *Emergence of Monasticism*, 67; and Smither, "'To Emulate and Imitate,'" 150–51.
13. Wilken, *First Thousand Years*, 102.
14. Cited in Harmless, *Desert Christians*, 421.
15. Goehring, "Monasticism," 770.
16. Ibid.
17. Ibid.

seems to have supervised monks."[18] Some anchoretic monks, like Evagrius of Pontus (345–399), admitted that withdrawal to isolation was a process because human beings—even monks—still needed other humans. In his personal ascetic journey, Evagrius "had gone from one end of the monastic spectrum, as a city dwelling monk-cleric in the coenobitic tradition, to being a more isolated, desert-dwelling anchorite (hermit). Evagrius was surely following the counsel of the abbas [monastic abbots or fathers][19] who 'approve highly of an anachoresis that is undertaken by degrees.'"[20]

The story of early and medieval Christianity includes many women ascetics as well. Some of these, such as Basil of Caesarea's grandmother and his sister (both named Macrina), proved to be quite influential in the development of early monasticism. Though some women lived as anchorites, most gathered in communal monasteries, many of which were parallel houses to a community of men. For example, when Pachomius (292–346) was instituting his *koinonia* (monastic settlements) in Egypt, his sister founded a monastic house for women.[21]

Given this basic description of the diversity within early monasticism, let us expand this further by briefly narrating the lives and contributions of some key monastic innovators. Although Antony was not the first anchoretic monk, he became a prominent symbol of this monastic form largely because of the successful distribution of Athanasius' *Life of Antony*.[22] Apparently, Antony was drawn to an ascetic lifestyle when he heard Jesus' words from Matthew 19:21 preached in church: "If you want to be perfect, go, sell your possessions and give to the poor, and you will have treasure in heaven. Then come, follow me."[23] Taking this text literally, he sold his possessions and gave what he had to the poor, while also taking care of his sister's material needs. Initially, he moved to the edge of his village and then eventually across the Nile to a more remote area to avoid human contact. Ironically, his withdrawal seemed to invite more and more pilgrims and

---

18. Dunn, *Emergence of Monasticism*, 13.

19. *Abba* (Aramaic) and *apa* (Coptic) is rendered "abbot" in English and refers to a monastic father or superior.

20. Smither, "Lessons from a Tentmaking Ascetic," 487; cf. Sinkewicz, *Evagrius of Pontus*, 56.

21. Dunn, *Emergence of Monasticism*, 45–47; also Harmless, *Desert Christians*, 121; and Laboa, *Historical Atlas*, 110.

22. Dunn, *Emergence of Monasticism*, 8–12; also Wilken, *First Thousand Years*, 100.

23. Unless otherwise indicated, all Scripture references in this book are from the New International Version.

visitors, which forced him farther into the wilderness near the Red Sea. After some twenty years living largely in isolation, he agreed to become the spiritual father of a loosely-related group of anchorites.[24]

Though certainly not the first coenobitic monk, Pachomius' name has been most associated with the rise of communal monasticism. Following his discharge from the Roman army, Pachomius returned home to Upper Egypt, where he was converted and later pursued an ascetic lifestyle under the mentorship of a hermit named Palamon. Pachomius' biographers reported that in response to a mystical voice calling, he left Palamon and formed a community of monks at Tabenessi. This later expanded into other settlements down the Nile River in Upper Egypt. According to Palladius' *Lausiac History*, Pachomius' monastic settlements included as many as three thousand monks.[25] Pachomius' contributions to coenobitic monasticism were twofold. First, he demonstrated innovation by organizing monastic settlements into what he called the *koinonia*. Each settlement included as many as forty houses and there was leadership at both the settlement and house level. This organizational structure, perhaps the fruit of Pachomius' training in the Roman military, facilitated both leadership development and growth of the overall *koinonia*.[26] Second, Pachomius drafted the first known monastic rule. This manual expressed the values of the *koinonia* and served as a guide for how the community of monks would carry out their daily lives. Pachomius' rule influenced later rules developed by Basil and Benedict.[27]

Another Egyptian monk Ammoun (d. ca. 350) founded a monastery at Mount Nitria near the Nile Delta. He was soon joined by others, including Macarius the Great (ca. 300–ca. 390) and, over time, three monastic settlements were started. This was also the region where the famous *Sayings of the Desert Fathers* were recorded. Ammoun was an innovator because of the semi-hermitic nature of his settlements—a loose association of anchorites who enjoyed isolation and community in their ascetic callings.[28]

---

24. Goehring, "Monasticism," 771; also Dunn, *Emergence of Monasticism*, 2, 8–9.

25. Smither, *Augustine as Mentor*; also Dunn, *Emergence of Monasticism*, 25–27; and Noll, *Turning Points*, 90.

26. Laboa, *Historical Atlas*, 47.

27. Harmless, "Monasticism," 494; also Harmless, *Desert Christians*, 115; and Wilken, *First Thousand Years*, 102–3.

28. Goehring, "Monasticism," 771.

Another monastic innovator who is often overlooked is Shenoute (334–450), who served as abba of the famous White Monastery in Upper Egypt. Shenoute led a coenobitic monastery in the tradition of Pachomius, and he was one of the greatest theologians of the Coptic Church in Egypt. He has been largely forgotten until recently because, unlike others, his works were never translated into Greek and his influence was limited to Coptic speakers.[29]

Originally from Georgia, Evagrius of Pontus was ordained a deacon in Caesarea (Asia Minor) where he also lived in community with other monks. After an apparent moral failure, he fled to Egypt and joined Ammoun's semi-hermitic settlement.[30] Evagrius became one of the earliest and greatest monastic theologians. Although his theology was forged in the Egyptian desert, it ultimately influenced the western Roman Catholic Church. As I have previously written: "Evagrius' greatest theological contribution was articulating his eight thoughts (*logismoi*) that inhibited spiritual progress—gluttony, lust, love of money, anger, dejection, *akedia* (listlessness), glory, and pride. These thoughts were introduced to the church by Evagrius' disciple John Cassian, and after Gregory the Great combined the ideas of vainglory and pride, they became known in the western medieval church as the seven sins."[31]

Outside of Egypt, other monastic innovators emerged in Syria and Palestine. Originally from Asia Minor, Symeon the Stylite (388–459) immigrated to Syria and became a symbol of rigorous Syrian monasticism. Symeon is largely remembered for spending the last thirty years of his life in isolation atop a column that reached as high at fifty feet off the ground.[32] Hilarion (293–371), whose sacred biography was recorded by Jerome, was a leader among anchorites in Palestine. He spent over twenty years alone and inspired the founding of monasteries in the Judean wilderness.[33]

Having been influenced in the ascetic life by his own family and by the monk bishop Eustathius of Sebaste (300–377), Basil of Caesarea emerged as a monastic innovator in Asia Minor.[34] A coenobitic monk who was also an ordained bishop, Basil articulated a monastic rule in his *Longer Rules* and

---

29. Ibid., 772; also Dunn, *Emergence of Monasticism*, 33–34.
30. Laboa, *Historical Atlas*, 166; also Harmless, "Monasticism," 502.
31. Smither, "Lessons from a Tentmaking Ascetic," 487–88.
32. Goehring, "Monasticism," 773; also Laboa, *Historical Atlas*, 49–51.
33. Goehring, "Monasticism," 773.
34. Wilken, *First Thousand Years*, 104–5.

Shorter Rules. He was convinced that community was a necessary means for spiritual growth and that the work of the Holy Spirit and application of Scripture in one monk's life could serve to edify others in the community. Basil's monastic theology was probably best summarized by Christ's teaching, "Love your neighbor as yourself" (Matt 22:39). As we will show, Basil was critical of monks who were so focused on the contemplative aspects of the ascetic life that they ignored opportunities to minister to the community. Basil's monastic thought and practice greatly shaped monasticism in the Eastern Orthodox tradition.[35]

Similar to Evagrius of Pontus, John Cassian (360–435) served as a broker between eastern and western Christianity and he influenced western monasticism with Egyptian values. Born in Scythia Minor (modern Bulgaria and Romania), Cassian lived among the Egyptian monks and recorded their dialogues in his work *Conferences,* which presented an anchoritic monastic vision. He also authored *Institutes* that outlined the coenobitic approach. Cassian was probably influenced by Basil and Pachomius' thoughts on communal monasticism through reading their rules and works in translation. He spent the latter part of his life in Gaul and established monasteries in Marseille, where he introduced many Egyptian practices. Cassian's influence extended beyond Gaul as his works (along with those of Basil and Jerome) were read by Celtic monastic innovators, Columba and Columban (543–615).[36]

Largely remembered in church history for his theology and philosophy, Augustine of Hippo served as a monk bishop in the North African context for the majority of his adult life. A contemporary of Cassian, he developed the first monastic rule in the western church and he trained clergy for ministry in the African church from his *monasterium clericorum* ("clergy monastery") in Hippo. While Augustine was committed to the value of monastic labor, some of the work of his monks included preaching, teaching, and writing theology for the church, and so his monastery was much more academic and intellectual than the more austere ones in Syria or Egypt.[37]

---

35. Harmless, "Monasticism," 496, 505; also Dunn, *Emergence of Monasticism,* 38–39, 70; and Laboa, *Historical Atlas,* 89.

36. Goehring, "Monasticism," 774; also Dunn, *Emergence of Monasticism,* 74–81, 88–89; and Harmless, "Monasticism," 495.

37. Smither, *Augustine as Mentor,* 134–57; also Dunn, *Emergence of Monasticism,* 64, 85–88; and Harmless, "Monasticism," 496.

A final monastic innovator, perhaps the most famous in the western tradition, was Benedict of Nursia. Originally a hermit who lived for a time in a cave, Benedict embraced a coenobitic approach and founded a monastery at Monte Cassino near Rome in 529. Influenced by Antony, Pachomius, Basil, Augustine, and Cassian, Benedict developed his own rule that focused on prayer and liturgy. Specifically, Benedict set a daily schedule for prayer and singing psalms, reading Scripture (*lectio divina*), and work.[38] More than any other monastic leader before him, Benedict brought balance and moderation to monastic living. Harmless asserts that the Benedictine rule became the "constitution of western monasticism."[39] There is also evidence that Benedict's monastic vision also influenced Columban and the Celtic monks and that Augustine of Canterbury and his monks took Benedict's rule with them on the mission to England in 596.[40]

The Rise of Missionary Monks

Intrinsic to the idea of monastic calling was separation from the world. Describing the architecture of Pachomius' *koinonia*, Harmless writes, "High walls were the most distinctive feature of a Pachomian monastery. These served as the very visible boundary separating monastery from the outside world."[41] Other monastic leaders, such as Benedict, worked to restrict the monks' contact with the outside world as much as possible. Given these tendencies within early monasticism, how did a missionary movement develop that would become the church's primary evangelistic arm in the early and medieval church?

Though a deliberate missionary emphasis was not prevalent in third- and fourth-century monasticism, there are some indications that monks did care about non-Christians. Harmless notes that Pachomius' original monastic vision was broader than merely caring for monks; it was to "minister to the human race" and "unite it to God."[42] Harmless adds that at least one of Pachomius' biographers portrayed the abba's work from a missional perspective:

38. Goehring, "Monasticism," 774; also Harmless, "Monasticism," 497; Harmless, *Desert Christians*, 373; and Dunn, *Emergence of Monasticism*, 114, 128.
39. Harmless, "Monasticism," 497; cf. Noll, *Turning Points*, 86–87.
40. Dunn, *Emergence of Monasticism*, 173, 192; also Laboa, *Historical Atlas*, 84.
41. Harmless, *Desert Christians*, 125; cf. Dunn, *Emergence of Monasticism*, 124–125.
42. Cited in Harmless, *Desert Christians*, 141.

Given that the Monastery of the Metanoia was built, quite literally, on the ruins of paganism, it was no accident that the author of the *First Greek Life* situates the work of Pachomius against the horizon of Christianity's worldwide mission. In the prologue, he explicitly quotes Matthew 28:19, in which the risen Jesus sends forth his apostles to go to all nations and baptize them in the name of the Father, Son, and Holy Spirit. He goes on to cite the divine promise made to Abraham, that his descendants will be as numerous as the stars (Gen 22:17). He then links the demise of paganism with the rise of monasticism in general and Pachomius in particular.[43]

Other Egyptian monks also showed some signs of missionary commitment. According to Palladius, Macarius the Alexandrian was concerned that his monks maintained a balance of prayer, work, and ministry in their daily lives, which at very least shows that he was concerned that they had a ministry.[44] For some fourth-century Egyptian monks, this meant cooperating with the church and serving as "evangelists to the countryside" and "winning people to Christianity."[45] Abba Shenoute was also engaged in evangelism among pagans and even aided in destroying some pagan temples.[46] Finally, the monks of Egypt as a whole were deeply committed to hospitality.[47] While many of the visitors to Egypt were Christian pilgrims, others were surely non-believers who were invited to table fellowship inside the monastic settlements. This tendency probably opened the door even more toward a missionary monasticism.

We can observe missional tendencies in western monasticism as well. Though Bishop Gregory's depiction of Benedict in his *Dialogues* has been questioned, it still suggests that Benedict was involved in mission. Dunn writes: "The *Dialogues* portray Benedict as an evangelist who uses the Subiaco house as a base for preaching in the surrounding countryside and Monte Cassino itself as a center of conversion. He destroys a pagan temple on the summit of the mountain to create churches and converts the pagan peasants of the neighborhood to Christianity."[48] Evidence likewise hints that Benedict had some contact with the Gothic King Totila and that he and his monks evangelized the people in the region of Monte Cassino during

43. Ibid., 140.
44. Ibid., 288.
45. Ibid., 16.
46. Ibid., 446.
47. Ibid., 118, 176–77, 275, 280–81; also Laboa, *Historical Atlas*, 42.
48. Dunn, *Emergence of Monasticism*, 132.

some turbulent days.[49] Like the monks of Egypt, Benedict taught his monks to practice hospitality: "All guests . . . are to be welcomed as Christ for he himself will say: 'I was a stranger and you welcomed me' (Matt 25:35)."[50]

While Gregory captured some of Benedict's missionary convictions in his writings, the monk bishop of Rome also spent many years wrestling with the tension between the contemplative life in the monastery and the active life in the community and world, especially as monks like himself were being increasingly ordained into church ministry. In a recent work on Gregory, George Demacopoulos argues that the Roman bishop's thoughts on the tension between the contemplative and active life were the most developed among the church fathers. Possessing "an ascetic vision that emphasized service to others as the climax of the spiritual and ascetic life," Gregory advocated a monasticism that celebrated the monk being interrupted from prayer, fasting, and other disciplines in order to serve others.[51] It seems that Gregory's leanings toward the active side of monasticism were what led him to ordain Augustine of Canterbury as a missionary bishop and send him along with forty monks to England in 596.[52] As monks were connected more to the work of the church, including community outreach, it seems that missionary activity also increased.

Up to this point in our discussion, the observed missionary work was largely an indirect by-product of monastic living and a secondary concern for most monks. However, the monastic vision of Basil of Caesarea seems to signal a turning point in the relationship between monasticism and mission. As shown, his monastic rule was centered on loving one's neighbor, including those outside of the church and the Christian faith. He was also "critical of self-absorbed hermits."[53] Laboa writes that for Basil, "Monastic life should not interpreted as a way of escaping from the world, of despising secular ways and habits, but merely as an attempt to form an eschatological community in our history."[54] It was an ascetic life built on the value of

---

49. See Gregory, *Dialogues* 2.8, 14–15, 21; cf. Laboa, *Historical Atlas*, 78; also Noll, *Turning Points*, 81.

50. Benedict, *Rule* 73 cited in Noll, *Turning Points*, 89.

51. Demacopoulos, *Gregory the Great*, 26.

52. Dunn, *Emergence of Monasticism*, 135–36; also Laboa, *Historical Atlas*, 114.

53. Wilken, *First Thousand Years*, 105; cf. Laboa, *Historical Atlas*, 52; and Harmless, *Desert Christians*, 429.

54. Laboa, *Historical Atlas*, 89.

serving others.[55] Robert Wilken adds, "And when he [Basil] was made a bishop he sought ways to adapt the monastic vision of radical devotion to God to life in the city. The solitary life of prayer would be complemented by the active life. Contemplation and service were to go hand in hand."[56] As we will show in the next chapter, Basil's missionary monastic vision included engaging the culturally diverse peoples who passed through Caesarea by showing hospitality, by offering practical help during humanitarian crises, and of course, by inviting non-believers to embrace the gospel. While Basil evangelized within the multi-cultural context of Asia Minor, it is not surprising that the evangelization of neighboring Armenia was accomplished in part through the witness of Cappadocian monks.[57] As we have also shown, later monastic thinkers reading Basil's rules were probably influenced by his outward mission focus.

Another significant turning point toward a missionary monasticism was the emergence of Celtic monasticism, especially with its notion of *peregrinus* or pilgrimage. Among the Celtic monks of Ireland and Wales, this practice of wandering was considered to be the highest form of penance and self-renunciation.[58] Yet, as these pilgrims mingled among pagans, non-Christians, and even lapsed Christians, they were compelled to minister to them. Dunn writes: "While wandering, *peregrini* might find themselves accepting the role of bishop and their monasteries serving as centers of conversion and baptism, officially-appointed bishops and missions to non-urbanized areas might use monasteries as bases for the same purpose."[59] Over time, the Celtic monks became more deliberate about mission. Dunn describes them as "*peregrini* on the peripheries of Christendom who believed that they were doing their Christian duty by preaching the word of God to pagans, apostates, or the very recently converted."[60] Laboa adds that, over time, gospel proclamation became "no less a vocation than the search for solitude" for them.[61] In short, the Celtic missionary conviction developed simply because the monks were living among non-believers and recognized their spiritual needs.

55. Dunn, *Emergence of Monasticism*, 41.
56. Wilken, *First Thousand Years*, 105.
57. Laboa, *Historical Atlas*, 160.
58. Dunn, *Emergence of Monasticism*, 140.
59. Ibid.
60. Ibid., 149–50.
61. Laboa, *Historical Atlas*, 120.

Missionary monasticism became much more recognizable in the medieval period through the deliberate preaching of the Dominican monks and the purposeful cross-cultural evangelism strategies of Francis of Assisi and Raymund Lull in the Muslim world.[62] In Europe, however, it seems that the monks' effectiveness in reaching the pagan population came through their presence and demonstrating the Christian life in word and in deed. Noll summarizes: "For a monastery to be established in a pagan area allowed the local population to see the application of Christianity to daily existence, as monks tilled the soil, welcomed visitors, and carried out the offices of study and daily prayer. So arose the saying that the monks civilized Europe *cruce, libro, et atro*—with cross, book, and plow."[63]

Summary

Wilken argues that because the monastic movement was "versatile, resilient, and adaptable," it served as the key organism in the Middle Ages for spreading the gospel outside of the Roman Empire and even eastward into Muslim-dominated areas.[64] In this chapter, we have attempted to narrate some of the backstory of missionary monasticism by grasping the meaning, origins, and development of monasticism in early and medieval Christianity. Given this foundation, in subsequent chapters, we will meet a variety of missionary monks, explore their contexts of service, and examine their approaches to and thoughts about mission.

---

62. Noll, *Turning Points*, 92.
63. Ibid., 92.
64. Wilken, *First Thousand Years*, 108.

CHAPTER 3

Basil of Caesarea

"THE HUNGRY ARE DYING. . . . The naked are stiff with cold. The man in debt is held by the throat."[1] This is how Basil described his city Caesarea of Cappadocia in the late fourth century, especially amid a lingering famine that plagued his region. As the twenty-first century global church continues to deal with problems such as hunger, usury, corruption, unemployment, displaced peoples, and even slavery, it seems useful to consider the model of Basil, the monk bishop missionary who sought to live out the gospel in the city. Following a brief survey of his life and call to monasticism and ministry and the context in which he ministered, I will discuss his practical strategies and theology of mission.

Basil's Life and Ministry

Basil was born into a wealthy Christian family and his grandparents were influenced by the ministry of Bishop Gregory Thaumaturgus, the most prominent evangelist in Asia Minor in the third century.[2] More than an average nominal Christian family in the post-Constantine era, Basil's family followed the example of his famous grandmother Macrina, practicing asceticism together as a household.[3] Basil was educated in the classical tradition and studied rhetoric (communication) and philosophy in Cappadocia, Constantinople, and later Athens. After a brief stint in

1. Basil, *Sermon* 6.6, cited in Holman, *Hungry Are Dying,* 103.
2. Rousseau, *Basil,* 1, 12.
3. Ibid., 4–5; also Sterk, *Renouncing the World,* 36; and Gregory of Nazianzus, *Oration* 43.12.

teaching, he traveled East in 356 pursuing the mentorship of the ascetic Bishop Eustathius of Sebaste, though Basil later broke fellowship with him because of Eustathius' Arianism.[4] Basil was baptized in 357 and then retreated with close friend Gregory of Nazianzus to his family's estate in Pontus in pursuit of a communal monastic experience. Basil was apparently convinced by his sister (also named Macrina) that a monastic way of life was superior to the academic path that he had begun to take following his return from Athens.[5]

Although a monk, Basil did not reject the opportunity to be ordained as a minister in the church at Caesarea and he was set apart as a reader in 360, a presbyter in 364, and then finally as bishop in 370. While his preference would have been to remain in ascetic retirement in Pontus, Basil was compelled to accept ordination in large part because of the Arian heresy that was threatening the churches of Asia Minor.[6] By combining his monastic and ecclesiastical callings, Basil played a part in one of the most intriguing developments of the fourth and fifth century—the phenomenon of the monk bishop—that included other leaders such as Eusebius of Vercelli (283–371), Martin of Tours, Gregory of Nazianzus (329–ca.390), John Chrysostom (347–407), and Augustine of Hippo. Unlike many monks in his day, Basil regarded the city as both his environment for monastic living and Christian mission.[7] While rejecting Eustathius' theology, Basil did emulate his mentor's concern for urban ministry and care for the poor.[8] In addition to leading the church in his city of Caesarea, which included the tasks of preaching, administering the sacraments, and ministering to the poor, Basil served as a metropolitan bishop, which meant that he oversaw the work of some fifty other bishops in Cappadocia.[9]

---

4. Basil, *Letter* 223; also Rousseau, *Basil*, 27; Sterk, *Renouncing the World*, 39–40; Ayres, "The Cappadocians," 121–24; and Hildebrand, *Basil*, 64, 101.

5. Rousseau, *Basil*, 9–11; also Sterk, *Renouncing the World*, 36.

6. Basil, *Letters* 207.2, 223.5; also Rousseau, *Basil*, 2, 68–69, 84–85, 93; and Sterk, *Renouncing the World*, 43, 74–76.

7. Hildebrand, *Basil*, 112, 126.

8. Sterk, *Renouncing the World*, 25–27.

9. Basil, *Letters*, 92, 98, 204–5; also Sterk, *Renouncing the World*, 44–46, 73–74; and Smither, *Augustine as Mentor*, 62–64.

Cappadocian Caesarea

Basil served in Caesarea, the capital of the Roman province of Cappadocia in Asia Minor. Originally called Mazaca, the city was renamed Caesarea by the Emperor Claudius and it became the provincial capital in AD 17. It remained the largest and most important city in Cappadocia through the fourth century. Although precise population statistics are not available, the presence of fifty bishops leading congregations in the region of Caesarea—a reflection of the Roman administrative system—suggests a significant population.[10]

Despite being large, from an economic perspective, Caesarea was not terribly prosperous. Olives, grapes, grain, and livestock were successfully harvested at times, but the Cappadocians struggled with agriculture.[11] In addition, the pre-Roman feudal system created such a sense of dependency that when the Romans did gain control of the region, the Cappadocians asked them for a king. These conditions were aggravated by multiple earthquakes in the third century that destroyed parts of Pontus and Cappadocia.[12] Despite these difficulties, Caesarea retained influence because of some key Roman roads—trade routes that stretched from Constantinople to Syria—that ran through the city. On one hand, this benefited Caesarea because travelling merchants would stop in the city, lodge there, and spend money in its establishments. On the other hand, the roads also brought the Roman army, including some troops that commandeered local food sources and other supplies, thereby creating stress for the local inhabitants. Understanding Caesarea's strategic geographic location, the Roman government established the city as one of its key administrative centers. Finally, the city's location made it an important intercultural crossroads as diverse peoples from Asia Minor, Armenia, Syria, Persia, and the northern Gothic regions regularly spent time and interacted in Caesarea.[13] In short, Basil ministered in an urban context frequented by peoples of diverse culture and belief systems.

Spiritually speaking, Caesarea was initially evangelized in the first century. However, the most significant church growth and expansion did not occur until the third, fourth, and fifth centuries. As mentioned, the

---

10. McHugh, "Cappadocia," 281.
11. Holman, *Hungry Are Dying*, 70; also Rousseau, *Basil*, 133.
12. McHugh, "Cappadocia," 213–14.
13. Rousseau, *Basil*, 133–34; also Holman, *Hungry Are Dying*, 69–70.

most effective third-century evangelist was Gregory Thaumaturgus, who enjoyed a fruitful ministry in Cappadocia.[14] Similar to the experience of pre-Constantine Christians in the Roman Empire, Cappadocian believers were persecuted for their faith by the Governor Serenianus in the mid-third century.[15]

What were the specific challenges that Basil faced in Caesarea in the fourth century? First, even though Christianity had been tolerated and even preferred in Rome in the fourth century, Basil still experienced conflicts with political leaders. The most obvious was with Emperor Julian (361–363), the so-called apostate, who attempted to revive paganism. Annoyed by the growing number of Christians in Cappadocia, Julian's revival also involved persecuting the church, which included confiscating church property and even drafting church leaders into the army.[16] While the conflict with Julian made sense, Basil also experienced conflict with the Arian Emperor Valens. During Basil's tenure as bishop, Valens divided Cappodocia in half, effectively limiting Basil's influence over the churches and citizens of the region. As we will see shortly, Basil had no problem confronting the political establishment over such decisions. In fact, if Basil had not been so popular with the people, he likely would have been spent time in exile as other fourth-century bishops like Athanasius and Ambrose did when they clashed with the authorities.[17]

Basil faced not only political challenges but theological ones as well. The Council of Nicaea of 325 had condemned Arius' heresy, however, Arianism was still quite prevalent and taught by many bishops in Asia Minor. As Basil and the other Cappadocian fathers (Gregory of Nazianzus and Gregory of Nyssa) battled Arianism through preaching, writing, and church councils, this theological conflict led to Basil's political conflicts with Valens.[18] Gregory of Nazianzus described the emperor as: "A cloud full of hail, with destructive roar, overwhelming every church upon which it

---

14. Basil, *On the Holy Spirit* 74; also Harakas, "Caesarea in Cappadocia," 201–2; and McHugh, "Cappadocia," 213.

15. Frend, *Rise of Christianity*, 309–10; also McHugh, "Cappadocia," 214.

16. Sozomen, *History of the Church* 5.4; also Holman, *Hungry Are Dying*, 70; and Ramsay, *Historical Geography of Asia Minor*, 304.

17. Basil, *Letters* 74–76; Gregory of Nazianzus, *Oration* 43.56; also Ramsay, *Historical Geography of Asia Minor*, 283; McHugh, "Cappadocia," 214; and Sterk, *Renouncing the World*, 72.

18. Basil, *Letters* 80, 82, 90.1, 91, 92.2–3, 203.1, 242.1, 243.4, 244.8, 256; Basil, *On the Holy Spirit* 30.76–77; also Sterk, *Renouncing the World*, 45.

burst and seized.... [He is] most fond of gold and most hostile to Christ."[19] Describing the struggle, Gregory added: "Furious indeed were his first acts of wantonness, more furious still his final efforts against us. What shall I speak of first? Exiles, banishments, confiscations, open and secret plots, persuasion, where time allowed, violence, where persuasion was impossible. Those who clung to the orthodox faith, as we did, were expelled from their churches; others were imposed upon, who agreed with the imperial soul-destroying doctrines, and begged for testimonies of impiety."[20]

A third major issue that Basil dealt with was poverty. In an insightful study on the nature of poverty in the early Christian centuries, Susan Holman writes:

> In the Greek texts of the first four centuries C.E., there are two common words for the poor person, *penes* and *ptochos*. *Ptochos* traditionally designated the destitute beggar who is outside or at the fringes of society, the "street person," the extreme poor. *Penes*, on the other hand, is used to indicate the individual whose economic resources were minimal but who functioned within society, the "working poor." The *penetes* differ from the *ptochoi* in that their social ties within the community remain intact: they retain their dwellings, families, and responsibilities, including their debts. *Penes* could also be a derogatory term for anyone forced to engage in manual labor for survival.[21]

Generally concurring with this distinction, Basil asserts, "I consider that a *ptochos* is he who falls from wealth into need; but a *penes* is he who is in need from the first and is acceptable to the Lord."[22] While both types of poor people lived in Caesarea, Basil's sermons (i.e., *Sermon 8*) suggest that the *ptochoi* represented the most common type of poverty. Sadly, this included desperate families who were abandoning children on the doorstep of the church at Caesarea.[23]

The biggest factor that contributed to Caesareans slipping into poverty was the famine that hit Cappadocia in 368. In fact, it is impossible to understand Basil's ministry without grasping this period of tragedy.

---

19. Gregory of Nazianzus, *Oration* 43.30 (Unless otherwise noted, all English translations are from *Nicene Post Nicene Fathers*).

20. Ibid. 43.36.

21. Holman, *Hungry Are Dying*, 5.

22. Basil, *Short Rules* 262, cited in Holman, *Hungry Are Dying*, 6.

23. Holman, *Hungry Are Dying*, 78–80.

Gregory of Nazianzus wrote: "There was a famine, the most severe one ever recorded. The city was in distress and there was no source of assistance.... The hardest part of all such distress is the insensibility and insatiability of those who possess supplies.... Such are the buyers and sellers of corn."[24] Holman adds:

> Basil's famine sermon refers back to an extremely cold, dry winter that had been followed by an unusually hot, dry spring, and this led to catastrophic agricultural crisis as wells and rivers dried up and crops failed. Those able to hoard grain increased their vigilance and the market prices. Laborers began to starve. Schools closed down. The populace came to church to pray for rain. The poor who worked in the fields and wandered along the roads took on the appearance of living cadavers. Possibly the poor resorted to exposing their children, or selling them, while the rich haggled with them over the purchase price. Gregory of Nazianzus implied that the situation was heightened by the difficulty of importing emergency food supplies to a landlocked region.[25]

Based on evidence from Basil's letters, the famine probably lasted for four years and resulted in additional difficulties. In 372, there was a riot in Caesarea. As shown, some responded by hoarding grain while others resorted to stealing.[26] From Basil's sermons, we are also given a picture of the slow and horrible death that some were dying from starvation.

Approaches to Mission

Given this historical, political, and cultural background of Cappadocian Caesarea as well as the specific challenges that Basil faced, let us now consider some key elements of his ministry. Four of these are most apparent: preaching and evangelism; a prophetic discourse toward oppressors; advocacy for the poor; and practical care for the poor in response to the famine and in the establishment of the *basileas* ("new city").

---

24. Gregory of Nazianzus, *Oration* 43.34, cited in Holman, *Hungry Are Dying*, 65.
25. Holman, *Hungry Are Dying*, 68–69.
26. Basil, *Letters* 31, 86; also Holman, "The Hungry Body," 339.

Preaching and Evangelism

Basil praised the ministry of Gregory Thaumaturgus, the bishop who helped transform Cappadocia in the third century through his evangelistic preaching. For Basil, an important element of his pastoral ministry was preaching in order to train believers and to reach non-believers with the gospel—aspects of ministry that he emphasizes to his disciples in his work *Morals*.[27] Finally, while describing Basil's humanitarian efforts, Gregory of Nazianzus suggested that spiritual teaching and gospel proclamation were his priorities:

> [Basil] provided the nourishment of the Word and that more perfect good work and distribution being from heaven and on high; if the bread of angels is the Word, whereby souls hungry for God are fed and given to drink, and seek after nourishment that neither diminishes nor fails but remains forever; thus [i.e., by his sermons] this supplier of grain and abundant riches [he who was] the poorest and most needy [person] I have known, provided, not for a famine of bread or a thirst for water, but a longing for the truly life-giving and nourishing Word, which effects growth to spiritual maturity in those nourished well on it.[28]

Prophetic Discourse

As social, economic, and political issues plagued Caesarea, Basil's preaching was also characterized by a prophetic discourse in which he challenged the rich, poor, and political leaders to pursue righteousness. Indeed, it was the famine of 368 that prompted Basil to preach his most famous sermons on hunger and poverty—*Sermons* 6 to 9 and two sermons on Psalm 14.[29]

Basil's audience included moneylenders—those who were exploiting the poor during the economic crisis and lending "to the financially desperate at highly usurious rates."[30] Declaring in one sermon that money lenders were worse than dogs, Basil argued from Psalm 14 that "usury involves the greatest inhumanity, . . . seeing a man by necessity bent down before his

---

27. Basil, *Morals* 70.9–11, 31–34.
28. Gregory of Nazianzus, *Oration* 43.36, cited in Holman, *Hungry Are Dying*, 65.
29. Holman, "Hungry Body," 338; also Daley, "Building a New City," 438.
30. Patitsas, "St. Basil's Philanthropic Program," 269–70; cf. Holman, *Hungry Are Dying*, 118, 121; also Rousseau, *Basil*, 136.

knees as a suppliant . . . [the creditor] does not pity him who is suffering misfortune; . . . he takes no account of his nature; he does not yield to his supplications."[31] He built his entire message around the single phrase, "[the righteous man] does not lend out his money at interest."[32] Similarly, in *Sermon 8*, Basil invited those involved in price gouging and usury to repent publically of their sin. Holman notes that Basil went even further and called on "usurers—anyone who lends at interest" to stop oppressing the poor and to offer interest-free loans instead.[33]

In the same sermons, Basil aimed part of his message at the poor themselves. He urged them to repay their debts, to refrain from borrowing more, and to be content in their simplicity.[34] Reiterating his understanding of how Caesareans slipped into poverty (*ptochoi*), Basil preached, "the debtor is . . . one who has borrowed and adopted a lavish lifestyle which he could not otherwise afford."[35] Finally, in *Sermon 8*, Basil reminded the poor that they were not so desperate that they could not be generous themselves.

A third group that Basil condemned were those who hoarded food during the famine. He preached that these hoarders "would rather burst themselves eating than leave a crumb for the hungry."[36] Though the rich were materially well off, Basil asserted that they were the truly poor ones: "You turn away from those you meet lest you be forced to let even a morsel escape your clutches. You have only one phrase: 'I have nothing to give; I am a poor man.' You are indeed poor; and in need of every good. You are poor in love for your fellow man; poor in humanity; poor in faith in God; poor in the hope of eternity!"[37] Instead of fearing the poor, Basil urged them to fear God who would judge those who fail to act justly. Further, he encouraged them to imitate God in his goodness and the Patriarch Joseph in his love for his fellow man. He added: "Make your brothers sharers of your grain; and what may wither tomorrow, give to the needy today. For it

---

31. Basil, *Sermon Ps.* 14b.1, cited in Holman, *Hungry Are Dying*, 120; cf. Basil, *Sermon* 2.2; also Ihssen, "Basil and Gregory's Sermons," 417.

32. Holman, *Hungry Are Dying*, 114.

33. Ibid., 78, 114.

34. Holman, *Hungry Are Dying*, 114; also Ihssen, "Basil and Gregory's Sermons," 420–21.

35. Basil, *Sermon Ps.* 14, cited in Ihssen, "Basil and Gregory's Sermons," 417.

36. Basil, *Sermon* 6.2, cited in Holman, *Hungry Are Dying*, 103.

37. Ibid.

is greed of the most horrible kind, to deny to the starving even what you must soon throw away!"[38]

Similarly, Basil chastised the wealthy for their failure to be generous with the poor. Preaching about the rich young ruler in Matthew 19, Basil largely addressed *Sermon 7* to the wealthy. Asserting that accumulating wealth was an indication of misguided love and ultimately a vain endeavor, Basil reminded them that they were merely stewards of their possessions and not owners.[39] He added, "Consequently, the one who loves his neighbor as himself possesses nothing in excess of his neighbor's. However, you obviously have many possessions . . . clearly your wealth and superabundance indicates a lack of charity."[40] Warning that hoarding wealth would lead to further social problems in Caesarea, Basil invited them to participate in the joy of giving—a sure outcome of their salvation in Christ. In this sense, he commended to them the example of the Good Samaritan and charged them to be good neighbors to the poor and oppressed in Caesarea.[41] In short, for Basil, authentic faith should transform Caesarea's economic system as generosity overcame greed and the rich and poor worshipped together in Christian community.[42]

While much of Basil's prophetic discourse addressed the issues of poverty and hunger, he also confronted the social sin of slavery. Slavery was not a new issue to Asia Minor, as the Goths had attacked the region in the fourth century and taken some Cappadocians captive, including the family of the famous Arian missionary Ulfilas (ca. 310–383).[43] While some parents were abandoning their children to the care of the church during the famine, others were selling their children into slavery. In *Sermon 8*, Basil called parents to repentance for these tragic choices.[44] Elsewhere, arguing that all creatures were subservient to God and not one another, Basil denounced slavery as a human condition.[45] Concurrent with his preach-

---

38. Basil, *Sermon 6.6*, cited in Holman, *Hungry Are Dying*, 103; cf. Holman, "Hungry Body," 349.

39. Daley, "Building a New City," 444–45.

40. Basil, *Sermon 7.1*, cited in Holman, *Hungry Are Dying*, 105.

41. Basil, *Sermon Ps. 14a.3*; also Holman, *Hungry Are Dying*, 105, 109, 112.

42. Basil, *Sermons 332.2, 323.5*; also Rousseau, *Basil*, 178–79.

43. McHugh, "Cappadocia," 214.

44. Holman, *Hungry Are Dying*, 81.

45. Basil, *On the Holy Spirit* 20.51; also Frend, *Rise of Christianity*, 570; and Ramsey, *Beginning to Read the Fathers*, 67.

ing against slavery, he likewise wrote a number of letters condemning this social sin.[46]

Finally, Basil was not opposed to confronting Roman officials in a prophetic manner, especially those with Arian leanings who were putting pressure on the church. Gregory of Nazianzus recorded an exchange between Basil and the Roman Prefect Modestus, who openly challenged Basil for not respecting the Emperor Valens. Basil related that he only followed the teachings of a true Sovereign—the Lord. When Modestus asked if Basil feared him, the following exchange occurred:

> "Fear of what?" said Basil. "How could it affect me? . . . confiscation, banishment, torture, death. Have you no other threat?" said he, "for none of these can reach me. . . . Because . . . a man who has nothing, is beyond the reach of confiscation; unless you demand my tattered rags, and the few books, which are my only possessions. Banishment is impossible for me, who am confined by no limit of place, counting my own neither the land where I now dwell, nor all of that into which I may be hurled. . . . As for tortures, what hold can they have upon one whose body has ceased to be? . . . Death is my benefactor, for it will send me the sooner to God." Amazed at this language, the prefect said, "No one has ever yet spoken thus, and with such boldness, to Modestus." "Why, perhaps," said Basil, "you have not met . . . a bishop . . . where the interests of God are at stake, we care for nothing else, and make these our sole object."[47]

Advocacy for the Poor

Basil went beyond merely preaching about the spiritual and physical needs in Caesarea. He used his position as a bishop to be an advocate for the poor, needy, and suffering in his city. In addition to integrating a monastic and ecclesiastical calling, Basil combined his pastoral office with that of a Roman patron—one endowed with authority and influence to impact society. While patrons were a normal part of the Roman social fabric, in the post-Constantine era, bishops were accorded a level of authority and often functioned as judges and mediators in the court system. In light of Caesarea's needs, Basil did not reject this opportunity to influence political

---

46. Basil, *Letters* 72, 73, 177–78, 273–75, 307.
47. Gregory of Nazianzus, *Oration* 43.48–50 *(NPNF)*.

leaders and even model for the government how to solve important social and economic problems.[48] Sterk writes: "In Basil's capacity as a patron he endeavored to act consistently with his understanding of both monastic vocation and episcopal responsibility [and] attempted to apply the principles of the gospel in confronting the social and political realities of his day, even . . . [using] . . . the tactics of petition and mediation."[49] Peter Brown adds, "Nowhere was the Christian representation of the church's novel role in society more aggressively maintained than in the claim of Christian bishops to act as 'lovers of the poor.'"[50] Through his letters and personal meetings, Basil lobbied to secure tax relief for the poor, tax-exempt status for priests, and tax exemption for his *basileas* ministry, which will be discussed shortly.[51] In addition, he appealed to the wealthy to gain an eternal perspective on material possessions and leave part of their estates to the poor.[52] Despite experiencing conflict with Valens, Basil still managed to secure a donation from the emperor for his ministry to the poor.[53]

Response to Famine

Andrew Dinan correctly notes that Basil's ministry was not limited to preaching and advocacy as "Basil's solicitude for the welfare of his people was manifest in concrete ways."[54] In an extended description, Gregory of Nazianzus remembers Basil's courageous leadership and generosity in response to the famine of 368:

> By his word and advice [Basil] opened the stores of those who possessed them, and so, according to the Scripture, dealt food to the hungry and satisfied the poor with bread. . . . [A]nd in what way? . . . He gathered together the victims of the famine with some who were but slightly recovering from it, men and women, infants,

---

48. Holman, *Hungry Are Dying,* 98; also Rousseau, *Basil,* 170–71; and Sterk, *Renouncing the World,* 66–69.

49. Sterk, *Renouncing the World,* 68–69.

50. Cited in Holman, *Hungry Are Dying,* 18.

51. Basil, *Letters* 88, 104, 110, 303, 308–9, 316–17; 86–87; 142–44; also Sterk, *Renouncing the World,* 67–68; and Rousseau, *Basil,* 142–43, 159.

52. Rousseau, *Basil,* 139; also Frend, *Rise of Christianity,* 569.

53. Gregory of Nazianzus, *Oration* 43.63; also Sterk, *Renouncing the World,* 70; Rousseau, *Basil,* 140; and Holman, *Hungry Are Dying,* 75.

54. Dinan, "Manual Labor," 135.

old men . . . and obtaining contributions of all sorts of food which can relieve famine, set before them basins of soup and such meat as was found preserved among us, on which the poor live. Then, imitating the ministry of Christ, . . . he attended to the bodies and souls of those who needed it, combining personal respect with the supply of their necessity, and so giving them a double relief. Such was our young furnisher of corn, and second Joseph. . . . [But unlike Joseph, Basil's] services were gratuitous and his succor of the famine gained no profit, having only one object, to win kindly feelings by kindly treatment, and to gain by his rations of corn the heavenly blessings.[55]

Basil upheld his conviction for generosity toward the poor and hungry during this period. Again, according to Gregory, Basil liquidated some of his own inherited assets to help meet the needs of the Caesareans. He writes: "[Basil] ungrudgingly spent upon the poor his patrimony even before he was a priest, and most of all in the time of the famine, during which he was a ruler of the church, though still a priest in the rank of presbyters; and afterwards did not hoard even what remained to him."[56] While Gregory of Nyssa (Basil's brother) likened him to Elijah, Gregory of Nazianzus described him as a Joseph for the people of Caesarea. Basil seemed to agree with the latter description. In *Sermon 6*, he interpreted and applied the Joseph narratives from Genesis toward his ministry in Caesarea: "I shall open my barns. I shall be like Joseph in proclaiming the love of my fellow man."[57]

The *Basileas*

A second concrete expression of Basil's ministry to the poor in Caesarea was the establishment of the *basileas* ("new city")—"a complex of buildings constructed at the edge of Caesarea during the early years of Basil's episcopate."[58] Built on land owned by Basil's family or perhaps donated by the emperor, this complex was first called the *basileas* by the fifth-century church historian Sozomen, who wrote: ". . . the *basileas*, the most celebrated

---

55. Gregory of Nazianzus, *Oration* 43.34–36, cited in Holman, *Hungry Are Dying*, 65.

56. Gregory of Nazianzus, *Against Eunomius*, cited in Holman, *Hungry Are Dying*, 65.

57. Basil, *Sermon* 6.2, cited in Holman, *Hungry Are Dying*, 128.

58. Sterk, *Renouncing the World*, 69.

hospice for the poor. It was established by Basil, bishop of Caesarea, from whom it received its name in the beginning, and retains it until today."[59] Though Basil was influenced by others to act on behalf of the poor (his pious family, his sister Macrina, and Eustathius), it seems that the devastation caused by the famine of 368 especially drove him to launch this project.[60]

What were the specific ministries of the *basileas*? First, the complex included a home for the poor. Some of the residents probably included children that had been abandoned by their parents during the famine.[61] Second, the facility had a hospital that cared for the sick. Sterk suggests that some patients suffered from leprosy.[62] Third, the *basileas* offered the poor an opportunity to work and to develop job skills.[63] Fourth, as noted, the complex included storehouses with food supplies administered by the "Joseph" of Caesarea.[64] Finally, with Caesarea being located on a crossroads between Asia Minor, Syria, Armenia, and the Gothic regions, the *basileas* included a guest house for travelers.[65] Basil insisted that his disciples be able to show hospitality to minister to other believers but also as a means to witness to non-Christians. In his *Long Rules*, he wrote:

> Has a guest arrived? If he is a brother . . . he will recognize the fare we provide as properly his own. What he has left at home, he will find with us. Suppose he is weary after his journey. We then provide as much nourishment as is required to relieve his weariness. Is it a secular person who has arrived? Let him learn through actual experience . . . and let him be given a model and pattern of frugal sufficiency in matters of food. . . . In every case, care must be taken for a good table, yet without overstepping the limits of the actual need. This should be our aim in hospitality—that the individual requirements of our guests may be cared for.[66]

---

59. Sozomen, *Ecclesiastical History* 6.34.9 *(NPNF)*.

60. Basil, *Letters* 94, 150, 176; also Daley, "Building a New City," 432; Patitsas, "St. Basil's Philanthropic Program," 269; Sterk, *Renouncing the World*, 40, 69; Dinan, "Manual Labor," 137–38; and Holman, *Hungry Are Dying*, 76.

61. Gregory of Nazianzus, *Oration* 43.35; also Holman, *Hungry Are Dying*, 80.

62. Sterk, *Renouncing the World*, 69.

63. Patitsas, St. Basil's Philanthropic Program," 269; and Holman, *Hungry Are Dying*, 74.

64. Rousseau, *Basil*, 142.

65. Ibid., 133.

66. Basil, *Long Rules* 20 (Unless otherwise noted, all English translations are from *Fathers of the Church*).

For Basil, the *basileas* ministry was perhaps the clearest expression of what it meant to be a monk bishop ministering in the city. His monasticism was characterized by voluntary poverty following the example of John the Baptist (if one has two coats, give the other away), Jesus (sell all you have and give it to the poor), and the early Christians in Acts (selling their goods and sharing everything in common).[67] In his instruction to Christian leaders in *Morals*, he stated, "one who is entrusted with the preaching of the gospel should possess nothing more than is strictly necessary for him."[68]

A coenobitic monk, Basil's ascetic vision was based largely on community. McGuire notes, "Basil is the first monastic writer in the East to be totally convinced that a common life provided the best way of bringing individual men to God."[69] Basil wrote plainly, "I observe that life spent in company with those of the same mind is of greater advantage in many ways."[70] In addition to the monasteries that Basil oversaw in Caesarea, the *basileas* also provided a communal context of spiritual growth for Basil's disciples.[71] Basil expected the monastery to be a community that served others. Distinguishing his monastic vision from those who withdrew into isolation, he simply asked: "Whose feet will you wash? For whom will you care? In comparison with whom will you be the least?"[72] Basil also regarded the community as a key vehicle for mission because, as the body of Christ, they possessed many gifts—far more than what one monk or Christian leader had. Stephen Hildebrand summarizes: "Thus, only the corporate Christians, the members acting as one, can simultaneously visit the sick, for example, welcome the stranger, feed the hungry, clothe the naked, rejoice with the joyful, and weep with the weeping."[73]

Finally, Basil was convinced that an important task of a bishop or Christian leader was caring for the poor. Basil instructed spiritual leaders in his *Morals* that "the preacher of the Word should be compassionate and merciful, especially toward those who are suffering distress of soul" and be

---

67. Basil, *Letter* 150; also Frend, *Rise of Christianity*, 631; and Daley, "Building a New City," 439.

68. Basil, *Morals* 70.27 (Unless otherwise noted, all English translations are from *Fathers of the Church*).

69. McGuire, *Friendship and Community*, 31; cf. Basil, *Letter* 150; also Smither, *Augustine as Mentor*, 56; and Hildebrand, *Basil*, 102, 108, 127–28.

70. Basil, *Long Rules* 7.1, cited in Hildebrand, *Basil*, 127.

71. Basil, *Letter* 150; also Smither, *Augustine as Mentor*, 56.

72. Basil, *Long Rules* 7, cited in Ramsey, *Beginning to Read the Fathers*, 180.

73. Hildebrand, *Basil*, 127.

"solicitous even with regard to the bodily needs of those in our charge."[74] While clergy in Caesarea were quite involved in administering the work of the *basileas*, Basil also encouraged church leaders in Cappadocia and Asia Minor to make ministry to the poor a priority in their churches. Despite some church leaders resisting this admonition at times, evidence suggests that other bishops under Basil's leadership initiated a number of smaller projects for the poor in Cappadocia.[75]

Sterk notes: "for Basil, then, involvement in such a foundation was what committed ascetics as well as bishops ought to be doing. Such activity on the part of monks, bishops, and laity alike made the gospel a living reality in the city."[76] Basil's efforts appeared to be sustainable as the *basileas* facility remained intact and ministry to the poor continued for over a century after his death.[77]

Summary

Basil died at the early age of forty-nine, but he lived a very full life. He was a theologian *par excellence* who also presented a winsome model for Christian leadership. Having discussed the political, theological, and social issues that he faced in fourth-century Caesarea, I have argued that Basil was a missionary monk bishop who was quite engaged with his context. Prioritizing the ministries of preaching and evangelism, he also ministered courageously to the needs of the poor in Caesarea. He read the Joseph narratives in quite a functional manner and found meaningful application for them in his context. Finally, his ministry to the poor was a concrete expression of his monastic and pastoral theologies. He chose a lifestyle of voluntary poverty in community with others and, in turn, this community lived out the gospel in word and deed in Caesarea.

---

74. Basil, *Morals* 70.19–20.

75. Basil, *Letters* 141.2; 142–44; 223.3; also Sterk, *Renouncing the World*, 69–70, 74; Patitsas, "St. Basil's Philanthropic Program," 269, 282; Daley, "Building a New City," 440; and Rousseau, *Basil*, 143, 149.

76. Sterk, *Renouncing the World*, 71.

77. Holman, *Hungry Are Dying*, 75.

CHAPTER 4

Martin of Tours

HAVING CONSIDERED BASIL'S LIFE and work as a missionary monk bishop, let us turn our attention to the first monk bishop in the western church who also demonstrated missionary convictions—Martin of Tours. Because Martin left no writings to the church, gaining an accurate picture of his life and thought is something of a challenge. Fortunately, his life and ministry were captured in the sacred biography *Life of Martin* and in a portion of *Dialogues*, both authored by Sulpicius Severus.[1] While these works do not fully stand up to the scrutiny of modern historiography and are considered questionable by scholars, our aim will be to glean as much as we can to construct an accurate picture of Martin, primarily relying on Severus' *Life*.[2] In this chapter, we will examine Martin's life story, including his conversion and monastic calling. In addition, we will consider the context of ministry in Gaul and his approach to mission.

---

1. In the sixth century, Gregory of Tours (ca. 538–ca. 594) authored *The Miracles of the Bishop St. Martin*, which recounted miracles associated with the Martin following his death. Given the scope of the present chapter, these accounts will not be considered.

2. Ironically, Hyppolyte Delahaye, in his critique of early Christian and medieval hagiography affirmed that Severus' *Life* was one of the more historically reliable accounts because of his direct contact with Martin. In a later chapter in the biography, Severus states his methodology: "At the same time, because already my mind was inflamed with the desire of writing his life, I obtained my information partly from himself, in so far as I could venture to question him, and partly from those who had lived with him, or well knew the facts of the case" (Severus, *Life of Martin* 25. All English translations are from *Nicene Post Nicene Fathers*). Cf. Delahaye, *Legends of the Saints*, 61; also Stancliffe, *St. Martin*, 6, 318–27, 341; and Smither, "'To Emulate and Imitate,'" 151–52.

Soldier, Monk, and Bishop

Martin was born in Sabaria in the province of Pannonia (Hungary) but grew up in Italy. Raised in a Roman pagan family, he apparently developed an interest in Christianity—and even monastic living—as a youth. Because his father was an officer in the Roman army, Martin was compelled to join the military at the age of fifteen.[3] Some five years later, he was converted in a rather dramatic fashion. According to Severus, after sharing part of his coat with a homeless man, he had a vision of Christ radiating himself on that coat. Though the account has been doubted by some scholars, Martin was apparently baptized at this time.[4] After several more years of military service, Martin announced his desire to be a "soldier of Christ," was released from his military obligations, and embraced a monastic lifestyle.[5]

During the mid-350s, Martin probably first traveled to Poitiers to be mentored by Bishop Hilary (ca. 300–ca. 368), who was likely already directing a group of disciples in an ascetic community.[6] Dunn notes, "When Hilary was exiled at the end of 356 for his opposition to Arianism, Martin embarked on a series of wanderings to Hungary, then the Balkans and Milan, finally settling on the island of Gallinara off the Ligurian coast [in northwest Italy]."[7] Here Martin established a monastic community—perhaps an act encouraged by Hilary to oppose Auxentius, the Arian bishop of Milan.[8] According to Severus, Martin encountered much conflict in northern Italy as the majority of church leaders were Arian-leaning in their theology.

Around 360, upon Hilary's return from exile, Martin left Milan and joined his mentor in Poitiers. Hilary had apparently wanted to ordain him as a deacon, but Martin's desire to remain a monk led him to refuse. Hilary did succeed in consecrating Martin to the lesser ecclesiastical post of exorcist perhaps because of Martin's aptitude for confronting the demonic—a characteristic of his mission work—had already been recognized. Hilary allowed Martin to establish a monastery at Ligugé outside of Poitiers in a facility that was likely a converted Roman villa with a church attached to

---

3. Severus, *Life of Martin*, 1.

4. Ibid., 2–3; also McHugh, "Martin of Tours," 724. Stancliffe (*St. Martin*, 343) accepts the account as reliable.

5. Ibid., 4.

6. Stancliffe, *St. Martin*, 22.

7. Dunn, *Emergence of Monasticism*, 62.

8. Ibid.

it.⁹ In some respects, this architecture symbolized Martin's career path as a monk cleric—a life of contemplation and service to the church. Similarly, the choice of Ligugé with its proximity to Poitiers shows that Martin, like Basil, was a monk who cared about the needs of the city and engaged its residents.¹⁰

Severus reported that when Bishop Lidorius' died in 372, the people of Tours pleaded with Martin to become their bishop. When he refused, a leading citizen of Tours lured him to the city on the pretense that his wife was sick and on the verge of dying and required Martin's prayers. When Martin arrived, he was rather forcefully ordained as bishop; a practice not terribly uncommon in the fourth century.¹¹ Accepting his new ministry and carrying it out with great seriousness, Martin also chose to remain a monk and established a monastery at Marmoutier, several miles from Tours in the Loire Valley, where he was again joined by a host of monks. Following the footsteps of Basil, Martin became the first monk bishop in the western church. Severus described the dual nature of his calling:

> He kept up the position of a bishop properly, yet in such a way as not to lay aside the objects and virtues of a monk. Accordingly he made use, for some time, of the cell connected with the church but afterwards, when he felt it impossible to tolerate the disturbance caused by the numbers of those visiting it, he established a monastery for himself about two miles outside the city. This spot was so secret and retired that he enjoyed in it the solitude of a hermit. . . . There were altogether eighty disciples, who were being disciplined after the example of the saintly master.¹²

Dunn correctly notes that Martin took a semi-hermitic approach to the ascetic life, valuing solitude and community. Though Martin did not develop or follow a particular monastic rule, Severus described the values that characterized Martin's community:

> No one there had anything which was called his own; all things were possessed in common. It was not allowed either to buy or to sell anything, as is the custom among most monks. No art was practiced there, except that of transcribers, and even this was assigned to the brethren of younger years, while the elders spent

---

9. Severus, *Life of Martin*, 5–6.
10. Stancliffe, *St. Martin*, 23–24.
11. Severus, *Life of Martin*, 9.
12. Ibid., 10.

their time in prayer. Rarely did any one of them go beyond the cell, unless when they assembled at the place of prayer. They all took their food together, after the hour of fasting was past. No one used wine, except when illness compelled them to do so. Most of them were clothed in garments of camels' hair.[13]

Martin's community renounced individual property and held everything in common. They prayed and fasted individually but took meals together. Despite living near the city of Poitiers and interacting with its inhabitants, the monks remained separate behind the walls at Marmoutier.[14] Manual labor was not a central value, for the church at Tours supported the monastery, though some younger monks copied manuscripts.[15] For Martin, intercultural ministry was likely becoming an increasing part of his monastic labor.

As a monk bishop, Martin also distinguished himself from other Gallic bishops through his modest dress and simple lifestyle. Irvin and Sunquist write, "He did not assume the trappings that were coming to characterize the episcopacy elsewhere in the Roman world in his day. Martin dressed more like a peasant . . . and he lived in the monastery that he founded outside the city rather than in the house set aside for the bishop."[16] A foreigner to Gaul who lacked the formal education of most of the Gallic clergy, Martin did not fit in that well with other church leaders and his choice of attire did not help those connections. On the other hand, his lower social status likely gave him a deeper burden for and affinity with Gaul's poor village populations.[17]

One final aspect worth noting is that Martin's monastery served indirectly as a training center for leaders for the greater Gallic church. In the *Life of Martin*, Severus asked rhetorically, "For what city or church would there be that would not desire to have its priests from among those in the monastery of Martin?"[18] Stancliffe confirms that Bishop Hero of Arles and

---

13. Ibid.

14. See Severus, *Life of Martin* 26 for further insights on Martin's personal ascetic practices.

15. Dunn, *Emergence of Monasticism*, 63; also Stancliffe, *St. Martin*, 26, 37.

16. Irvin and Sunquist, *History of the World Christian Movement*, 225; cf. Dunn, *Emergence of Monasticism*, 62.

17. Stancliffe, *St. Martin*, 350, 352.

18. Severus, *Life of Martin*, 10.

possibly Lazarus of Aix were trained in the monastery at Marmoutier before being set apart to their ministries.[19]

Fourth-Century Gaul

What do we know about the context of fourth-century Gaul? First, there was a great deal of political instability in Gaul during Martin's lifetime. Beginning in the mid-third century, Germanic invaders had already ravaged much of Gaul. Dunn writes, "the frontiers of the Roman Empire began to give way under barbarian pressure and German incursions across the Touraine led to the slaughter of its inhabitants and the destruction or abandonment of many settlements."[20] Stancliffe adds that the city of Tours itself was probably besieged, and by 406, Gaul had been completely overrun by the Germanic tribes.[21] Though Gaul did not fall completely until after Martin's death, the political and social environment in which he served as a bishop and missionary was quite unstable.

Second, Roman paganism dominated the religious context of Martin's service. Despite the fact that Constantine had given peace and favor to the church in the early fourth century, Ramsay MacMullen argues that a pagan worldview and its associated practices remained vibrant through the empire until the eighth century.[22] Since Theodosius did not introduce anti-pagan legislation until the late fourth century, pagan temples and rituals continued to be tolerated during most of Martin's lifetime.[23]

Finally, Martin's ministry was also affected by doctrinal issues within the church. Following the Council of Nicaea of 325, Arian teaching continued to influence many of the western Roman emperors and probably most of the bishops. As shown, Martin stood with Hilary of Poitiers in the battle against Arianism and he probably accepted ordination as bishop at Tours to insure that the church maintained sound doctrine.

---

19. Stancliffe, *St. Martin*, 351.
20. Dunn, *Emergence of Monasticism*, 62.
21. Stancliffe, *St. Martin*, 2–3.
22. See MacMullen, *Christianity & Paganism*.
23. Stancliffe, *St. Martin*, 330.

Approaches to Mission

Given the pagan context of fourth-century Gaul, a large part of Martin's mission focus involved actively confronting paganism. One strategy that Martin employed that might seem strange or even troubling to the modern reader was physically demolishing pagan temples. Prior to Theodosius' legislation around 391–392, Martin's actions were actually illegal; however, this power-encounter approach seemed effective in the Gallic context. Severus recounted one such instance:

> Martin returned to the village; and while the crowds of heathen looked on in perfect quiet as he razed the pagan temple even to the foundations, he also reduced all the altars and images to dust. At this sight the rustics, when they perceived that they had been so astounded and terrified by an intervention of the Divine will, that they might not be found fighting against the bishop, almost all believed in the Lord Jesus. They then began to cry out openly and to confess that the God of Martin ought to be worshiped, and that the idols should be despised, which were not able to help them.[24]

While in some cases, there were violent reactions to Martin's actions, in this account the pagan audience, perceiving that Martin's God was more powerful than their own deities, embraced the gospel. Evaluating Martin's actions missiologically, Irvin and Sunquist posit that Martin was "accommodating forms of missionary outreach that sought to transfer people's allegiances from their traditional local deities to Jesus Christ."[25]

A second approach, ironically related to the first, was Martin's preaching. Severus wrote: "Very frequently, too, when the pagans were addressing him to the effect that he would not overthrow their temples, he so soothed and conciliated the minds of the heathen by his holy discourse that, the light of truth having been revealed to them, they themselves overthrew their own temples."[26] In these instances, Martin did not have to destroy their buildings because, after hearing his message, the Gallic pagans were willing to do it themselves. Stancliffe argues that Martin's destruction of pagan temples was closely linked to his itinerant preaching ministry.[27] Martin was clearly interested in realizing worldview transformation through

---

24. Severus, *Life of Martin*, 14. For other accounts, see *Life of Martin*, 13, 15.
25. Irvin and Sunquist, *History of the World Christian Movement*, 226.
26. Severus, *Life of Martin*, 14.
27. Stancliffe, *St. Martin*, 329.

his preaching and in no way tolerated vestiges of pagan belief or practice among his converts.

A third aspect of Martin's mission was his commitment to sound doctrine. As shown, many of the church leaders in the western church were taken with Arian teaching. Through his preaching and teaching, part of Martin's mission was to cross boundaries of belief—especially heretical teaching—in order to evangelize and purify the church.

A fourth aspect of Martin's work generally related to the miraculous. While many modern historians have rejected Severus' sacred biography of Martin and others accounts because of supernatural claims, Stancliffe rightfully shows that the average fourth-century Christian, including some brilliant church fathers, had no objections to the miraculous in their worldview.[28]

In addition to the accounts related to Martin and destroying temples, Severus also recorded some other power encounters. In one instance, a robber attempted to beat Martin with a hammer, but was supernaturally kept from doing so. This led him to ask Martin about spiritual matters and the robber ended up converting.[29] In another account, Martin intended to cut down a pine tree that was sacred to the local pagan populace. He agreed to place himself in the way of the falling tree. When it fell in another direction, the onlookers perceived God's power and put their faith in Martin's God.[30]

Severus also mentioned a number of instances where Martin cast out demons as part of his mission work.[31] In one example from the *Life of Martin*, Severus described Martin's ministry with a pagan Roman official.

> At the same time the servant of one Tetradius, a man of proconsular rank, having been laid hold of by a demon, was tormented with the most miserable results. Martin, therefore, having been asked to lay his hands on him, ordered the servant to be brought to him; but the evil spirit could, in no way, be brought forth from the cell in which he was: he showed himself so fearful, with ferocious teeth, to those who attempted to draw near. Then Tetradius throws himself at the feet of the saintly man, imploring that he himself would go down to the house in which the possessed of the devil was kept. But Martin then declared that he could not visit the house of an unconverted heathen. For Tetradius, at that time, was

28. Ibid., 205–56; also Smither, *Mission in the Early Church*, 140–45.
29. Severus, *Life of Martin*, 5.
30. Ibid. 13.
31. Ibid., 17–18, 22–24.

still involved in the errors of heathenism. He, therefore, pledges his word that if the demon were driven out of the boy, he would become a Christian. Martin, then, laying his hand upon the boy, cast the evil spirit out of him. On seeing this, Tetradius believed in the Lord Jesus, and immediately became a catechumen, while, not long after, he was baptized.[32]

As shown, Martin's ability to minister to those afflicted by evil spirits was probably the reason why Hilary ordained him to the office of exorcist at Poitier.[33]

Severus' *Life of Martin* also contains a number of accounts of physical healing.[34] Severus wrote: "the gift of accomplishing cures was so largely possessed by Martin, that scarcely any sick person came to him for assistance without being at once restored to health."[35] Some of the healings clearly benefited those who were already Christians; however, in other instances, they accompanied Martin's gospel preaching to pagan audiences. For instance, in his *Dialogues,* Severus recorded the following account:

> As we pass by a certain village . . . an enormous crowd went forth to meet us, consisting entirely of heathen. . . . [Martin] at once began to preach to the heathen the word of God. . . . [W]hile an incredible multitude had surrounded us, a certain woman, whose son had recently died, began to present, with outstretched hands, the lifeless body to the blessed man, saying, "We know that you are a friend of God: restore me my son, who is my only one." . . . Martin perceiving, as he afterwards told us, that he could manifest power, in order to the salvation of those waiting for its display, received the body of the deceased into his own hands; and when, in the sight of all, he had fallen on his knees, and then arose, after his prayer was finished, he restored to its mother the child brought back to life. Then, truly, the whole multitude, raising a shout to heaven, acknowledged Christ as God, and finally began to rush in crowds to the knees of the blessed man, sincerely imploring that he would make them Christians. Nor did he delay to do so. As they were in the middle of the plain, he made them all catechumens, by placing his hand upon the whole of them.[36]

32. Ibid., 17.
33. Stancliffe, *St. Martin,* 345.
34. Severus, *Life of Martin,* 7–8, 16, 18–19.
35. Ibid., 16.
36. Severus, *Dialogues* 2.4 (all English translations are from *Nicene Post Nicene Fathers*).

Stancliffe helpfully concludes, "with Martin, healing miracles are linked closely with evangelism."[37]

One final element of Martin's overall approach to mission was that he apparently involved his monks in the ministry. In two instances in *Life of Martin*, Severus indicated that members of Martin's community accompanied him as he confronted pagans and dismantled pagan temples.[38] Since Marmoutier has already been shown to be a place where church leaders were trained, it seems reasonable that Martin also valued training other monks for mission as he involved them in the work.

Summary

During difficult, volatile times in fourth-century Gaul, Martin defied what it meant to be a bishop and "simply clad in a rough cloak, [he] strode across his diocese, preaching, healing, exorcising and destroying pagan shrines."[39] Based in Tours, Martin's itinerant ministry extended to Chartres, Paris, Trier, Bordeaux, and Vienne and he is rightly remembered as the "great evangelist of Gaul."[40] A semi-hermitic monk who seemed to value involving other monks in the work of ministry, Martin combined the offices of monk and bishop and was a catalyst for Christian mission in the fourth-century western church.

---

37. Stancliffe, *St. Martin*, 162.
38. Ibid., 161.
39. Dunn, *Emergence of Monasticism*, 62.
40. Stancliffe, *St. Martin*, 340.

CHAPTER 5

Patrick of Ireland

EVERY MARCH 17, MILLIONS of Americans wear green and take part in a variety of celebrations in honor of St. Patrick's Day. There is probably no figure from the early church as well known to the modern western world as Patrick, and no person with as many legends associated with his name. It may come as a shock to some modern readers that Patrick was not actually Irish; rather, he was most likely from the Roman province of Britannia (roughly the area of modern England and Wales), but spent much of his adult life as a missionary bishop among the Irish. Thomas O'Loughlin writes, "Patrick was a fifth-century Christian of the Roman Empire, who crossed the sea to an alien land to bring its people Christianity."[1]

Because of the number of legends connected with Patrick and the abundance of unreliable ancient texts making claims about him, gaining an accurate picture of him is no small task. The best sources for knowing about Patrick are actually the ones written by him. Probably published toward the end of his life, Patrick's *Confessions* was written to "vindicate against defamers [probably British and Irish bishops] his missionary calling and career."[2] His other surviving work, *Letter to the Soldiers of Coroticus*, was addressed to the army of a monarch—probably a Pictish apostate Christian—who had brutally murdered and enslaved some of Patrick's disciples.[3] While each work was written for a specific occasion and purpose, both offer us a window of understanding into Patrick's world and his work as a bishop, missionary, and monk.

1. O'Loughlin, *St. Patrick*, 48.
2. McNeill, *Celtic Churches*, 55; cf. O'Loughlin, *Discovering Saint Patrick*, 62.
3. McNeill, *Celtic Churches*, 55; O'Loughlin, *Discovering Saint Patrick*, 36.

In this chapter, I will begin by presenting some background on the Celtic peoples and the early church in Ireland in order to understand Patrick's context for mission. After, I will present Patrick's background and journey to faith and ministry, including his thoughts about and approaches to mission in Ireland. Finally, I will argue that Patrick went about his work as a missionary and bishop while also living as a monk.

Celtic Peoples and Early Irish Christianity

Given the modern fascination with Celtic civilization, it would be good to first ask, who were the Celts? As the Greeks encountered this network of tribal peoples, they referred to them as *keltoi,* meaning "strangers" or "hidden peoples," or *Gallatai* because they inhabited the region of Galatia. Part of this isolation may have been because the Celts were given to warfare and did not mix very well with their neighbors, especially in the pre-Christian period. Because of their geography, the Romans called them *Galli* and Gaul (modern France) was an area occupied by many Celtic tribes.[4] In addition to Gaul, the Celts lived throughout the British Isles including Wales, Ireland, and Scotland. More than shared geography, what unified this group of tribal peoples was a shared language comprising two major dialects: P-Celtic, spoken by the Welsh and Cornish; and Q-Celtic, spoken by the Irish and Scottish.[5] In terms of religion, the pre-Christian Celts adhered to their own form of paganism and worshipped as many as four hundred gods, while also venerating certain animals, sacred places, and sacred dates. A priestly class known as the Druids facilitated their rituals. More than mere religious practitioners, the Druids occupied an important place in Celtic society as "judges, teachers, healers, politicians, and astronomers."[6] It was probably the arrival and acceptance of Christianity that ultimately ended their influence in Celtic religion and society.[7]

The earliest Christian mission among the Celts was very likely Paul's first-century work in Galatia. In the second century, Irenaeus of Lyons devoted a portion of his ministry in Gaul to rural Celtic peoples, and in the

---

4. McNeill, *Celtic Churches*, 1–7; also Olsen, *Christianity and the Celts*, 12.

5. McNeill, *Celtic Churches*, 6; also Olsen, *Christianity and the Celts*, 18; and Freeman, *St. Patrick*, 9–11.

6. Olsen, *Christianity and the Celts*, 28.

7. Ibid., 26–28; also McNeill, *Celtic Churches*, 7–9; and Freeman, *St. Patrick*, 94–105.

third century, seven bishops from Rome were sent to minister in Gaul. As eastern Britain became more Romanized in the fourth century, the Celts migrated toward the western side of the British Isles. During this period, the most significant Christian witnesses to the Celts were captured slaves.[8]

In the fifth century, prior to Patrick's mission to Ireland, a certain Palladius was set apart by the church at Rome to be a missionary bishop to Ireland. Little is known about Palladius except that his focus was probably ministering to established groups of Christians. O'Loughlin argues that these were congregations made up of slaves from outside of Ireland as well as other Irish Christians. During his short tenure in Ireland, Palladius most likely did not engage the larger pagan populous as Patrick did.[9]

Patrick's Life and Conversion

Born (ca. 389) in western Roman Britain, Patrick grew up in a village near the coast called Bannavem Berniae. Ethnically British and a citizen of the Roman Empire, Patrick was born into a family of means: his family owned their own estate and they were part of the local nobility. Patrick was raised as a Christian. His father Calpornius served as a deacon in the church, and his grandfather Potitus was a priest.[10]

When Patrick was sixteen years old, he was captured along with a large number of fellow Britons by a band of Irish raiders and began a six-year journey as a slave.[11] On one hand, Patrick immediately identified with thousands who were enslaved in his day—perhaps as many as a quarter of the world's population.[12] On the other hand, John McNeill muses: "How little did Patrick's barbarous captors guess what they were doing to their country when they hustled into one of their ships amid a throng of bound captives this badly brought up and bewildered teenager."[13]

---

8. Olsen, *Christianity and the Celts*, 30–33, 48; also McNeill, *Celtic Churches*, 10, 14, 50; and O'Loughlin, *Discovering Saint Patrick*, 33.

9. O'Loughlin, *Discovering Saint Patrick*, 37–42; also O'Loughlin, *Saint Patrick*, 16, 31; and McNeill, *Celtic Churches*, 51.

10. Patrick, *Coroticus*, 10; Patrick, *Confessions*, 1; also Olsen, *Christianity and the Celts*, 60; O'Loughlin, *Saint Patrick*, 21; McNeill, *Celtic Churches*, 56; and Freeman, *St. Patrick*, 3.

11. Patrick, *Confessions*, 1.

12. Freeman, *St. Patrick*, 25.

13. McNeill, *Celtic Churches*, 58.

Patrick was raised in a Christian home, but had apparently rejected his family's faith. During his time in captivity, however, he was afforded much time to think about spiritual matters. Spending his days tending flocks of sheep, Patrick struggled a great deal with loneliness, which he attempted to counter with prayer. According to his *Confessions,* he began to rise early for prayer and then spent much of the rest of the day at work in prayer.[14] Within this environment of reflection, Patrick began to embrace the gospel for himself.[15] Freeman notes that while Patrick was growing spiritually during his six-year-long enslavement, he was also receiving valuable intercultural training for future ministry in Ireland: "Even though Patrick scarcely realized it at the time, all his experiences as a slave on an Irish farm were training him for his future career. Every day he picked up more of the language. . . . He became familiar with the customs and gods of the foreign land."[16] Patrick reported that after six years in Irish captivity, he received a vision directing him to escape, board a ship, and return home, where he successfully rejoined his family.[17]

After a few years home, Patrick related that he received new visions—only this time they were telling him to go back to Ireland. In the first of three visions, a man named Victoricus held a bundle of letters and called out with the voice of the Irish, "O holy boy, we beg you to come again and walk among us."[18] Patrick's parents, of course, found it inconceivable that their recently liberated son would go back to the very people who had enslaved him. Later in his life, Patrick interpreted these initial visions in light of his missionary call to the Irish: "The one and only purpose I had in going back to the people from whom I had earlier escaped was the gospel and the promises of God."[19] From one perspective, Patrick had simply followed in the footsteps of his father and grandfather and embraced Christian ministry. From another, he demonstrated the value of being a *peregrinus* (wanderer) on Christian mission who was willing to encounter danger and suffering.[20]

14. Patrick, *Confessions,* 1–2, 16.
15. McNeill, *Celtic Churches,* 58–59; also Olsen, *Christianity and the Celts,* 61.
16. Freeman, *St. Patrick,* 28–29.
17. Patrick, *Confessions,* 17.
18. Ibid. 23 (all English translations are from O'Loughlin, *St. Patrick*); cf. Wilken, *First Thousand Years,* 270.
19. Patrick, *Confessions,* 61.
20. Freeman, *St. Patrick,* 54.

Patrick's Missionary Narrative

Though Patrick responded to the vision and went back to Ireland, his return was not immediate but "after many years had gone by."[21] Traditional sources have claimed that he went to Gaul and studied under the Bishop Germanus of Auxerre; however, it was more likely that he trained for ministry under local clergy in Britain.[22] Tradition further asserts that he arrived in Ireland in 432—a question that has been significantly debated, especially regarding the timetable of Palladius' service in Ireland. Although dating his arrival and life in Ireland is difficult, it is certain that Patrick's was a fifth-century mission.[23] Interestingly, Patrick was set apart, presumably by Pope Celestine, as a missionary bishop. O'Loughlin asserts that unlike the bishops in the fourth and fifth century, who were appointed as organizers of established communities of Christians, Patrick's "missionary work is explicitly aimed at those Irish who are not Christians" and that he saw himself as "the final missionary to Ireland, the one who went to mop up the last pockets of paganism so that Ireland could be wholly Christian."[24]

Patrick's Mission Context

Despite the seventh-century hagiographer Muirchu's claim that Patrick focused his ministry on the northern part of Ireland, his preaching was likely much more widespread.[25] Serving outside of the established church, Patrick was ministering largely within an Irish pagan context. During his time in captivity, Patrick surely observed Irish paganism firsthand, and he also encountered pagan practices on board a ship following his initial escape.[26] While Christians were present in Ireland before Patrick arrived to preach

---

21. Patrick, *Confessions*, 15.

22. For the traditional view see Muirchu, *Life of St. Patrick* 1.6; cf. Olsen, *Christianity and the Celts*, 66. About his training happening in Britain, see O'Loughlin, *Discovering Saint Patrick*, 58 and Freeman, *St. Patrick*, 62–63.

23. O'Loughlin, *Saint Patrick*, 15–19; also O'Loughlin, *Discovering Saint Patrick*, 58–59.

24. O'Loughlin, *Discovering Saint Patrick*, 58–59.

25. McNeill, *Celtic Churches*, 5; also Freeman, *St. Patrick*, 73.

26. Patrick, *Confessions* 18; also Freeman, *St. Patrick*, 36–38; and Robert, *Christian Mission*, 147.

the gospel, he described his life in Ireland as living "among Gentiles, in the midst of barbarian worshippers of idols."[27]

In addition to this religious environment, Patrick also served in a context of hardship and persecution, including threats from pagans. Referring regularly to instances of persecution in his *Confessions,* Patrick added that God gave him grace to preach and also to "put up with the insults from unbelievers . . . [and to endure] many persecutions even including chains."[28] In one instance, he reported that he and some fellow missionaries spent fourteen days in jail because of their work.[29] Patrick's hardships were not always on account of pagans and unbelievers, as he reported being ridiculed by other church leaders who did not appreciate his mission work.[30] Finally, the violence committed by Coroticus' soldiers against Patrick's disciples could be considered Christian-on-Christian violence as the monarch and his men were nominal or perhaps apostate Christians.[31]

Theology of Mission

Let us consider his values and thoughts about mission as a way into grasping his theology of mission. First, visions played an important part in his call to mission. As shown, he responded to visions to escape slavery in Ireland as well as to go back to the Irish as a missionary. In his *Confessions,* largely a defense of his missionary call, Patrick mentioned visions and his favorable response to them on seven different occasions. Summarizing the missionary nature of his dreams, Dana Robert writes: "What made Patrick's calling unique was not that he was called by God through dreams, but that he was called to cross cultures so as to communicate the knowledge of the Christian God."[32]

Second, Patrick believed that the scope of his mission work was the whole world. In *Coroticus,* he wrote of being "predestined to preach the gospel even to the ends of the earth."[33] In one sense, this involved continuing

---

27. Olsen, *Christianity and the Celts,* 66.

28. Patrick, *Confessions,* 37; cf. Patrick, *Confessions,* 46; Olsen, *Christianity and the Celts,* 71; and Freeman, *St. Patrick,* xix, 94.

29. Patrick, *Confessions,* 52; also McNeill, *Celtic Churches,* 65.

30. Patrick, *Confessions,* 47.

31. Olsen, *Christianity and the Celts,* 74; cf. McNeill, *Celtic Churches,* 65.

32. Robert, *Christian Mission,* 148; cf. Freeman, *St. Patrick,* 33, 50, 146.

33. Patrick, *Coroticus,* 6 (all English translations are from O'Loughlin, *St. Patrick*).

the mission that Jesus gave to the apostles. O'Loughlin notes: "[Patrick's] work of evangelization belongs to the final, and most difficult, phase of a process that began with the sending out of the apostles by Christ to the whole world (Matthew), starting with Jerusalem and reaching out to every nation out to the very ends of the earth (Luke/Acts)."[34] Given Ireland's geographic location in the far western end of the known world, Patrick literally saw Ireland as the ends of the earth. In *Confessions,* he wrote of his commitment to reaching those that the Lord had purchased for salvation in the "in the farthest ends of the earth"[35] and of his need to physically go to them.[36] Finally, he saw the Irish mission as part of the bigger picture of "making disciples of all nations" (Matt 28:19-20). Patrick affirmed that he carried out his work among Irish pagans because he had "sworn to [his] God to teach the nations"[37] in the conviction that "believers will come from the whole world."[38] Because the text of Matthew 28:18-20 figured prominently into Patrick's mission thought, Richard Fletcher makes the insightful point that Patrick was probably the earliest Christian leader or missionary to take seriously the task of completing the Lord's "Great Commission."[39]

Third, in addition to the global scope of his ministry, Patrick also believed that he was ministering in the last days. A key recurring text in his writings was Matthew 24:14: "And this gospel of the kingdom will be preached in the whole world as a testimony to all nations, and then the end will come." In *Confessions,* he wrote that he was "in the last days" and involved in such a "holy and wonderful work, imitating those who [were sent to] preach the gospel for testimony to all nations before the end of the world."[40] This eschatological perspective certainly motivated him to proclaim the gospel among the Irish. Freeman adds, "There was simply no reason for God's judgment to be delayed once the Irish had heard the good news. . . . [Patrick] saw it as his mission to spread the Christian message

---

34. O'Loughlin, *Saint Patrick,* 47; cf. O'Loughlin, *Discovering Saint Patrick,* 72-74; and McNeill, *Celtic Churches,* 59.

35. Patrick, *Confessions,* 58.

36. Patrick, *Confessions,* 1, 34, 43; *Coroticus* 9; also McNeill, *Celtic Churches,* 59; Freeman, *St. Patrick,* 123.

37. Patrick, *Coroticus,* 1.

38. Patrick, *Confessions,* 39.

39. Cited in Robert, *Christian Mission,* 150.

40. Patrick, *Confessions,* 34 cited in McNeill, *Celtic Christians,* 59; cf. O'Loughlin, *Saint Patrick,* 2; O'Loughlin, *Discovering Saint Patrick,* 74-77.

to as many Irish souls as possible before it was too late."[41] This future hope probably also helped him to endure the hardship and suffering he encountered in ministry. O'Loughlin notes that Patrick reflected deeply on Matthew 10:23 and applied it to his context: that he should continue preaching, flee to neighboring towns when needed, and complete the task in expectation of the Lord's return.[42]

A final key element of Patrick's missionary thought was that he saw himself as a stranger in a foreign land in Ireland. His words in *Coroticus* captured a sentiment repeated in his writings: "I live as an alien among the barbarians and as a wanderer for the sake of the love of God."[43] Given Patrick's experience of being taken from his home as a slave and then returning to Ireland of his own accord, his feelings of being a stranger living in another culture among non-believers made much sense. Though he had spent six years learning the Irish culture and language, part of the missionary reality was feeling like an outsider. While painful in one sense, Patrick also seemed to yearn for this status of being a "wanderer"—a precursor to the *peregrinus* value that characterized much of the Celtic monastic missionary story in the centuries that followed.

Approaches to Mission

Given these underlying values, how did Patrick approach mission in Ireland? First, Patrick began new ministry work in a given area by first approaching tribal or political leaders. Robert Wilken asserts, "In Ireland the basic social unit was a tribe or clan under a king without any fixed territory. . . . [B]y making alliances with the local dynasties Patrick was able to advance the Christian mission."[44] Part of working within this social structure involved offering gifts to local leaders, especially to gain safe passage through the area.[45] Freeman adds that "Patrick would have first visited the local king and sought his permission to work with the Chris-

---

41. Freeman, *St. Patrick*, 125.

42. O'Loughlin, *Discovering Saint Patrick*, 79. The complete text of Matthew 23:10 reads: "When they persecute you in one town, flee to the next, for truly, I say to you, you will not have gone through all the towns of Israel before the Son of Man comes" (ESV).

43. Patrick, *Coroticus*, 1; cf. Patrick, *Confessions* 1, 9, 12, 23, 43, 48; O'Loughlin, *Saint Patrick*, 36–40; and O'Loughlin, *Discovering Saint Patrick*, 65–68.

44. Wilken, *First Thousand Years*, 271.

45. Patrick, *Confessions*, 52–53.

tians within the tribal borders—a request accompanied by generous gifts of silver and gold and promises of more to come."[46] As Patrick continued to mix with such leaders and build relationships, some leaders embraced the gospel themselves, which Freeman adds "would have made Patrick's work immeasurably easier."[47] Patrick also recruited the sons of some kings to travel with him as guides and mediators on potentially treacherous journeys. While the modern reader might conclude that Patrick's mission was advanced through Christendom or political power, Patrick's actions actually reveal that he was serving in contexts of violence and he understood how to navigate the social and power structures of fifth-century Ireland in order to preach the gospel.[48]

Second, as Matthew 28:18–20, Mark 16:15, and Matthew 24:14 ("make disciples," "proclaim the gospel," "gospel . . . will be proclaimed") were central texts in his mission thinking, itinerant preaching was a key part of Patrick's ministry. In his *Confessions*, he declared he had "travelled everywhere" to preach and baptize and that "we are now witnesses to the fact that the gospel has been preached out to beyond where anyone lives."[49] Building on Jesus' promise that his disciples would be "fishers of men" (Matt 4:19), Patrick added an Irish spin to his evangelistic vocation and referred to himself as a "hunter" of men.[50] The fruit of his preaching included "many peoples" being "reborn" and also new local church leaders set apart for ministry.[51]

Third, though Patrick's evangelistic sermons have not survived, we know something about the content of his preaching because his evangelism was organically related to catechesis—a thorough period of instruction prior to baptism—and baptism itself. O'Loughlin points out that the confession of faith in the opening paragraphs of Patrick's *Confessions*, which surely informed his catechesis, was based on a creed that greatly resembled that of Nicaea.[52] A hunter of men in Ireland, Patrick described the fruit of his ministry: "many thousands, my brothers and sisters, sons

---

46. Freeman, *St. Patrick*, 91.

47. Ibid., 92.

48. Robert, *Christian Mission*, 153.

49. Patrick, *Confessions* 51, 34; cf. O'Loughlin, *Discovering Saint Patrick*, 60; and O'Loughlin, *Saint Patrick*, 45.

50. Patrick, *Confessions*, 6; cf. Robert, *Christian Mission*, 150, 154.

51. Patrick, *Confessions*, 38.

52. Ibid., 4; also O'Loughlin, *Saint Patrick*, 54–55.

and daughters, I have baptized in the Lord."[53] Patrick further rejoiced that new church leaders had been raised up who shared those values—"clergy everywhere to baptize and preach to a people who are in want and need."[54] Patrick's commitment to catechesis and baptism were also evident in the letter to Coroticus' soldiers as he mourned the deaths of new disciples: "the anointed neophytes—still wearing their white baptismal garb and with the fragrance of the chrism on their foreheads still about them."[55] In sum, Patrick's mission work was church-centered as new believers were instructed according to a creed that resembled Nicene confession, they were baptized, and they became a part of the church. Like the church fathers of the fifth century, Patrick could not have conceived of an unbaptized Christian or a church-less Christianity.

Fourth, Patrick's preaching also addressed the social sin of slavery. Having personally endured this indignity, his letter to Coroticus' men was prompted by the enslavement of some of his disciples. Appealing to his own authority as a bishop and condemning Coroticus' actions, Patrick demanded that the captured believers be freed. Despite being a foreigner himself, Patrick identified with the Irish and denounced slavery as a clear violation of human rights.[56]

Fifth, although Patrick denounced the injustice of slavery, he acknowledged that suffering and persecution were an expected part of mission in Ireland. Despite the hardship that he already endured, including imprisonment and the uncertainty of dangerous roads, he continued to preach and baptize. Though denouncing the actions of Coroticus and his men, Patrick praised the faith of the martyrs who lost their lives: "still thanks be to God, it is as faithful baptized people that you have left this world to go to Paradise . . . you will reign with the apostles, the prophets, and martyrs and take possession of the eternal kingdom."[57]

Finally, in Patrick's approach to mission, he was committed to working with ministry teams. This point goes without saying because the sheer breadth of his ministry made it impossible for him to do it alone. In his *Confessions*, Patrick referred to assistants who were apparently serving with

---

53. Patrick, *Confessions*, 14; also ibid., 50–51.
54. Ibid., 40.
55. Patrick, *Coroticus*, 3; cf. ibid., 19.
56. Freeman, *St. Patrick*, 134–37; also Robert, *Christian Mission*, 156.
57. Patrick, *Coroticus*, 17–18.

him in ministry and spent two weeks in prison with him.[58] While Patrick did not mention them, the Annals of Ulster of 439 recorded that three additional bishops were set apart to serve with Patrick.[59] Finally, as noted, Patrick valued setting apart new church leaders who surely became part of Patrick's network of co-laborers in Ireland.

Though Muirchu and other sources made claims about Patrick's missionary strategies and their outcomes, they have not been consulted for their lack of credibility. Reliable primary sources about Patrick's work are limited at best, but there is enough to describe him as a "warm-hearted, alert, zealous, diligent, and courageous biblical preacher, and the faithful bishop intensely conscious of his unique mission and pastoral responsibility."[60]

Was Patrick a Monk?

Since this book is concerned with the work of missionary monks, it would be good to establish that Patrick was in fact a monk. In his survey of Christian history, Mark Noll clearly identifies Patrick as a monk; however, scholars such as Philip Freeman are more tentative and argue that just because Patrick had ascetic tendencies, that did not necessarily make him a monk.[61] Also, the most reliable sources about Patrick's life do not explicitly claim that he was a monk. That said, let us consider several pieces of evidence that suggest that Patrick was at least a monk of some sort.

First, Patrick demonstrated monastic values throughout his entire life. Once converted to the gospel during captivity in Ireland, his practice of rising early for prayer and then praying as many as a hundred times a day while engaged in manual (albeit forced) labor was quite ascetic in nature. Later, in *Coroticus*, he effectively argued for a Christian faith in which there was no dichotomy between belief and action—a view of the Christian life that was ascetic and that shaped a developing Irish monasticism.[62] This approach seems best captured in the "Hymn to St. Patrick" attributed to Patrick's fifth-century colleague Secundius:

> Out of the love of God he guards his chaste flesh

---

58. Patrick, *Confessions*, 37.
59. McNeill, *Celtic Churches*, 66.
60. Ibid., 67.
61. Mark Noll, *Turning Points*, 79; also Freeman, *St. Patrick*, 117.
62. O'Loughlin, *Saint Patrick*, 92; also Olsen, *Christianity and the Celts*, 76.

> that flesh which he prepares to be a temple of the Holy Spirit
>
> by whom he is constantly possessed with pure actions
>
> which he offers to the Lord as an acceptable and living sacrifice.[63]

Patrick showed further evidence of pursuing a monastic calling by praising the ascetic life and through serving as a monk bishop. O'Loughlin argues: "the fact that Patrick mentions 'monks and virgins' (*Confessio* 41; *Epistola* 12), that he praises women who have remained virgins (*Confessio* 42), and his use of the phrase 'the religious chastity which I have chosen for Christ' (*Confessio* 44), all incline me to think that Patrick was one of those fifth-century clerics who believed that a perfect minister of grace would be celibate."[64] McNeill adds that while growing up and during his ministry training prior to returning to Ireland, he was very likely exposed to the monk bishop examples of Martin of Tours and Ninian (ca. 360–ca. 432) and that these models shaped Patrick's vision of the episcopate.[65]

The most compelling evidence for Patrick's monastic leanings were the outcomes of his mission work. He celebrated the fact that many of his converts adopted ascetic lifestyles. Interestingly, this included many "Irish leaders' sons and daughters . . . seen to become the monks and virgins of Christ."[66] Freeman notes that as young people from prominent families were embracing ascetic lifestyles, there was a strong negative reaction from their families.[67] McNeill adds that when Patrick planted new churches around Ireland that he also "formed [ascetic] groups under vows."[68] Irvin and Sunquist assert that he deliberately "sought to establish monasteries in the regions of his missionary labors."[69] In short, the reason that Patrick celebrated these monastic commitments for his converts was because he had already adopted this way of living for himself.

---

63. Cited in O'Loughlin, *Discovering Saint Patrick*, 188.
64. O'Loughlin, *Discovering Saint Patrick*, 50.
65. McNeill, *Celtic Churches*, 69.
66. Patrick, *Confessions*, 41; also Patrick, *Coroticus* 2, 12; cf. McNeill, *Celtic Churches*, 65; Olsen, *Christianity and the Celts*, 76; and Dunn, *Emergence of Monasticism*, 156. O'Loughlin (*Saint Patrick*, 77) notes that when Patrick uses the term "virgin" in *Confessions* 41, it most likely refers to a type of nun.
67. Freeman, *St. Patrick*, 113–16.
68. McNeill, *Celtic Churches*, 69.
69. Irvin and Sunquist, *History of the World Christian Movement*, 236.

Patrick's monastic convictions also influenced the leadership structure of the developing Irish church. As there were no towns to speak of in Ireland prior to Patrick's mission, the monasteries filled that void and became the first towns. While the Irish church had bishops, monastic abbots were the primary leaders. This monastic form of church polity made the Irish church distinct from the broader church in the world and it eventually led to conflict between the Celtic and Roman churches.[70]

Despite the fact that the most reliable sources about Patrick are limited and they do not explicitly claim that he was a monk, the evidence presented shows that he practiced an early form of ascetic renunciation and living.[71] This was a way of life that he advocated for his disciples and that they embraced on a significant level and that shaped Irish Christianity for centuries to come.

Summary

Born into a family of privilege in Roman Britain, Patrick was an ex-slave who became a bishop. His life and journey were characterized by a missionary call and commitment to the very people who had mistreated him. In Patrick, we observe both a bishop set apart for the purpose of mission, and a type of monk who embraced a life of prayer, service, hardship, and leading others toward monastic living. Irvin and Sunquist correctly note: "The end result was a network of missionary monasteries under Patrick's direction, where students were learning Latin, studying the Scriptures, and working among the local population."[72] In terms of his lasting legacy, McNeill adds that the "life of the monasteries offered an outlet to native talent and energy" toward "missionary adventure by which Ireland was to make its great medieval contribution to the Christian West."[73] In the following chapter, we will continue to explore Patrick's legacy and the work of Celtic missionary monks.

---

70. McNeill, *Celtic Churches*, 69–70.
71. Dunn, *Emergence of Monasticism*, 143.
72. Irvin and Sunquist, *History of the World Christian Movement*, 237.
73. McNeill, *Celtic Churches*, 70–71.

CHAPTER 6

Celtic Monks

MODERN INTEREST IN CELTIC Christianity and spirituality has at times turned into a fascination that is quite disconnected from reliable historical accounts. While careful historical work must continue to be done, one piece of Celtic Christian history that merits further exploration is its contribution to medieval Christian mission. Continuing the legacy of Patrick, Celtic missionary monks moved about Europe between the sixth and ninth centuries with this wandering (*peregrinus*) spirit and facilitated one of the most remarkable missionary movements in the region. In this chapter, we will probe more into this movement by exploring three representative examples of Celtic missionary monks—Columba (520–597), Aiden (d. 651), and Columban (543–615)—providing a brief biographical sketch of each of these men, describing their context of ministry, as well as their approaches to mission.

Columba

Columba was born into a wealthy family and descended from Irish royalty. Like many wealthy children in his day, he was educated by monks in a monastery. However, unlike most of his peers, he wound up embracing a monastic calling for his own life and was given the name Colum Cille ("dove of the church") because of his love for the Psalms and commitment to the church. During his monastic journey, he was mentored by a number of abbots, particularly Finnian, who served as leader of the community at Clonard. After the Clonard monastery was abandoned in 543, Columba founded a community at Ulster and then later started monasteries in

Durrow and Kells—evidence of his ability to attract monks and lead monastic communities in Ireland.[1]

Iona

Around 560, Columba's monastic itinerary took a decidedly different turn as he was expelled from Ireland. One account claimed that he clashed with Finnian over a manuscript that he (Columba) had allegedly copied, which got him expelled from the monastery. Another account stated that, following conflict with his relative King Diarmat of Tara, he rallied his clan and apparently killed more than three thousand of Diarmat's men. Columba was exiled from Ireland and, as an act of penance, was ordered to convert as many people as he had killed to the gospel.[2] Regardless of the actual reason for his departure, McNeill notes that this became an opportunity for Columba to become a *peregrinus* and "devote his life to a mission beyond the shores of Ireland."[3] Initially, he traveled to the Irish kingdom of Dalriada around 563 and started a monastery on the Inner Hebrides island of Hinba.[4] Columba's missionary work began in earnest around 565 when he made contact with the Pictish King Brute. Bede recorded that Columba "came to Britain to preach the word of God to the kingdoms of the northern Picts.... Columba came to Britain when Bridius [Brute]..., a most powerful king, had been ruling over them for over eight years. Columba turned them to the faith of Christ by his words and example and so received the island of Iona from them in order to establish a monastery there."[5] Bede's claim that King Brute gave Columba and his monks the island on which to build a monastery and establish a base for their ministry is quite plausible. In fact, Columba was not even the first monk to live at Iona, as Oran (d. 549) and other monks had previously resided on the island.[6]

The tiny island itself measured just three miles long and a half-mile wide and contained two thousand acres of land—only 500 of which could

1. McNeill, *Celtic Churches*, 87–88, also Olsen, *Christianity and the Celts*, 105.

2. Olsen, *Christianity and the Celts*, 103–6; also Snyder and Tabbernee, "Western Provinces," 467.

3. McNeill, *Celtic Churches*, 90.

4. Bede, *Ecclesiastical History* (all English from Bede are from McClure and Collins), 386, n. 115.

5. Ibid., 3.4.

6. McNeill, *Celtic Churches*, 91–92.

be farmed.[7] In terms of structures, the monks lived in huts and the other buildings included "a refectory with a kitchen; a scriptorium with a library; a guesthouse (*hospitium*) for the use of surprisingly numerous visitors from near and far; a smithy, a kiln, a mill, and two barns; and a small church."[8] All of this was surrounded by a protective wall. As interest in Columba's community increased, particularly from Christians from nearby Ireland, it became necessary to cap membership in the monastery at 150 persons.[9] The size of the island and capacity of its structures probably drove these constraints.

Though Bede asserted that Columba and his monks observed a monastic rule, there is no evidence that Columba developed his own rule. Rather, given the semi-hermitic tendencies of the Iona community, Columba likely adopted practices inherited from Syrian and Egyptian ascetic movements. Also, Columba's community was surely influenced by Patrick's monastic vision, which had probably been shaped to some degree by Martin of Tours.[10] The Iona monks slept in individual cells but spent much of the day in communal worship, work, and meals. On Wednesdays and Fridays, the community fasted, while Saturday was set aside for rest. Older monks were responsible for leading liturgical assemblies and copying books while other brothers supported the material needs of the community through fishing and farming, which included tending to livestock in the *machair* (grassy field) on the island. Younger monks, including those in training, studied and performed other tasks to help the community.[11] Of course, as we will show, the community was involved in the work of evangelism and catechesis among the Pictish peoples.

Context and Approach to Mission

Iona's geographic location put Columba and his monks in close contact with two distinct peoples in the region—the Dalriada and the Picts. The Dalriada were an already evangelized Celtic people who had moved into the region of western Scotland and had largely controlled the Pictish people

---

7. Olsen, *Christianity and the Celts*, 108.

8. McNeill, *Celtic Churches*, 92.

9. Olsen, *Christianity and the Celts*, 108; also McNeill, *Celtic Churches*, 92.

10. Bede, *Ecclesiastical History*, 3.4; also McNeill, *Celtic Churches*, 85; and Mayr-Harting, *Coming of Christianity*, 78–93.

11. McNeill, *Celtic Churches*, 92–94.

until the reign of King Brute.[12] McNeill writes that Brute had "effectively stopped the expansion of the Irish kingdom in Scotland but also had regained some territory on its northern frontier."[13] Because of the history of conflict between the Dalriada and Picts, Columba's cultural affinity with the Dalriada certainly made ministry to the Picts a potentially dangerous endeavor for him. On the other hand, Olsen correctly notes that Iona's location made it an "almost a perfect place for launching an evangelistic mission to the Picts."[14]

Who were the Picts? McClure and Collins describe them as "a preliterate society composed of Celtic and pre-Celtic elements . . . the indigenous inhabitants of most of northern and central Scotland in the Roman and post-Roman periods."[15] Cummins adds that they were "the first British nation to emerge from the tribal societies. . . . [F]rom the fourth to the ninth century, they flourished and were the dominant power in the north [of Britain]."[16] The Picts were comprised of northern and southern clans. While the southern group was evangelized in part by Ninian in the fourth and fifth centuries, Columba's ministry was focused on the northern Picts, who had remained pagan.[17] As we will discuss further, the Picts were quite famous for their artistic innovations, which included silver work, book art, and most notably stone monuments.

Following in the footsteps of Patrick, one of Columba's initial mission strategies involved approaching leaders, sometimes ministering to them, but also receiving their favor to proclaim the gospel among their subjects. As we have seen, Columba's first contact with the Picts came when he called on King Brute, who was himself converted, but also gave Iona to the abbot as a physical base for monastic living and for mission among the Pictish peoples. Although not as celebrated as his work among the Picts, Columba also stayed in contact with the kings of Dalriada and ministered to them as well.[18] Columba was certainly more comfortable in the political realm than other monks of his day. McNeill notes that "by his royal lineage and his superior personal gifts . . . [Columba] . . . was well qualified for the

12. Ibid., 94; also Olsen, *Christianity and the Celts*, 108.
13. McNeill, *Celtic Churches*, 91.
14. Olsen, *Christianity and the Celts*, 108.
15. McClure and Collins editorial remarks in Bede, *Ecclesiastical History*, 386.
16. Cummins, *Age of the Picts*, 1.
17. Smither, *Mission in the Early Church*, 118.
18. Olsen, *Christianity and the Celts*, 113–14.

political aspects of his role."[19] Indeed, despite the physical isolation at Iona, Columba did not shy away from influencing political issues in Scotland and Ireland. In addition, his biographer Adomnan wrote that on one occasion he prayed openly for a certain Aiden to become king.[20] While Columba's political savvy has been noted, his motivation for making these connections seemed to be spiritually driven.

A second observable approach in Columba's mission work was preaching. In one instance, Adomnan remembered Columba preaching to an old Pictish captain on the island of Skye who received the gospel and was baptized just prior to his death.[21] In the narrative of Columba's visit to Brute, Bede recounted that "Columba turned them to the faith of Christ by his words," a clear reference to his preaching.[22] Bede also added that Columba's preaching was integrated with a holy example—a quality of monastic mission work that will continue to be observed through the medieval period.[23]

Columba's preaching was also accompanied by power encounters (confronting demons and evil spirits) as well as healing. In one account, Adomnan told of a certain well that was inhabited by a demonic presence. Despite the fact that those who touched or drank the water became sick with leprosy, blindness, or other ailments, the well became a center for pagan devotion. Adomnan wrote:

> When St. Columba learned of this, he made his way fearlessly to the well. The wizards, whom he had often driven away in confusion and defeat, saw what he was doing and were glad, for they expected that he too should suffer the effects of touching the harmful water. The saint first raised his hands and called on the name of Christ before washing his hands and feet. Then he and his companions drank from the water that he had blessed.[24]

---

19. McNeill, *Celtic Churches*, 90.
20. Adomnan, *Life of St. Columba* 1.8; 3.5.
21. Ibid. 1.33; and McNeill, *Celtic Churches*, 95.
22. Bede, *Ecclesiastical History*, 3.4.
23. Mayr-Harting (*Coming of Christianity*, 43–44) argues that one of Bede's primary aims in *Ecclesiastical History* is to show concrete examples of faith, including those of monks and missionaries.
24. Adomnan, *Life of Columba* 2.11 (all translations of *Life of Columba* are from Sharpe).

Adomnan added, "Since that day, the demons have kept away from the well. Instead, far from harming anyone, after the saint had blessed it and washed in it, many ailments among the local people were cured by that well."[25] In this report, we observe an interesting combination of both power encounter and healing as demons were cast out of the well and the Picts were no longer made sick by the water.

In another account of healing, Adomnan noted that following the conversion of a Pictish man and his family, his son fell sick and died. As pagan religious leaders were mocking the family, Columba was called to the home. Adomnan wrote:

> Seeing their great distress, St. Columba comforted [the family] and assured them that they should not in any way doubt that God is almighty. . . . Having gone inside, St. Columba immediately knelt and, with tears streaming down his face, prayed to Christ the Lord. After these prayers on bended knee, he stood up and turned his gaze to the dead boy, saying: "In the name of the Lord Jesus Christ, wake up again and stand upon thy feet." At the saint's glorious word, the soul returned to the body, and the boy that was dead opened his eyes and lived again. . . . He gave the boy, now restored to life, back to his parents, and a great shout went up from the crowd.[26]

Columba's biographer concluded by noting that this power encounter, marked by evangelical proclamation, resulted in more Pictish people embracing the gospel: "Mourning gave way to celebration and the God of the Christians was glorified."[27]

A final aspect of Columba's mission practice was training other missionary monks. Bede reported that out of the Iona community "sprang very many monasteries which were established by his disciples in Britain and Ireland."[28] Like other monastic communities, the Iona monastery was a center of spiritual discipline and learning centered on prayer, worship, and Scripture memory, as well as studies in theology and other disciplines. As these monastic values were transferred to newly-established communities,

---

25. Ibid.
26. Ibid. 2.32.
27. Ibid.
28. Bede, *Ecclesiastical History*, 3.4.

such as Lindisfarne and others, conviction for cross-cultural mission was passed on as well.[29]

Iona Monks' Visual and Oral Strategies

Though the historical record of Columba and his community's mission work is limited, scholars such as McNeill believe that much of the evangelization of the northern and western Scottish islands was accomplished through the monks of Iona.[30] One final approach to mission that was perhaps initiated by Columba but continued through the ongoing mission work of the Iona monks was engaging Pictish art forms to communicate the gospel and teach Scripture through visual and oral media.

For years, art historians have been intrigued by the Pictish contribution to Insular Art, the predominant style of art in the British Isles from ca. 600–900. While also known for their book art, the Picts were especially adept at metal work and stone art. Employing many symbols and as many as fifty different animal figures, the Picts constructed gravestones as well as monuments to narrate their history, including things like military victories.[31] Henderson and Henderson have grouped Pictish stone art into three periods or classes that also coincide with their spiritual history. They argue that the Class I artifacts belong to the "pre-conversion" or pre-Christian period because of their "pagan symbolism."[32] In the Class II period, the primary goal of Pictish stone art was to represent the cross, which the Hendersons regard as "a consequence of [their] conversion." In fact, they argue that in this period, the primary function of Insular sculpture in greater Britain was "to display the cross publicly."[33] Finally, Class III stone art contained images of the cross that were completely free of pagan images.[34]

While the three periods of stone art show evidence that the Picts accepted Christianity and were apparently growing in their devotion to it, there is also evidence that Columba and his missionary band were deliberate in using this art form to communicate the gospel. The Hendersons argue that the cross-marked stone "originated, without a doubt, in Irish

29. McNeill, *Celtic Churches*, 123.
30. Ibid., 97.
31. Henderson and Henderson, *Art of the Picts*, 125–27, 134–35.
32. Ibid., 10.
33. Ibid., 28.
34. Ibid., 10.

missionary work among the Picts in the sixth and seventh centuries. . . . [T]he conformity in every respect with the cross-marked stones on Iona, and in the West of Scotland generally, is in itself evidence for the period at which Christianity began, literally, to make its mark on Pictland."[35] Simply put, Insular stone crosses communicated the essence of the gospel—the death, burial, and resurrection of Christ. The Hendersons add:

> [W]hen the first Irish or British missionaries introduced to the Picts the idea of carving a cross on a stone they will also have explained how the Christian symbol could function in a Christian society. It would primarily be as the embodiment of the central belief of the church that Christ's sufferings on the cross and his subsequent resurrection gave mankind the hope of eternal life. The cross was the basic aid for instruction and devotion.[36]

In short, Columba and his monks used this key text of Pictish culture, not only to communicate the essence of the gospel, but also to offer the Pictish church a visual catechism as it instructed new believers.

As these initial stone crosses aided the monks in communicating the gospel through a medium familiar to the Picts, over time other crosses were constructed that communicated more of the overall story of Scripture. One example is St. Martin's cross, a large stonework cross built between 750 and 800 at Iona, which still stands there today. At the center of the cross, the birth of Christ is depicted with Mary holding the baby Jesus. Continuing down the cross appear the stories of Daniel in the lions' den, Abraham raising his sword to sacrifice Isaac, David fighting Goliath, and David playing his harp. The latter image seems especially contextual with David joined by another musician playing triple pipes. In short, in viewing St. Martin's cross, Pictish visitors to Iona could contemplate the meaning of the cross and also engage in a visual Bible study.[37]

The gospel was further communicated through one of the most famous artifacts of Insular Art, the Book of Kells, which was developed at Iona around 800. Though it only included the four Latin Gospels, a mix of both Old and Vulgate Latin, the work was much longer because of its

---

35. Ibid., 159.

36. Ibid., 161.

37. Ritchie, *Iona Abbey and Nunnery*, 9; also Snyder and Tabernee, "Western Provinces," 472–73.

beautiful calligraphy and many pages of colorful illustrations, especially those relating New Testament stories.[38]

Let us consider how the Book of Kells was influenced by Pictish art and, in turn, how it became a significant means of clarifying the gospel for the Picts. First, while it was a book, the style of art in the Book of Kells greatly resembled the features of Pictish stone art. The many crosses displayed throughout the book look like the crosses at Iona and around the Pictish region. According to Meehan, the function of the crosses was to offer the reader a regular reminder of the death, burial, and resurrection of Christ.[39] Second, the Book of Kells is rich in animal imagery, including snakes, birds, and lions, which also resemble the animals used in pre-Christian Pictish art. These are especially important for conveying the person and work of Christ. Depicted as a human being at his birth, Christ is rendered as a calf in his death, as a snake shedding skin in the process of his resurrection, and as a lion in the resurrection. He is likewise presented as a peacock because of his perfect, authentic flesh and later as a fish because of having gone through the waters of baptism. The last image was probably particularly meaningful to those near the island of Iona where fishing was still a way of life.[40] The human depictions of Christ were also very contextual as he was rendered "blond, youthful, and radiant"; that is, he looked very Pictish and Irish in the pages of the Book of Kells.[41]

It should be remembered that the Book of Kells was forged in a liturgical and catechetical context. Though small and portable enough to be carried on mission trips through the Pictish areas, the Book of Kells probably stayed at Iona for the most part. However, since there were many visitors who came to the island, including those who participated in the liturgical assemblies, the visual themes conveyed in the books (the person and work of Christ, the cross, as well as other Eucharistic imagery) served to instruct new believers.[42] In turn, these Bible stories and their truths traveled throughout the Scottish highlands in a manner that was meaningful and relevant to Pictish culture and their visual and oral memory. Obviously, one of the reasons the Book of Kells was effective in this way was because it was an excellent and beautiful work of art. In 1185, Giraldus Cambrinsus com-

---

38. Meehan, *Book of Kells*, 78.
39. Ibid., 30–33.
40. Ibid., 41, 50–65.
41. Ibid., 50.
42. Adomnan spoke of visitors to the island (*Life of Columba* 1.4, 25–27, 30, 32).

mented to that end: "if you take the trouble to look closely, and penetrate your eyes to the secrets of the artistry, you will notice such intricacies, so delicate and so subtle, so close together, and well-knitted, so involved and bound together, and so fresh still in their colorings that you will not hesitate to declare that all these things must have been the work, not of men, but of angels."[43]

In short, the influence of Pictish stone and book art is quite apparent when we study the symbols of Pictish Christianity, particularly artifacts such as St. Martin's cross and the Book of Kells. Further, because Columba and the generations of Ionan monks that followed embraced these art forms, it seems evident that they were being deliberately contextual in their mission strategy to convey the gospel through the building material of local Pictish culture.

Aiden

Aiden was a member of the monastery at Iona in the early seventh century after Columba passed away. Around 635, King Oswald of Northumbria returned from exile to reclaim his throne. Having spent nearly twenty years in exile at Iona where he was converted, the restored king was quite interested in having Christian missionaries come to Northumbria to teach his people.[44] Responding to the king's invitation, the monks at Iona "sent him Bishop Aiden, a man of outstanding gentleness, devotion, and moderation who had a zeal for God."[45] Not unlike Columba's experience with King Brute and Iona, Bede recorded that upon Aiden's arrival, "the king gave him a place for his episcopal see on the island of Lindisfarne," which was located off the Northumbrian coast near the royal castle of Bamburgh.[46] Though Bede referred to Aiden as a bishop, Aiden probably saw himself more as a monk teacher missionary. Mayr-Harting asserts that Aiden was "a wandering missionary bishop (an *episcopus vagans*) and Lindisfarne was merely his monastic center."[47]

Aiden's context for ministry was rather turbulent, as evidenced by Oswald's political struggle to regain his throne. Later, the king was killed in

43. Cited in Meehan, *Book of Kells*, 89.
44. McNeill, *Celtic Churches*, 104–5.
45. Bede, *Ecclesiastical History*, 3.3.
46. Ibid.
47. Mayr-Harting, *Coming of Christianity*, 94–95.

battle against the pagan King Penda of Mercia. Despite continued missionary work, this event resulted in an increase of Germanic pagan influences in the region.[48]

Approaches to Mission

Given this brief background, what were Aiden's strategies for mission in Northumbria? First, Aiden went beyond merely approaching political leaders to receive favor to minister; rather, he collaborated with Oswald in evangelizing the Northumbrians. As noted, the initiative for the mission work came from the English king. Bede reported that King Oswald "humbly and gladly listened to . . . [Aiden's] . . . admonitions in all matters, diligently seeking to build up and extend the church of Christ in his kingdom."[49] More specifically, it appears that Oswald, having learned Irish fluently during his twenty-year exile at Iona, served as Aiden's personal translator and was directly involved in public preaching to his subjects at court.[50] Outside of the palace, Oswald further assisted Aiden by giving him access to the king's country homes, which facilitated itinerant preaching. Further, Oswald vouched for Aiden to other monarchs in the region allowing the missionary monk even more favor to minister. Mayr-Harting notes that for Aiden "missionary work could not succeed without the support of the king."[51]

Second, and quite related, Aiden's mission work included much itinerant preaching. Bede reported that Aiden "used to travel everywhere, in town and country, not on horseback but on foot. . . . [A]s he walked along, whenever he saw people whether rich or poor, he might at once approach them, and if they were unbelievers, invite them to accept the mystery of the faith."[52] This on-foot approach probably allowed him to connect more personally with his audience and to be more attuned to their spiritual needs. According to Bede, Aiden was not the first monk that Oswald invited to Northumbria; however, the first missionary was apparently abrasive in his tone and also preached in such a sophisticated manner that was over the

---

48. McNeill, *Celtic Churches*, 102–6.
49. Bede, *Ecclesiastical History*, 3.3.
50. Ibid., 3.5.
51. Mayr-Harting, *Coming of Christianity*, 98.
52. Bede, *Ecclesiastical History*, 3.5; also 3.17.

heads of his listeners. Aiden, on the other hand, communicated with gentleness and kindness and shared with them "the milk of simpler teaching."[53]

Third, also similar to Columba and other monks, Aiden's preaching gained credibility through his holy lifestyle. Bede speaks of his "abstinence," "self-control," and that "he neither sought after nor cared for worldly possessions."[54] He further described Aiden's "love of peace and charity, temperance and humility; his soul which triumphed over anger and greed and at the same time despised pride and vainglory; his industry in carrying out and teaching the divine commandments, his diligence in study and keeping vigil."[55] Apparently Aiden's simplicity and modesty proved to be an example to other English clergy and Christians as well. This quality of Aiden's life was supported by the monastic value of studying Scripture. Bede noted that in the context of his ministry, Aiden not only spent much meditating on Scripture himself, but "all who accompanied him . . . had to engage in some form of study . . . to occupy themselves with reading the Scriptures or learning the Psalms."[56]

Miracles also accompanied Aiden's preaching and ministry.[57] At one point during the Mercian King Penda's siege of Northumbria, the king set fire to the city of Bamburgh. Bede reported that Aiden responded with a prayer that revealed to the Mercians the power of Aiden's God: "He raised his eyes and hands toward heaven and said with tears, 'Oh Lord, see how much evil Penda is doing.' As soon as he had uttered these words, the winds veered away from the city and carried the flames in the direction of those who had kindled them, so that, as some of them were hurt and all of them terrified, they ceased to make any further attempt on the city, realizing it was divinely protected."[58]

A fifth observable value in Aiden's work was caring for the poor and disenfranchised. Though his relationship with King Oswald certainly facilitated his mission work and could have resulted in a more comfortable life for Aiden, he apparently resisted those temptations. In fact, upon receiving

---

53. Ibid., 3.5.

54. Ibid.

55. Ibid., 3.17.

56. Ibid., 3.5.

57. See Mayr-Harting (*Coming of Christianity*, 47–50) for a discussion on Bede's worldview regarding miracles and his comfort level about reporting them, which has been a troubling aspect for modern readers of Bede.

58. Bede, *Ecclesiastical History*, 3.16; also Mayr-Harting, *Coming of Christianity*, 99.

a gift of a horse from Oswald's brother King Oswiu, Aiden seemingly refused this status symbol of nobility and gave the horse to a beggar.[59] While pursuing a simple lifestyle as a missionary monk, Aiden was remembered for being "kind and generous to the poor and to strangers" and showing "tenderness in comforting the weak, in relieving and protecting the poor."[60] Some of those included slaves and Bede reported that Aiden used money "for the redemption of those who had been unjustly sold into slavery" and "many of those . . . he afterwards made his disciples."[61] Resisting the material temptations of being acquainted with royalty, Aiden actually influenced Oswald to think about the poor among his subjects. On one occasion, probably due to Aiden's influence, the king had food that had been prepared for a royal banquet at Easter distributed to the poor.[62]

McNeill writes that by 663, "the greater part of England . . . had become permanently Christian under the influence of the Celtic mission and was being served by preachers and bishops trained under Irish teachers at Lindisfarne."[63] Bede added that Aiden's preaching influenced the church as it expanded among four language groups—Britons, Picts, Irish, and the English.[64] While the outcomes of Aiden's mission work are evident here, it also reveals that he was committed to training and setting apart other missionary monks and church leaders through the monastery at Lindisfarne.

Columban

Columban represented a group of sixth- and seventh-century Celtic monks that came from Ireland to minister across the continent of Europe. Contrasting the monks with the kings and armies marching around Europe at this time, McNeill writes: "The new invaders were unarmed, white-robed monks with books in their satchels and psalms on their lips, seeking no wealth or comfort but only the opportunity to teach and pray."[65] Birthed from the Irish monastic confederations (*paruchiae*) originating with Patrick, these *peregrini* were sent off by their monasteries to never return but

59. Bede, *Ecclesiastical History*, 3.14; also Mayr-Harting, *Coming of Christianity*, 97.
60. Bede, *Ecclesiastical History*, 3.5; 3.17.
61. Ibid., 3.5.
62. Ibid., 3.6.
63. McNeill, *Celtic Churches*, 108.
64. Bede, *Ecclesiastical History*, 3.5.
65. McNeill, *Celtic Churches*, 155.

to serve God and begin more monastic networks. Though some scholars debate whether these monks ought to be considered cross-cultural missionaries, some went out with clear missionary intentions while others were *peregrini* who ministered to the peoples they encountered when the need and opportunity arose.[66]

Columban was born in Leinster around 543. The sources for his life and thought are based on his surviving sermons and letters, his monastic rule, as well as the *Life of St. Columban* penned by the seventh-century monk Jonas.[67] Columban apparently received a fine education; however, as a young man, he withdrew from the world and initially joined a monastery at Gleenish before moving to another community at Bangor (Ireland), where he spent twenty-five years.[68] Around 590, moved by the text of Genesis 12:1–3—"Go from your country, your people and your father's household to the land I will show you"—Columban and a group of twelve monks were released by the monastery and began their pilgrimage. Jonas wrote, "So they embarked, and began the dangerous journey across the channel and sailed quickly with a smooth sea and favorable wind to the coast of Brittany. Here they rested for a while to recover their strength and discussed their plans anxiously, until finally they decided to enter the land of Gaul."[69] Highlighting their missionary motivations as they entered the Kingdom of Burgundy, Jonas added, "They wanted zealously and shrewdly to inquire into the disposition of the inhabitants in order to remain longer if they found they could sow the seeds of salvation; or in case they found the hearts of the people in darkness, go on to the nearest nations."[70]

Columban's Context and Monastic Itinerary

Though Irenaeus, Martin of Tours, and others had previously evangelized Gaul, and though established churches still remained, McNeill notes that by the time of Columban's ministry, "political conditions were deplorable."[71] Jonas likewise asserted that "the Christian faith had almost

---

66. Mayr-Harting, *Coming of Christianity*, 78; also McNeill, *Celtic Churches*, 156, 168–75.
67. McNeill, *Celtic Churches*, 158.
68. Jonas, *Life of Columban*, 7–9 (all English translations are from Dana Munro).
69. Ibid., 10.
70. Ibid.
71. McNeill, *Celtic Churches*, 158.

departed from that country."[72] After gaining favor with the Frankish King Sigibert, Columban and his monks established a monastery in an old abandoned military fort at Anegray. During this period, Columban developed his own monastic rule based on those of his mentors at Bangor who were influenced by the semi-hermitic visions of John Cassian and the Egyptian monks.[73] As their monastic community at Anegray attracted more and more monks, Columban opened additional monasteries at Luxeuil and Fontaines. By the end of his life, his monastic network included some sixty monasteries in Gaul.[74]

A charismatic figure, Columban attracted many followers to his community; however, his charisma often resulted in conflicts as well. He struggled with established church leaders, especially the Frankish Roman bishops with whom he argued over the date of Easter. Although he initially received favor from a Gallic monarch to enter the region, he struggled to maintain good relationships with political leaders. Ultimately, Columban was expelled from Burgundy for angering the monarch Brunhilda because he refused to bless the illegitimate children of her son, King Theuderic. Escorted from the kingdom, he traveled through Gaul to what is now Switzerland before arriving in Italy where he dreamed of preaching to the Arian-leaning Lombards. Eventually, he established a final monastery at Bobbio in northern Italy where he remained for the rest of his life.[75]

Approaches to Mission

Like Columba, Columban also engaged with political and social leaders in the work of mission. In addition to his initial contact with the king of Burgundy at the outset of his work in Gaul, Columban also met with other European monarchs following his expulsion from Burgundy as he considered a place to settle, set up a monastery, and minister to the local people. Columban's engagement at these levels also included intervening and mediating a conflict between two feuding brothers, Theuderich and Theudebert of Burgundy. Aside from political encounters, Columban also

---

72. Jonas, *Life of Columban* 10.

73. Ibid. 12, 16; also McNeill, *Celtic Churches*, 159, 166.

74. Jonas, *Life of Columban*, 17; also Olsen, *Christianity and the Celts*, 132; and Dunn, *Emergence of Monasticism*, 158–59.

75. Jonas, *Life of Columban*, 31–38; also McNeill, *Celtic Churches*, 160–64; and Olsen, *Christianity and the Celts*, 134–35.

influenced social leaders as quite a number of the seventh-century Frankish nobility embraced his monastic vision.[76]

A second aspect of Columban's work was itinerant preaching. Jonas reported, "Everywhere that he went the noble man preached the gospel. And it pleased the people because his teaching was adorned by eloquence and enforced by examples of virtue."[77] According to Jonas, the virtuous example that supported Columban's preaching and impacted the Frankish people included the collective witness of Columban's community and the quality of life that they exhibited. Interestingly, Columban's expulsion from Burgundy served as a catalyst for more itinerant preaching as the *peregrinus* responded by preaching among the Swabian and Slavic peoples.[78]

In the midst of itinerant preaching, Columban imitated the practices of Martin of Tours and openly confronted paganism in Gaul. This included physically destroying pagan idols and sacred places in Switzerland. Columban was accompanied by a colleague named Gall, who continued ministering in Switzerland after Columban's departure; however, Gall chose a more peaceful and persuasive approach among pagans in the years that followed.[79]

Evangelizing nominal and heretical Christians was another element of Columban's ministry. Jonas wrote that in Mainz, he reached out to those "who were already baptized but still lived in the heathenish unbelief, like a good shepherd, he again led by his words to the faith and into the bosom of the church."[80] As noted, his motivation for ministering to the Lombards in Italy was due to their wayward, Arian beliefs. Jonas continued, "[Columban] was received with honor by Agilulf, king of the Lombards. The latter granted him the privilege of settling in Italy wherever be pleased; and he did so, by God's direction. During his stay in Milan, he resolved to attack the errors of the [Arian] heretics . . . , which he wanted to cut out and exterminate with the cauterizing knife of the Scriptures."[81]

Finally, Columban's mission work also included the miraculous—healing the sick and confronting demons and evil spirits. Jonas described

---

76. McNeill, *Celtic Churches*, 158, 162; also Dunn, *Emergence of Monasticism*, 162–63; Jonas, *Life of Columban*, 57.

77. Jonas, *Life of Columban*, 11.

78. Ibid., 11, 56; also McNeill, *Celtic Churches*, 158, 163, 167.

79. McNeill, *Celtic Churches*, 162, 168–69.

80. Jonas, *Life of Columban*, 53.

81. Ibid., 59.

the groups of sick people who gathered outside of the monastery at Luxeuil: "Then crowds of people and throngs of the infirm began to crowd about St. Columban in order that they might recover their health and in order to seek aid in all their infirmities. . . . [T]hrough his prayers and relying upon the divine aid, he healed the infirmities of all who came to him."[82] Following his departure from Burgundy and Luxeuil, Columban had further opportunities to lay hands on and heal the sick and liberate others from demonic oppression.[83] Finally, among the pagan Swabians, Columban engaged in a display of power against a pagan, demonic practice, and communicated the gospel through it. Jonas wrote:

> Once as he was going through this country, he discovered that the natives were going to make a heathen offering. They had a large cask that they called a cupa, and that held about twenty-six measures, filled with beer and set in their midst. On Columban's asking what they intended to do with it, they answered that they were making an offering to their God Wodan (whom others call Mercury). When he heard of this abomination, he breathed on the cask, and . . . it broke with a crash and fell in pieces so that all the beer ran out. Then it was clear that the devil had been concealed in the cask, and that through the earthly drink he had proposed to ensnare the souls of the participants. As the heathens saw that, they were amazed and said Columban had a strong breath, to split a well-bound cask in that manner. But he reproved them in the words of the gospel, and commanded them to cease from such offerings and to go home. Many were converted then, by the preaching of the holy man, and turning to the learning and faith of Christ, were baptized by him.[84]

While Columban was on the move quite a bit throughout his missionary career—an itinerant, preaching *peregrinus*—he still retained a clear commitment to the church and his converts were catechized, baptized, and some became part of newly formed monastic communities. As new monasteries were formed, more Irish *peregrini* moved out and preached among pagans and heretics in Europe and continued Columban's legacy.[85]

---

82. Ibid., 14.
83. Ibid., 39–41, 49.
84. Ibid., 53.
85. Dunn, *Emergence of Monasticism*, 162–63.

Summary

The Irish missionary monastic narrative is a rich one. Certainly, some of the Irish monks were accidental missionaries: that is, after departing their monasteries as ascetic pilgrims (*peregrini*), they encountered non-believers and pagans and they proclaimed the gospel, instructed new believers, and baptized them. In other cases, including the ones discussed in this chapter, they took a more deliberate approach to the task of mission. Regardless, wherever they went, the Celtic monks engaged local people—monarchs and noblemen, pagans, artistic peoples, the demon possessed, and the sick and poor. Their verbal witness was made credible by exemplary lifestyles characterized by prayer, discipline, and redemptive labor. Many pagans were drawn to the gospel because of the collective witness of these semi-hermitic communities. Finally, the monks' ascetic rigor prepared them to endure hardship—hunger, expulsion, politically and socially turbulent areas—and to press on to establish new monasteries from which they proclaimed the gospel.

CHAPTER 7

Gregory the Great and Augustine of Canterbury

According to an eighth-century biography of Bishop Gregory I (540–604) of Rome, one day, before his days as bishop, Gregory observed boys "with fair complexions, handsome faces, and lovely hair" being sold in the slave market in Rome.[1] Inquiring about their identity and background, he was told that they were *angli* (Anglo or English). Responding with a play on words, he declared, "they have the face of angels [*angeli*] and such men should be fellow-heirs with the angels in heaven."[2] Although the accuracy and truthfulness of this particular story is highly doubted by scholars, what is undeniable is that around 596, several years after becoming bishop of Rome, Gregory sent Augustine of Canterbury (d. 604) and a group of about forty monks on a mission to evangelize the English. It was the first cross-cultural mission effort to a non-believing people initiated by a Roman bishop.

In this chapter we will begin by briefly examining the life and career of Gregory, including his monastic journey and his burden and motivation for mission. Next, we will narrate the missionary journey of Augustine and company to England. Finally, we will discuss the primary approaches to mission employed by Gregory and Augustine in this late sixth- and early seventh-century mission effort.

---

1. This story is also recounted by Bede in *Ecclesiastical History* 2.1.

2. Bede in *Ecclesiastical History* 2.1; cf. Mayr-Harting, *Coming of Christianity*, 57–58.

Gregory

Gregory is regarded as one of the greatest popes in the history of the church—known for both his deep spirituality as well as administrative efficiency. Born into a family of Roman patricians, Gregory was appointed Prefect of Rome in 573, making him the highest-ranking civil administrator in the city.[3] However, the following year, he left it all behind and became a monk. Initially, he founded the monastery of St. Andrew on his family's estate in Rome while, later, he initiated six other similar communities. For the first four years of his monastic journey, Gregory had no leadership roles but lived as a simple monk. When looking back, he considered these the best years of his life. In 578, Bishop Benedict appointed Gregory as a deacon and put him in charge of distributing material aid throughout the city. Later, Gregory was sent as a papal envoy to Constantinople that included the unintended experience of having theological disputes with the eastern Patriarch Eutychius. After returning to Rome, Gregory spent five more years at the St. Andrew's monastery until 590 when he became the first monk in church history to be set apart as the bishop of Rome.[4]

Describing Gregory's semi-hermitic monastic vision, Mayr-Harting asserts that "like the Irish, Gregory was spiritual heir to the hermits and monasteries of Syria and Egypt."[5] Although he probably did not adopt Benedict's rule for his communities, it seems that Gregory was greatly influenced by the Italian abbot's monastic ideals. This was probably most apparent in Gregory's missionary vision. Mayr-Harting adds, "Gregory's missionary zeal . . . sprang from his monasticism, from his knowledge that St. Benedict had converted pagans, and from his general emphasis that monastic contemplation should bear fruit in action."[6] Hence, similar to Benedict and Basil, Gregory rejected an ascetic program that focused on contemplation without activism.[7]

His work as a deacon surely alerted him to the great spiritual and material needs of the Romans. A decline in agricultural productivity coupled with a plague that broke out after the Tiber River flooded created many social and economic problems in the city. In addition, an attack by the

---

3. Markus, *Gregory the Great*, 8–9.

4. Zinn, "Gregory I the Great," 488; also Markus, *Gregory the Great*, 10–13.

5. Mayr-Harting, *Coming of Christianity*, 54.

6. Ibid.; cf. Markus, *Gregory the Great*, 68–69.

7. Markus, *Gregory the Great*, 17–26; 69–70; also Demacopoulos, *Gregory the Great*, 21, 26, 28–30.

neighboring Lombards in the Italian countryside in 586 caused the Romans to live in constant fear of another invasion. It was in this context of social, economic, and political tension that Gregory served as a monk and church leader.[8] Despite the great needs on his doorstep that could have easily occupied all of his energy, Gregory's missionary vision was bigger than Rome and he turned his eyes to the English.[9]

So why was Gregory particularly burdened for England? Though the story of Gregory encountering *angli* boys in the slave market is considered unreliable, it is quite plausible that Anglo-Saxon slaves were being sold in Rome. We also know that Gregory was involved in purchasing the freedom of teenage slave boys and educating them in the monastery and it is possible that some of these could have been English. This leads Mayr-Harting to conclude that "it is at least likely, therefore, that Gregory's interest in preaching the gospel to the Anglo-Saxons was aroused by his encountering pagan slaves of that race in Rome either before or during his pontificate."[10]

Gregory was probably also interested in the English because they represented the last vestiges of paganism within the Roman Empire. Though the Roman British had been evangelized since the fourth century, there was much conflict between them and the Anglo-Saxons and the British made very little effort to make the gospel known among their adversaries. During the sixth century, the Anglo-Saxons began to exert more dominance over their British neighbors, and their paganism became more widespread.[11] In short, following Constantine's peace to the church in 313, Theodosius I's declaration of Christianity as the imperial religion around 390, and Justinian's closure of the final pagan temples in 529, Gregory seemed motivated to complete Rome's Christianization by reaching the pagan Anglo-Saxons.

Finally, it is very possible that Queen Bertha, the wife of the English King Ethelbert and a Christian from Gaul, had reached out to Gregory for missionaries. Gregory's letters reveal much interaction with Gallic monarchs and so it is possible that he was acquainted with Bertha.[12] While each of these three reasons for engaging the English are quite plausible,

8. Markus, *Gregory the Great*, 2–8; 97–107.

9. Mayr-Harting, *Coming of Christianity*, 54, 57; also Zinn, "Gregory I the Great," 489–90.

10. Mayr-Harting, *Coming of Christianity*, 59; cf. Wood, "Mission of Augustine," 2; and Markus, *Gregory the Great*, 177–78.

11. See Mayr-Harting, *Coming of Christianity*, 13–16, 22–30, for a description of Anglo-Saxon pagan beliefs and practices; cf. Markus, *Gregory the Great*, 80–82.

12. Markus, *Gregory the Great*, 178, 185–86.

ultimately Gregory's motivations for initiating toward the Anglo-Saxons were pastoral: "He wanted the English to have the benefit of the gospel."[13]

Mission to England

Our main sources for understanding and evaluating the mission to England are Gregory's pastoral letters and Bede's *Ecclesiastical History*. While Bede offered the most complete narrative, it is evident that there are some shortcomings with his chronology; as a result, our timeline for the mission is tentative at best.[14]

Bede began the narrative by stating simply: "Gregory, prompted by divine inspiration, sent a servant of God named Augustine and several more God-fearing monks with him to preach the word of God to the English race."[15] In all, the band of missionary monks may have been as large as forty persons. Because Bede's account presents Gregory as a strong and assertive bishop and Augustine as a rather weak and uncertain monk, one might wonder why Augustine was chosen to lead the effort. The most likely reason was that since Augustine was already serving as the abbot of Gregory's St. Andrew's monastery, the pope had a great deal of confidence in him. In addition, the monks in his charge on the English mission had made a vow of obedience to Augustine—the same vow that Augustine had made to Gregory. It seems that obedience to spiritual authority was a strong value in this missionary effort, especially as the group of monks faced difficulties that came with cross-cultural ministry among a pagan people.[16]

Sometime after setting out from Italy *en route* to England, the community either experienced dissension or became overwhelmed by the hardship of the journey and the task before them. Bede wrote that "they began to contemplate returning home rather than going to a barbarous, fierce, and unbelieving nation."[17] Augustine apparently left the group for

---

13. Mayr-Harting, *Coming of Christianity*, 60; cf. Snyder and Tabbernee, "Western Provinces," 460.

14. See Gregory, *Letters* 6.51–59; 8.30; 9.11; 9.108–9; 11.61; 11:63–66; 14.16; Bede, *Ecclesiastical History* 1.23—2.3; also Markus, "Chronology of the Gregorian Mission," 16–30; and Wood, "Mission of Augustine," 3.

15. Bede, *Ecclesiastical History* 1.23.

16. Mayr-Harting, *Coming of Christianity*, 61.

17. Bede, *Ecclesiastical History* 1.23; also McHugh, "Augustine of Canterbury," 154–55.

a time and returned to Rome to convince Gregory that the mission should be abandoned. The strong-willed bishop demonstrated pastoral care for his struggling abbot; however, he refused to allow the monks to return. Instead, he sent Augustine back with a brief letter to encourage the group. Gregory wrote:

> You must, most beloved sons, fulfill the good work which with the help of the Lord, you have begun. Let, then, neither the toil of the journey nor the tongues of evil-speaking men deter you; but with all [urgency] and all fervor go on with what under God's guidance you have commenced, knowing that great toil is followed by the glory of an eternal reward. Obey in all things humbly Augustine your provost (*præposito*), who is returning to you, whom we also appoint your abbot, knowing that whatever may be fulfilled in you through his admonition will in all ways profit your souls. May Almighty God protect you with His grace, and grant to me to see the fruit of your labor in the eternal country; that so, even though I cannot labor with you, I may be found together with you in the joy of the reward; for in truth I desire to labor. God keep you safe, most beloved sons.[18]

As the journey continued, Augustine and the monks entered Gaul at Marseilles and continued on through Tours (presumably to visit the shrine of St. Martin) before arriving at Kent. Gregory sent letters of commendation to a number of Gallic bishops as well as to members of the Frankish monarchy, particularly Queen Brunhild, who seemed to show an interest in the mission to England.[19]

Upon arriving at Kent, Augustine and company were greeted by King Ethelbert. However, the king chose to meet the monks outdoors on the island of Thanet to protect himself from any harmful "magic" that they might attempt. Having been married to a Christian wife for thirty years and remaining unmoved by the gospel, unsurprisingly, Ethelbert did not respond immediately to the monks' message. However, the king did allow them to settle at Canterbury and gave the monks freedom to preach among his subjects. According to Gregory, in the first year of their ministry, over ten thousand Anglo-Saxons believed the gospel and were baptized. Though

---

18. Gregory, *Letter* 6.51 (all English translations are from *Nicene Post Nicene Fathers*).

19. Gregory, *Letters* 6.52–55, 57–59; Bede, *Ecclesiastical History* 1.24; also Wood, "Mission of Augustine," 6–8.

it is difficult to know exactly when Ethelbert was converted, the king eventually embraced the gospel for himself.[20]

After the initial wave of ministry and the fruitful response, two monks named Laurence and Peter were sent back to Rome to give a full report to Gregory. At some point after the initial efforts in England, Augustine traveled to Gaul where he was set apart as a bishop for the work among the English. Later, he was promoted to metropolitan bishop, which meant that he supervised the work of other bishops.[21] Around 601, Gregory sent more monks to assist in the ministry, including Mellitus who would later be set apart as the bishop of London, and Paulinus who would serve as bishop of Kent.[22]

Ethelbert granted the monks some space at Canterbury to establish a base for their lives and ministry. Initially, this was probably a compound where monks and clergy lived together and where the monastery and church functioned as one entity—similar to the Celtic monastic and church structures. However, Augustine later restored a church and built a monastery and established a clear division between monastery and church, which reflected more of the Roman, Gregorian tradition.[23]

Approaches to Mission

What characterized the Roman mission to England? First, as shown, obedience proved to be one of the team's strongest values. The monks were obedient to Augustine and all were obedient to Gregory, who had initiated the mission effort.[24] After Augustine's trip back to Rome, Gregory rejected his request to abort the mission and sent Augustine back with a

---

20. Bede, *Ecclesiastical History* 1.25–26; Gregory, *Letter* 8.29; cf. Mayr-Harting, *Coming of Christianity*, 62–64; Wood, "Mission of Augustine," 12; and Markus, "Chronology of the Gregorian Mission," 19–24.

21. Markus, "Chronology of the Gregorian Mission," 24–28; also Markus, *Gregory the Great*, 180.

22. Bede, *Ecclesiastical History* 1.27; also Wood, "Mission of Augustine," 6; Snyder and Tabbernee, "Western Provinces," 462–63; and Irvin and Sunquist, *History of the World Christian Movement*, 327–39.

23. Bede, *Ecclesiastical History* 1.33; also Snyder and Tabbernee, "Western Provinces," 462–63; Mayr-Harting, *Coming of Christianity*, 62–63; and Markus, *Gregory the Great*, 70–71.

24. Bede, *Ecclesiastical History* 1.23.

letter telling the monks to "humbly obey [Augustine] in all things."[25] While Gregory seemed intent on seeing his vision for the English fulfilled, his sincere pastoral care for Augustine and the monks should not go unnoticed.[26] Gregory's demand for obedience did not end with Augustine or the monks, as he also wrote to the recently converted Ethelbert urging that the king obey Augustine's teachings, saying, "so whatever counsel he gives you, listen to it gladly, follow it earnestly and carefully keep it in mind."[27]

Second, similar to the practice of other missionary monks, Augustine and the team began their work in England by first approaching the king. Although Ethelbert did not initially embrace the gospel for himself, he did give the monks space to build a monastery as a place of worship and base for ministry and the king also granted them the freedom to preach among his people. Gregory's act of sending monks to England may very well have come at the invitation of Queen Bertha, who surely influenced her non-believing husband to consider the gospel. In addition to his wife, other Christian monarchs of Gaul may have also influenced Ethelbert spiritually, particularly the neighboring Merovingians who had developed a strong kingdom based on Christian principles.[28]

Once Ethelbert was converted, Gregory took the opportunity to exhort the English leader toward growth in his new faith. Likening him to the Roman Emperor Constantine, Gregory encouraged him to put an end to idolatry in his kingdom and to destroy all pagan temples. The Roman bishop added, "So, my illustrious son, watch carefully over the grace you have received from God and hasten to extend the Christian faith to those who are subject to you."[29]

A third aspect of their mission work was combining preaching with holy living. Bede described the monks' task as primarily "preach[ing] the word of God."[30] This value reflected Gregory's pastoral theology in which he believed that a minister's duty was to preach the gospel to believers and

25. Ibid; also Markus, *Gregory the Great*, 179.

26. Bede, *Ecclesiastical History* 1.23, 25. This tension between Gregory's authority and pastoral care is discussed further in Markus, *Gregory the Great*, 26–32.

27. Bede, *Ecclesiastical History* 1.32.

28. Bede, *Ecclesiastical History* 1.25; also Wood, "Mission of Augustine," 10; Irvin and Sunquist, *History of the World Christian Movement*, 327–28; and Tyler, "Reluctant Kings and Christian Conversion," 146, 154–57.

29. Bede, *Ecclesiastical History* 1.23; Gregory, *Letters* 11.66; cf. Wood, "Mission of Augustine," 11.

30. Bede, *Ecclesiastical History* 1.23.

non-believers alike.³¹ Describing this proclamation ministry that was integrated with godly living, Bede wrote: "They began to imitate the way of life of the apostles and of the primitive church. They were constantly engaged in prayers, in vigils and fasts; they preached the word of life to as many as they could; they despised all worldly things as foreign to them; they accepted only the necessaries of life from those whom they taught; in all things they practiced what they preached. . . . [S]ome, marveling at their simple and innocent way of life and sweetness of their heavenly doctrine, believed and were baptized."³² This mission approach was likely influenced by Gregory's *Pastoral Rule*, in which Gregory taught that an ideal minister was "a spiritual model who preaches . . . by word and example."³³

Bede also reported that their message was "confirmed by performing many miracles."³⁴ As Augustine related back to Gregory miraculous accounts, the Roman bishop freely shared this news with others in his correspondence.³⁵ Gregory himself may have instilled in Augustine and the monks the expectation that miracles would accompany their ministry. In a few of his works that pre-dated the English mission—including *Homilies on the Gospels* (ca. 591), *Dialogues* (ca. 593–594), and *Moralia on Job* (ca. 595)—Gregory celebrated the place of miracles in ministry. He seemed convinced that miracles were intimately linked to the virtuous life of the minister. In this case, it was the holy examples of preaching monks imitating Christ among the English. For Gregory, miracles also demonstrated the power of God to a pagan people, which helped them become convinced of the truth of the Christian message. Finally, the Roman bishop was convinced that outward miracles corresponded closely to the process of conversion within a non-believer as they heard the gospel being preached—"leading the Angles to interior grace through exterior miracles (*per exterior miracula ad interiorem gratiam*)."³⁶ While celebrating and even advocating the role of miracles in mission, Gregory was also careful to warn Augustine not to become prideful or arrogant about such acts of power. He wrote:

---

31. Markus, *Gregory the Great*, 80.
32. Bede, *Ecclesiastical History* 1.26; cf. Dunn, *Emergence of Monasticism*, 196–97.
33. Zinn, "Gregory I the Great," 490.
34. Bede, *Ecclesiastical History* 1.26.
35. See for example Gregory, *Letters* 8.30.
36. Wood, "Mission of Augustine," 14; Bede, *Ecclesiastical History* 1.31; cf. Mayr-Harting, *Coming of Christianity*, 74.

> I know, most beloved brother, that Almighty God, out of love for you has worked great miracles through you for the [English]. . . . It is therefore necessary that you should rejoice with trembling over this heavenly gift and fear as you rejoice. You will rejoice because the souls of the English are drawn by outward miracles to inward grace: but you will fear lest among these signs which are performed, the weak mind may be raised up by self-esteem and so the very cause by which it is raised to outward honor may lead through vainglory to its inward fall.[37]

A fifth noticeable element of Gregory and Augustine's mission practice was contextualizing Christianity in light of the English pagan context, especially as it related to places of worship and religious festivals. Originally, Gregory instructed Mellitus, who joined Augustine in 601, to destroy all of the pagan temples.[38] Similarly, in a letter to Ethelbert, he urged the king to "suppress the worship of idols; overthrow their buildings and shrines."[39] However, in a follow-up letter to Augustine communicated via Mellitus, Gregory apparently changed his mind about pagan temples and wrote:

> The idol temples of that [English] race should by no means be destroyed, but only the idols in them. . . . For if the shrines are well built, it is essential that they should be changed from the worship of devils to the service of the true God. When this people see that their shrines are not destroyed they will be able to banish error from their hearts and be more ready to come to the places they are familiar with, but now recognizing and worshipping the true God.[40]

Though Gregory was clearly intolerant of the continued presence of pagan idols and ordered them destroyed, he did believe that the pagan sacred space could be redeemed and transformed into a suitable place for sincere Christian worship. Seeing nothing inherently evil about the physical structures themselves and showing little concern that pagan memories of worship would overcome the English as they entered these buildings, Gregory showed much sensitivity to the local people in giving this direction. He wanted them to feel comfortable, worshipping as Christians in familiar

---

37. Bede, *Ecclesiastical History* 1.31.

38. For the broader context of Gregory's thought see Bede, *Ecclesiastical History* 1.29–30; 2:3–7.

39. Bede, *Ecclesiastical History* 1.32; also Gregory, *Letters* 11.66.

40. Bede, *Ecclesiastical History* 1.30. On the apparent change of mind, see Markus, "Gregory the Great and a Papal Missionary Strategy," 36.

surroundings. Indeed, Gregory was asserting a form of contextualization by redeeming sacred space rather than by destroying it and building new spaces.

Similarly, Gregory believed that pagan festivals could also be transformed into opportunities for Christian worship. Referring to a certain festival where cattle were sacrificed, he advised Augustine and the monks: "And because they are in the habit of slaughtering much cattle as sacrifices to devils, some solemnity ought to be given them in exchange for this.... Do not let them sacrifice animals to the devil, but let them slaughter animals for their own food to the praise of God, and let them give thanks to the Giver of all things for His bountiful provision."[41] Again, with no tolerance for idolatry, which he likened to worshipping the devil, Gregory stated that a festival like this could continue if the object of worship (the one true God) and the heart of worship (thanksgiving) were properly oriented.

In short, Gregory was urging Augustine and his team of monks to contextualize Christian worship in familiar English forms given their pagan past. Gregory appears to show much sensitivity to and even appreciation for the host culture; however, he was also a bit of a realist and acknowledged that the conversion of a people takes time and that missionaries must be patient. He wrote: "it is doubtless impossible to cut out everything at once from their stubborn minds. As when one climbs a high mountain, one does not advance in great strides, but slowly and surely by small steps."[42]

Despite demonstrating these contextual values, in other aspects of the English mission—particularly church structures and organization—Gregory advocated a very Roman approach. This is evident in the fact that Augustine was consecrated as a bishop for his work and that two other missionary monks, Mellitus and Justus, were made bishops for theirs. Though these tendencies resulted in conflict with the Celtic missionary monks, Roman forms of worship and organization became prevalent in the English church following the Synod of Whitby in 664.[43]

Finally, the English mission was distinct because of the strength and personality of its sender, Gregory. Bede wrote: "It is true that he sent other preachers, but he himself helped their preaching to bear fruit by his

---

41. Bede, *Ecclesiastical History* 1.30.

42. Ibid.; cf. Snyder and Tabbernee, "Western Provinces," 462.

43. Bede, *Ecclesiastical History* 1.27; 2.3; Gregory, *Letter* 11.65; also Markus, *Gregory the Great*, 180–181.

encouragement and prayers."[44] The mission to England is rightly called the Gregorian or Roman mission because Gregory dominated the narrative through his initiative for the work, and his correspondence with Frankish monarchs, church leaders, King Ethelbert, and, of course, with Augustine and the team of monks. His communication with the monks demonstrated his passion for the work, his expectation of their absolute obedience, as well as his genuine care for the missionary team—a leadership model worth reflecting on further. According to Bede, Gregory's model for mission continued to influence missionary efforts in the British Isles in the generations after his death.[45]

Summary

The story of the English mission is dominated by Gregory the Great—a monk bishop who clearly had a vision for the pagan Anglo-Saxons but also possessed the drive to see the work come to fruition. While this mission was distinct because of the character and conviction of the sender, the mission was still accomplished by a team of monks who obeyed their leader, endured hardship, preached the gospel, lived exemplary lives among the English, and allegedly performed miracles, while establishing a Christianity that was in some ways contextual to England, but also foreign in its organization. As missionary monks established Christianity in England, mission efforts from England would also be the work of monks.

---

44. Bede, *Ecclesiastical History* 2.1
45. Ibid. 4.2

CHAPTER 8

Willibrord and Boniface

THOUGH THE ENGLISH WERE not evangelized until a relatively late period in European church history, Anglo-Saxon monks were actively on mission to the rest of Europe by the eighth-century. Probably influenced by the *peregrinus* value of Celtic missionary monks as well as the missionary vision of Gregory the Great that brought Christianity to them in the first place, English missionary monks were particularly key in the evangelization of the Germanic peoples of northern Europe. To make that case, in this chapter, we will focus on the work of two innovative missionary monks—Willibrord (ca. 658–737) and Boniface (ca. 680–754) and their companions—and narrate their journeys in mission and discuss their approaches to making disciples in northern Europe.

Willibrord

While most of what we know about Willibrord comes from Bede's *Ecclesiastical History* and a sacred biography written by his fellow priest and relative Alcuin, a letter from Boniface offers a concise picture of Willibrord's life:

> In the time of [the Roman Bishop] Sergius (687–701) . . . there came . . . a Saxon priest of great holiness and self-denial, by name Willibrord, called also Clement. The aforementioned pope consecrated him bishop and sent him to preach to the heathen Frisians by the shores of the western sea. For fifty years he preached to the Frisian people, converted a great part of them to the faith of Christ, destroyed their temples, and holy places, and built churches, establishing an episcopal see with a church in honor of the Holy

Savior in a fortified place called Utrecht. In that see and in the church which he had built he continued preaching up to his feeble old age.[1]

According to Alcuin, Willibrord joined the monastery at Ripon in Northumbria as a child and was raised and educated there by the famous Abbot Wilfrid. During those years, he was apparently exposed to and inspired by the lives of Celtic missionary monks—permanent pilgrims dwelling among pagan peoples. Willibrord was especially encouraged to pursue mission by the monk bishop Egbert, who had spent some time living at Iona and had considered becoming a missionary himself.[2] Describing Willibrord's initial venture into ministry, Alcuin writes:

> Accordingly, in the thirty third year of his age the fervor of his faith had reached such an intensity that he considered it of little value to labor at his own sanctification unless he could preach the gospel to others and bring some benefit to them. He had heard that in the northern regions of the world the harvest was great but the laborers few. [He] decided to sail for those parts and, if God so willed, to bring the light of the gospel message to those people who through unbelief had not been stirred by its warmth. So he embarked on a ship, taking with him eleven others who shared his enthusiasm for the faith.[3]

Willibrord focused his ministry on the Frisians—a Germanic people group who lived in what is now Holland and northern Germany. The Frisians were adherents to Germanic paganism, which included belief in gods and goddesses, ancestors and spirits, and honoring their deities through rites and feasts.[4] Willibrord's work was facilitated by the encouragement and protection of the Frankish leader Pepin of Herstal who, around the time of Willibrord's arrival, "had just driven King Radbod out of nearer Frisia and had taken it over."[5] The Frankish leader sent Willibrord and his companions to "preach there; at the same time he gave them the support

---

1. Boniface, *Letter*, 48 (all English translations are from Talbot).

2. Alcuin, *Life of Willibrord*, 3–4; Bede, *Ecclesiastical History* 4.10; also Mayr-Harting, *Coming of Christianity*, 129–47, 265; and Neill, *History of Christian Missions*, 63.

3. Alcuin, *Life of Willibrord*, 5 (all English translations are from Talbot).

4. Some indication of their belief system is conveyed through Bishop Daniel of Winchester's letter to Boniface (Boniface, *Letter*, 11) in the early years of his mission.

5. Bede, *Ecclesiastical History* 4.10.

of his royal authority so that none should molest them as they preached."[6] In 695, after a decade of preaching among the Frisians, Willibrord was selected by Pepin (with the bishop of Rome's blessing) to serve as the bishop of Utrecht. Despite his new role as a missionary bishop, Willibrord, now renamed Clement by the Roman bishop, continued to live as a monk, and established new monasteries at Utrecht and Epternach. Although life in Frisia could be turbulent at times, the greatest tensions came because the Frisians associated Willibrord and the monks with their enemies, the Christianized Franks.[7]

Approaches to Mission

What were Willibrord's key approaches to mission? First, like many missionary monks already surveyed, Willibrord was well connected with political leaders. Willibrord was able to access Frisia because of Pepin's protection and dominance over the Frisians. Bede noted that Pepin was willing to give "favors to those [Frisians] who were willing to receive the faith"[8]—a rather troubling development for sure. In light of this, Alcuin remarked that part of Willibrord's work was "attempt[ing] to bring into the church by baptism the people that had recently been won by the sword."[9] This statement seems to indicate that Willibrord had his own ideas about how the gospel ought to be spread. Nevertheless, Pepin remained Willibrord's benefactor and used his authority to make Willibrord a bishop and to give him land in Utrecht on which to build a monastery.[10]

Aside from Pepin, Willibrord apparently had contact with other non-Christian monarchs during his missionary career. According to Alcuin, Willibrord had his own positive encounter with the Frisian King Radbod, who had been defeated and pushed back by Pepin. Apparently, Willibrord was afforded some opportunity to witness to the king about Christ; however, Radbod showed no interest. In another instance, Willibrord approached the Danish King Ongendus seeking favor and the opportunity to minister

---

6. Ibid.; also Alcuin, *Life of Willibrord*, 5; and Neill, *History of Christian Missions*, 63.

7. Alcuin, *Life of Willibrord*, 6; cf. Talbot, *Anglo-Saxon Missionaries*, viii; and Neill, *History of Christian Missions*, 64.

8. Bede, *Ecclesiastical History* 4.10.

9. Alcuin, *Life of Willibrord*, 13.

10. Bede, *Ecclesiastical History* 4.10.

among the Danes. Finally, he engaged the pagan king of Fositeland and proclaimed the gospel to him.[11]

Second, Willibrord was deliberate about establishing new monasteries—"communities of monks and nuns whom he gathered together in various localities"—as part of his missionary work.[12] The monastic foundations, of course, made possible a common life where like-minded ascetics could live together and pursue spiritual disciplines. This way of life also served as a collective witness to the surrounding non-believing population with whom Willibrord and the monks interacted regularly. Describing Willibord's monastic witness, Alcuin wrote: "His personal life can be inferred from his vigils and prayers, his fasting and singing of psalms, the holiness of his conduct and his many miracles. His charity is made manifest in the unremitting labors, which he bore daily for the name of Christ."[13] Finally, the new monasteries that he established across northern Germany served as bases for itinerant preaching among the Frisians.

Despite the pressure that Pepin put on the Frisians to accept Christianity, Willibrord's ministry was centered on preaching and persuasion. Bede asserted that Willibrord "preached the word of faith far and wide, recalling many from their errors,"[14] while Alcuin added that his primary focus was to "preach the gospel to others and bring some benefit to them."[15] Describing Willibrord's intensity for preaching and some favorable outcomes that resulted, Alcuin wrote: "The more clearly the man of God saw the need of overcoming the ignorance and arresting the spiritual famine in these districts, the more vigorously he preached the Word of God. How great was the success which, through the help of divine grace, attended his labors is attested even in these days by the people whom in the cities, villages, and fortified towns he brought to a knowledge of the truth and the worship of almighty God by his holy admonitions."[16]

In addition to preaching, Willibrord's mission was also characterized by power encounters and miracles accomplished before his pagan audience. Alcuin described an instance where the English monk was driven ashore to an island that was a center for pagan worship—a place generally avoided

11. Alcuin, *Life of Willibrord*, 9–10.
12. Ibid. 8; also ibid., 12.
13. Ibid., 24.
14. Bede, *Ecclesiastical History* 4.11.
15. Alcuin, *Life of Willibrord*, 5.
16. Ibid., 8.

by the local population because of their fear of the gods and spirits. When Willibrord and his companions emerged unscathed, the local king angrily called them to his presence to condemn them for upsetting the island's deities. According to Alcuin, while demonstrating the Christian God's power over other spiritual beings, Willibrord proclaimed:

> The object of your worship, O King, is not a god but a devil, and he holds you ensnared in rank falsehood in order that he may deliver your soul to eternal fire. For there is no God but one, who created heaven and earth, the seas and all that is in them; and those who worship Him in true faith will possess eternal life. As His servant I call upon you this day to renounce the empty and inveterate errors to which your forebears have given their assent and to believe in the one almighty God, our Lord Jesus Christ. Be baptized in the fountain of life and wash away all your sins, so that, forsaking all wickedness and unrighteousness, you may henceforth live as a new man in temperance, justice, and holiness.[17]

Devoting much of the last half of *Life of Willibrord* to miracles, some that benefited Christians and others that served as a witness of God's power to non-believers, Alcuin regarded this as a significant part of Willibrord's ministry. However, Alcuin still regarded Willibrord's preaching as the most important aspect of his work: "Many miracles were also wrought by divine power through His servant. While the ministry of preaching the gospel is to be preferred to the working of miracles and the showing of signs, yet, because such miracles are recorded as having been performed, I think mention of them ought not to be suppressed."[18]

A final significant part of Willibrord's ministry involved setting apart leaders to continue the work of mission. Bede wrote: "He appointed in those parts [Frisia] a number of bishops from among the brothers who had come with him or had followed him there for the purpose of preaching."[19] One of the purposes of establishing monasteries was to train, equip, and send out other laborers among the Frisians. In other cases, this included setting apart new bishops and church leaders.

---

17. Ibid., 10–11.
18. Ibid., 14. See ibid., 14–22 for a full account of miracles attributed to Willibrord.
19. Bede, *Ecclesiastical History* 4.11.

Boniface

Boniface was the most well-known eighth-century missionary and perhaps the greatest influence on European Christianity in the medieval period. Most of what we know about him comes from his disciple Willibald's *Life of Boniface*, a source that must be evaluated carefully, as well as a corpus of surviving letters. Originally named Wynfrith, he spent the first forty years of his life in monasteries at Exeter and Nursling. According to Willibald, he was attracted to ascetic living as a boy through the influence of traveling preachers and clergy; and once in the monastery, he demonstrated a great desire and aptitude for learning.[20] While living at Nursling, where he was also probably inspired by the accounts of the Celtic *peregrini*, Boniface felt the initial urge to leave the cloister and move out among pagans for the purpose of pilgrimage and mission. Initially opposed to Boniface's ideas, the abbot at Nursling eventually released him to go. With no monastic or ecclesiastical sending structure in place, this initiative to mission seemed to rest squarely on Boniface's vision.[21]

Boniface's missionary career began around 719 when he joined Willibrord's work among the Frisians for about one year. Upon the death of Abbot Winbert of Nursling, Boniface was called upon to lead that community; however, he declined due to his deepening commitment to mission. Instead of returning to England, Boniface journeyed to Rome where he was set apart by Bishop Gregory II as a missionary envoy to the Frisians. It was at this point that Wynfrith was given the Roman name Boniface.[22]

After another season of ministering with Willibrord, Boniface returned to Rome in 722, and Gregory II set him apart as a missionary bishop for all of Germany. Boniface took a vow of allegiance to the pope and made a commitment to propagate a Roman form of Christianity among the Germanic peoples. Commenting on the uniqueness of Boniface's episcopal appointment, Talbot writes: "This was not a case of becoming a bishop like anyone else. Boniface had no diocese, no episcopal see, no attachment or

---

20. Willibald, *Life of Boniface*, 1–2; cf. Mayr-Harting, *Coming of Christianity*, 262; also Neill, *History of Christian Missions*, 64.

21. Willibald, *Life of Boniface*, 4; also Talbot, "St. Boniface and the German Mission," 45–46.

22. Blocher and Blandenier, *Evangelization of the World*, 74; also Talbot, "St. Boniface and the German Mission," 48.

subordination to a metropolitan. His sphere of work was the whole of Germany beyond the Rhine."[23]

The most celebrated account of Boniface's ministry among the Germans came in 724 when he confronted pagan ritual and belief head on by cutting down the sacred oak tree of Jupiter in the town of Geismar. Willibald described the encounter:

> With the counsel and advice of the latter persons, Boniface in their presence attempted to cut down, at a place called Geismar, a certain oak of extraordinary size called in the old tongue of the pagans the Oak of Jupiter. Taking his courage in his hands (for a great crowd of pagans stood by watching and bitterly cursing in their hearts the enemy of the gods), he cut the first notch. But when he had made a superficial cut, suddenly, the oak's vast bulk, shaken by a mighty blast of wind from above crashed to the ground shivering its topmost branches into fragments in its fall. As if by the express will of God (for the brethren present had done nothing to cause it) the oak burst asunder into four parts, each part having a trunk of equal length. At the sight of this extraordinary spectacle the heathens who had been cursing ceased to revile and began, on the contrary, to believe and bless the Lord. Thereupon the holy bishop took counsel with the brethren, built an oratory from the timber of the oak and dedicated it to Saint Peter the Apostle.[24]

While this approach will be discussed more shortly, it is worth noting here that this was not Boniface's only ministry strategy, and he appears to have backed away from such confrontational tactics as he continued serving among the Germans.[25]

As his mission work continued and as churches were established, Boniface's gifts as an administrator became evident. In 737 and 738, following another trip to Rome, he was given authority over all of the churches of Bavaria. He also organized several new churches and appointed bishops in the region. Despite Boniface's desire to move away from administration and back toward pioneering mission efforts, Gregory III of Rome ordered Boniface to stay in this role. Between 741 and 747, his administrative tasks only

---

23. Talbot, "St. Boniface and the German Mission," 49; cf. Boniface, *Letter,* 16; Willibald, *Life of Boniface,* 5.

24. Willibald, *Life of Boniface,* 6 (all English translations are from Talbot).

25. Wilken, *First Thousand Years,* 277.

grew as the pope tasked him with bringing reform to the existing Frankish churches, dealing with such issues as immoral clergy and financial abuses.[26]

Neill writes, "As Boniface grew older, he withdrew more and more from the field of administration; at the end the spirit of the missionary prevailed, and drove him out again into the lands where Christ had not been named."[27] In 753, when he was well into his seventies, Boniface headed out to a part of Frisia where there were still unbaptized pagans. In the midst of this new work of preaching, baptizing, and teaching, Boniface and a team of his companions were attacked by an angry mob and were martyred in 754.

Approaches to Mission

First, following the example of Willibrord and others, Boniface was also engaged with political leaders. Having celebrated Charles Martel's military victories over the Frisians, which Boniface believed served to advance the gospel among the Germans, Boniface was dependent upon Charles and other Frankish leaders for protection in his mission work. Writing on Boniface's behalf, Gregory II asked the Frankish leader "to grant [Boniface] your constant protection against any who may stand in his way."[28] Charles later responded, "Let it be known that the apostolic father Bishop Boniface has come into our presence and begged us to take him under our protection. Know then that it has been our pleasure to do this."[29] Boniface kept in close contact with Frankish leaders and even participated in the coronation of Pepin when he became king of the Franks in 752.[30]

In addition to Frankish leaders, Boniface also appears to have had relationships with non-Christian German leaders. At the outset of his ministry, he followed Gregory II's lead and directed his message toward German leaders, speaking "to the senators of each tribe and the princes of the whole people with words of spiritual exhortation, recalling them to the true way

---

26. See Boniface, *Letters*, 23–24, 27–29, 35; also Talbot, "St. Boniface and the German Mission," 53–55; and Neill, *History of Christian Missions*, 65.

27. Neill, *History of Christian Missions*, 66.

28. Boniface, *Letter* 9.

29. Boniface, *Letter* 10.

30. Willibald, *Life of Boniface* 5; Boniface, *Letter* 26, 45; also Neill, *History of Christian Missions*, 66; and Talbot, "St. Boniface and the German Mission," 45.

of knowledge and the light of understanding that for the greater part they had lost through the perversity of their teachers."[31]

Second, despite the advantages that came from his relationships with Frankish leaders Charles Martel, Carloman, Griffo, and Pepin, Boniface kept preaching as the central element of his ministry. In a letter from Bishop Daniel at the outset of his work, Boniface was encouraged to avoid arguments and disputes and instead pose questions and engage the Frisians in a reasonable manner.[32] Bishop Gregory II sent the English monk from Rome with the imperative to preach and this theme resounds throughout their ongoing correspondence. For instance, Gregory wrote: [we] "decree that you go forth to preach the word of God to those people who are still bound by the shackles of paganism. You are to teach them the service of the kingdom of God by persuading them to accept the truth in the name of Christ, the Lord our God. You will instill into their minds the teaching of the Old and New Testaments, doing this in a spirit of love and moderation, and with arguments suited to their understanding."[33] Boniface seems to have taken these admonitions seriously. Willibald repeatedly referred to Boniface's itinerant preaching ministry. He wrote, "By preaching the gospel and turning their minds away from evil toward a life of virtue and the observance of canonical decrees [Boniface] reproved, admonished, and instructed to the best of his ability the priests and the elders, some of whom devoted themselves to the true worship of Almighty God."[34] Though Bishop Daniel had encouraged Boniface to avoid arguments with the Frisians, Boniface's preaching was characterized by an anti-pagan polemic. As his preaching bore fruit through the conversion of many Frisians, Boniface followed up the work through teaching, catechesis, and the establishment of new churches.[35]

Related to his preaching, confronting paganism was a third aspect of Boniface's mission work. According to Willibald, when Boniface joined Willibrord, the two "destroyed pagan temples and shrines, built churches and chapels, and . . . gained numerous converts to the church."[36] Boniface's zeal to destroy pagan places of worship was very likely a reaction to

---

31. Willibald, *Life of Boniface*, 5.
32. Boniface, *Letter* 11; also Mayr-Harting, *Coming of Christianity*, 263.
33. Boniface, *Letter* 3; see also *Letter* 12.
34. Willibald, *Life of Boniface*, 5; see also Boniface, *Letter,* 15.
35. Willibald, *Life of Boniface*, 5–6.
36. Ibid., 5.

Gregory the Great and Augustine of Canterbury's practice in his homeland of leaving pagan temples intact in the hopes of transitioning them into churches, which may have resulted in syncretism. When Boniface cut down the sacred oak at Geismar, one of the groups deeply affected were the "half-Christianized peoples of that area"[37]—those that still held some allegiance to Germanic paganism.

Though Boniface's actions seemed to have a purifying effect on German Christians, he was also contextualizing the gospel for the eighth-century Frisian pagans. Because the sacred oak was their key symbol of power, Boniface's actions demonstrated a "conflict not between men but between the gods" and they connected with the German traditions of "trial by ordeal."[38] Neill explains: "The Germans were convinced that anyone who infringed the sacredness of the sanctuary would be destroyed by the gods; Boniface affirmed that he would be unscathed. The oak was felled; nothing happened. The watchers were at once convinced that Boniface was right and that the God he proclaimed was really stronger that the gods of their fathers."[39] Reminiscent of Elijah's standoff with the prophets of Baal (1 Kgs 8:17–40), Boniface's actions seemed to connect with the German appreciation for spiritual power encounters, and they perceived that Boniface's god was more powerful than their deities. These factors doubtless contributed to their conversions.[40]

Another quality of Boniface's mission work was that he worked in teams and also set apart other laborers for the work among the Frisians. This value was perhaps first encouraged by Gregory II, who asked the existing German churches to provide Boniface with co-laborers at the outset of the mission.[41] In his final years of service in Germany, Willibald reported that Boniface was joined by a Bishop Eoban and was also "assisted in his labors by a number of priests and deacons."[42]

Boniface's missionary teams were largely comprised of other monks. As word of his ministry spread, monks from around Europe were drawn to join his monastery and serve in the work among the Frisians. Willibald notes: "By this means the report of his preaching reached far-off lands so

---

37. Neill, *History of Christian Missions*, 64.
38. Ibid., 65.
39. Ibid.
40. Irvin and Sunquist, *History of the World Christian Movement*, 345–46.
41. Boniface, *Letter* 6.
42. Willibald, *Life of Boniface*, 8.

that within a short space of time his fame resounded throughout the greater part of Europe. From Britain an exceedingly large number of holy men came to his aid, among them readers, writers, and learned men trained in the other arts. Of these a considerable number put themselves under his rule and guidance, and by their help the population in many places was recalled from the errors and profane rites of their heathen gods."[43] Following the example of Willibrord, Boniface expanded his ministry and community of missionaries by starting new monasteries. Talbot argues that mission work in the German context required disciplined and well-trained teachers and the monastery was the best environment to cultivate such leaders. Also similar to the monasteries of Willibrord and other missionary monks, the monastic community itself served as a witness to the Frisians. Talbot adds: "The monasteries would provide perfect examples of the Christian life to people living in the neighborhood, so that if they could not learn through words, they could imbibe through example."[44]

As Boniface was innovative in recruiting missionary teams, he was probably the first to involve women in the work of ministry. From the earliest years of his ascetic journey, Boniface had been involved in teaching both men and women, which apparently convinced him that women had something to contribute to cross-cultural ministry. The most famous missionary-nun recruited by Boniface was Leoba. Her journey to mission was recounted by her biographer:

> When Boniface found that the [Frisian] people were ready to receive the faith and that, though the harvest was great, the laborers who worked with him were few, he sent messengers and letters to England, his native land, summoning from different ranks of the clergy many who were learned in the divine law and fitted both by their character and good works to preach the word of God.... Likewise, he sent messengers with letters to the abbess Tetta, of whom we have already spoken, asking her to send Leoba to accompany him on this journey and to take part in this embassy: for Leoba's reputation for learning and holiness had spread far and wide and her praise was on everyone's lips.[45]

Her primary tasks in ministry included overseeing the women's house of the monastery, pursuing a collective witness among the Germanic

---

43. Ibid., 6.
44. Talbot, "St. Boniface and the German Mission," 50–51.
45. Rudolph of Fulda, *Life of Leoba* (all English are from Talbot).

peoples, and inviting female converts to join their community. Since she was well educated in the Scriptures, her ministry also included teaching the Bible and a Christian worldview.[46] Summarizing the contribution of Leoba and her companions to the German mission, Talbot argues: "Never, perhaps, has there been an age in which religious women exercised such great power, for it is extremely doubtful if even Boniface without their help would have enjoyed the measure of success in every field which attended his labors."[47]

Following both the examples of Augustine of Canterbury and Willibrord, Boniface's mission work was also characterized by its distinct Romanness. This was initially evident when Wynfrith was given the name Boniface upon his consecration as missionary bishop, just as Willibrord had been renamed Clement.[48] In an early letter, Boniface communicated that he saw himself being sent to Germany based on the authority of the Roman church: "by the authority of St. Peter, prince of the apostles, whose government we administer in this [Roman] See by the dispensation of God."[49]

Boniface also demonstrated a strong loyalty to the bishop of Rome. In his work, particularly the organization of new German churches, he sought to align them with the authority, teaching, and practices of Rome.[50] In Gregory II's initial letter to Boniface, the bishop encouraged him to assimilate German believers into the church according to Roman customs: "we command you that in admitting within the church those who have some kind of belief in God, you will insist upon using the sacramental discipline prescribed in the official ritual formulary of the Holy Apostolic See."[51] In commending Boniface to the existing German churches, Gregory II communicated that Boniface's task was to reach German pagans and to "instruct them in the teachings of this Apostolic See and confirm them in the Catholic faith."[52] According to Willibald, on a follow-up visit to Rome after

---

46. Talbot, "St. Boniface and the German Mission," 51.
47. Talbot, *Anglo-Saxon Missionaries in Germany*, xiii.
48. Mayr-Harting, *Coming of Christianity*, 268–69.
49. Boniface, *Letter* 3.
50. See Boniface, *Letters* 23, 25, 37, 46–47.
51. Boniface, *Letter* 5.
52. Boniface, *Letter* 6.

the German mission was underway, the Roman bishop scrutinized Boniface over his doctrine to insure that he was in line with Rome's teachings.[53]

Similar to Augustine of Canterbury's interactions with Gregory I about the mission to England, Boniface also corresponded with the Roman bishops for specific instructions on how to organize and lead the new German churches.[54] Since Boniface received direction on questions related to ordinations, marriage, and the liturgy among other things, Roman theology and approaches to church certainly prevailed, which surely inhibited the German churches from becoming fully indigenous.[55]

A final characteristic of Boniface's mission practice was his willingness to suffer. Though Boniface had enjoyed the protection of the Frankish leaders, ultimately his *peregrinus* instinct and passion to preach the gospel among non-believing pagans led him to move beyond the boundaries of safety to engage the Frisians once more. Capturing the hardships of the journey for the seventy-something missionary monk, Willibald wrote:

> After the lapse of a few days, he still persevered in his decision to set out on the journey, and so, taking with him a few companions, he went on board a ship and sailed down the Rhine. Eventually, he reached the marshy country of Frisia, crossed safely over the stretch of water . . . and made a survey of the lands round about, which up till then had borne no fruit. After bravely hazarding the perils of the river, the sea and the wide expanse of the ocean, he passed through dangerous places without fear of danger, and visited the pagan Frisians, whose land is divided into many territories and districts by intersecting canals.[56]

This hardship only continued as Boniface and his companions were attacked and martyred in 754 while preaching and baptizing new believers in Frisia. Willibald concluded:

> When . . . the faith had been planted strongly in Frisia and the glorious end of the saint's life drew near, he took with him a picked number of his personal followers and pitched a camp on the banks of the river Bordne. . . . Here he fixed a day on which he would

---

53. Willibald, *Life of Boniface*, 6.

54. It is interesting to note that Boniface (*Letter* 19) also wrote to Archbishop Nothelm of Canterbury asking for his own copy of the correspondence between Gregory I and Augustine.

55. Boniface, *Letters* 14, 16; also Talbot, "St. Boniface and the German Mission," 51–52; and Mayr-Harting, *Coming of Christianity*, 269.

56. Willibald, *Life of Boniface*, 8.

confirm by the laying on of hands all the neophytes and those who had recently been baptized. . . . But events turned out otherwise than expected. When the appointed day arrived and the morning light was breaking through the clouds after sunrise, enemies came instead of friends, new executioners in place of new worshipers of the faith. A vast number of foes armed with spears and shields rushed into the camp brandishing their weapons, . . . the frenzied mob of pagans rushed suddenly upon them with swords and every kind of warlike weapon, staining their bodies with their precious blood.[57]

Summary

Willibrord and Boniface were the face of eighth-century monastic missions from England to northern Europe and particularly to the German peoples. Clearly influenced by the sixth- and seventh-century Celtic monks, they were also quite accustomed to and comfortable with the developing Christendom of the eighth century. Their ministries were sponsored and protected by Frankish leaders and they propagated a Roman form of Christianity. Despite this, preaching remained central to their mission work and, in the case of Boniface, his *peregrinus* motivation pushed him beyond the bounds of military protection, which ultimately resulted his martyrdom.

---

57. Ibid.

CHAPTER 9

Anskar

AROUND 793, MUCH OF western Europe began to encounter the Vikings. Seeking wealth and swift military victories, these sea-going Scandinavian peoples regularly attacked and pillaged monasteries and other soft targets along the coasts of England, Ireland, and Germany. Naturally, their actions drew the serious attention of European monarchs such as the Frankish King Charlemagne, his son Louis the Pious, and the English monarch Ethelred, all eager to protect their kingdoms. Much of the European Christian literature from the ninth to eleventh centuries portrays the Scandinavians as barbaric, pillaging pirates—"Northmen"—who were driven by their Norse pagan beliefs.[1] Within this understandable environment of fear, there were some sincere attempts at Christian mission toward the Scandinavian peoples. One intriguing example was the missionary monk Anskar of Corbie (801–865) who ministered in Denmark and Sweden while also serving as a missionary bishop in the northern regions of the Frankish empire. In this chapter, we will examine Anskar's background and monastic journey, narrate his story in mission, and also discuss his approaches, values, and innovation in mission among the Vikings.

Background

Anskar was born in the Frankish town of Amiens in 801. Most of what we know about his life comes from the *Life of Anskar*, a sacred biography written in 875 by his disciple and Bishop Rimbert, who succeeded Anskar as bishop

---

1. Winroth, *Conversion of Scandinavia*, 121.

of Bremen and was also involved in mission work to Sweden.[2] Some corroborating insights can also be gleaned from Adam of Bremen's eleventh-century work, the *History of the Archbishops of Hamburg-Bremen*.[3]

Raised in a noble Frankish family, Anskar entered the monastery at Corbie at a young age and he received an excellent education there. Founded by Columban's disciples from Luxeuil two centuries prior, the Corbie monastery followed a modified Benedictine rule and was surely influenced by Columban's missionary vision.[4] Around 822, Anskar was sent with a group of monks to set up a new monastery at Corvey (New Corbie) in Saxony, where his primary role was beginning a school and teaching. Commenting on Anskar's skills in this area, Rimbert noted: "God's servant was first sent in company with other brethren in order that he might perform the office of a teacher. In this task he was found so commendable and agreeable that, by the choice of all, he was appointed to preach the word of God to the people in church. So it came about that in this same place he became the first master of the school and teacher of the people."[5]

Danish Mission

In 826, after meeting with the Frankish King Louis the Pious, the exiled Danish King Harald Klak was baptized along with his wife and four hundred members of their court. Clearly desiring to regain his kingdom and to forge an alliance with the Franks, Harald's conversion was politically motivated. As Harald planned his return to Denmark, Louis urged him to take missionaries with him to teach the Christian faith to his people.[6] The Scandinavians had had previous contact with the gospel through the ministry of Ebo, the archbishop of Reims, who had preached in Denmark

---

2. While Eric Knibbs has offered a critical evaluation of Rimbert's *Life of Anskar* and cast doubt on some of the traditionally accepted details of Anskar's life and work as bishop of Hamburg-Bremen, the narrative that we present of Anskar's journey in and approach to mission remains faithful. Cf. Nibbs, *Ansgar, Rimbert and the Forged Foundations*, 175–207.

3. Blocher and Blandenier, *Evangelization of the World*, 83; also Sawyer, *Kings and Vikings*, 26.

4. Rimbert, *Life of Anskar*, 2; cf. Cardoza-Orlandi and Gonzalez, *To All Nations from All Nations*, 102.

5. Rimbert, *Life of Anskar*, 6 (all English translations by C. H. Robinson).

6. Adam of Bremen, *History of the Archbishops* 1.17; also Winroth, *Conversion of Scandinavia*, 16, 53, 105–6; and Blocher and Blandenier, *Evangelization of the World*, 83.

just a few years before. Beyond that one campaign, the "Northmen" had also encountered the gospel through the numerous believing merchants, soldiers, and even slaves who frequented Scandinavia.[7]

Rimbert reported that Harald took Louis' suggestion seriously to return home with missionaries: "He began to make diligent enquiry in order that he might find a holy and devoted man who could go and continue with him, and who might strengthen him and his people, and by teaching the doctrine of salvation might induce them to receive the faith of the Lord."[8] Rimbert added that Wala, the abbot at Corvey, recommended Anskar for the mission because he "burned with zeal for true religion and was eager to endure suffering for the name of God."[9] That is, Anskar believed that he was called to be a martyr. After Anskar agreed to accept the assignment, some of his fellow monks reacted strongly and some even tried to dissuade him from going. He responded: "I am asked whether I am willing on God's behalf to go to pagan nations in order to preach the gospel. So far from daring to oppose this suggestion I desire, with all my strength, that the opportunity for going may be granted to me, and that no one may be able to divert me from this design."[10] Perhaps inspired by Anskar's resolve, another monk named Autbert agreed to join him in the work.

What was the political, social, and religious landscape of Scandinavia that Anskar and his co-laborers were entering? As shown, violence marred the initial Scandinavian encounters with Europe. Vikings attacked, raided, and pillaged Europeans towns, enslaving their people. As a natural result, most Europeans feared the "Northmen"; therefore, Louis the Pious' actions to receive King Harald and send back missionaries with him were surely a calculated risk. In fact, the Frankish alliance with Harald was short-lived since the Dane did not regain his kingdom and later resorted to pirating himself, including an attack on the Franks.[11] In short, Anskar and his colleagues were being asked to minister in a context of violence.

---

7. Nelson, "Frankish Empire," 20; also Sørensen, "Religions Old and New," 204, 218; Sawyer, *Kings and Vikings*, 65–77, 134–35; and Winroth, *Conversion of Scandinavia*, 9, 90–92, 105.

8. Rimbert, *Life of Anskar*, 7.

9. Ibid., 7 and 3.

10. Ibid., 7.

11. Adam of Bremen, *History of the Archbishops* 1.16; also Nelson, "Frankish Empire," 19–24; Sawyer, *Kings and Vikings*, 1–2, 6, 78–97; and Winroth, *Conversion of Scandinavia*, 24–40.

Although not a great deal is known about ninth-century Scandinavian social organization, it appears that the Danes, Swedes, and others were organized in something of a tribal structure and were led by various family and monarchial leaders. With no unifying king or leader under which the Scandinavian peoples could rally, kings such as Harald often fought against neighboring monarchs. One of the clear roles of Viking kings was leading their people in military expeditions, particularly during the noted raids against the rest of Europe. Also, these tribal structures were evident at sea as the Vikings organized themselves into fellowships around particular ships.[12]

Little is known about Scandinavian religious beliefs and practices in the pre-Christian period, but Viking worship probably resembled the Germanic paganism that Willibrord and Boniface had encountered in Frisia. Arguably the best source for understanding Viking religion was the vast body of Norse poetry—narratives that venerated the warrior gods Oden, Thor, and Ullr, along with Freyr, the god of fertility. The Scandinavians paid homage to these deities through offering sacrifices, both animals and humans. Though the Scandinavians constructed temples and other shrines for the purpose of honoring the dead, these sacred places were not essential to Norse paganism as family and tribal leaders often conducted rituals in the open air.[13]

Anskar and his team began their work in Schleswig in the northern most region of Denmark. His ministry included public preaching and evangelizing the Danes, while also starting a school for children—an extension of his previous work as a teacher in the monastery at Corvey. He was also allowed to build a church facility in Schleswig and to hold services. Anskar was probably granted this freedom because of the tolerance of some Danish kings and because, at this point, revering the Christian God was not seen as incompatible with Norse pagan practices.[14] Despite these initial signs of openness to their work, Anskar's team was quickly met with hardship as Autbert became sick and died. Also, in the second year of their ministry, they encountered some anti-Christian backlash from local pagans and were forced to leave the area and return to Corvey. In the end, King Harald was

---

12. Sawyer, *Kings and Vikings*, 54–55.

13. Sawyer, *Kings and Vikings*, 131–33; also Winroth, *Conversion of Scandinavia*, 3–4, 146–50.

14. Rimbert, *Life of Anskar*, 8; also Blocher and Blandenier, *Evangelization of the World*, 83; and Sørensen, "Religions Old and New," 223.

unable to regain his kingdom and Anskar seemed discouraged at the political nature of the mission.[15]

Swedish Mission

Around 830, King Bjorn of Sweden sent ambassadors to Louis the Pious and requested that Christian teachers be sent to the Swedes.[16] According to Rimbert, the emperor summoned Anskar to lead the mission and the monk committed to the task before being asked. Describing Anskar's continued willingness to suffer and embrace martyrdom, Rimbert wrote: "If in a journey of this kind any harm or misfortune should befall him, he was resolved to bear it patiently for Christ's sake."[17] Anskar seemed motivated to engage in mission and even suffer because of some compelling dreams and visions. Rimbert added that Anskar had "no hesitation in undertaking this task, as he was comforted by the heavenly vision which he had previously seen" and that in another vision he was commanded to "Go, and declare the word of God unto the nations."[18]

A fellow monk named Witmar, who had served with him at the Corbie and Corvey monasteries, accompanied Anskar on the journey to Sweden. The trip was filled with many difficulties: their ship was attacked by pirates and they were robbed of nearly all of their possessions, including Bibles and liturgical books, as well as gifts for the Swedish king. According to Rimbert, some members of the team wanted to turn back, but Anskar encouraged them to persevere and continue with the mission. Eventually, they made it to Sweden where they were received by the king and allowed to establish a base of operations, presumably a monastery, on the island of Birka on Lake Mälar near modern Stockholm.[19]

Part of Anskar's strategy in Sweden was connecting with those who were already Christians. Many of these were slaves, and Anskar considered it part of his ministry to secure their release. In addition to this work, he proclaimed the gospel to Swedish pagans and saw a number believe the

---

15. Rimbert, *Life of Anskar*, 8; also Neill, *History of Christian Missions*, 70; and Tucker, *From Jerusalem to Irian Jaya*, 52.

16. Rimbert, *Life of Anskar*, 9; also Neill, *History of Christian Missions*, 70.

17. Rimbert, *Life of Anskar*, 9.

18. Ibid.

19. Rimbert, *Life of Anskar*, 6, 10–11; also Blocher and Blandenier, *Evangelization of the World*, 83; and Tucker, *From Jerusalem to Irian Jaya*, 52.

gospel and be baptized, including some members of the nobility and local government. He also started a church as well as another school. After a year and a half of successful ministry, Anskar, Witmar, and their colleagues returned back to Frankia.[20]

Mission Base in Hamburg and Bremen

Rimbert wrote that Louis the Pious "began to enquire by what means he might establish a bishop's see in the North within the limits of his own empire, from which the bishop who should be stationed there might make frequent journeys to the northern regions for the sake of preaching the gospel."[21] Pleased with Anskar's work among the Swedes, in 832 the emperor appointed Anskar to lead a school and a mission base in Hamburg—a staging point for mission to the "Northmen." Affirming this move, Bishop Gregory IV of Rome set apart Anskar as a papal legate among all the "neighboring races of the Swedes and Danes, also the Slavs and the other races that inhabited the regions of the North."[22] Similar to Boniface's appointment in the previous century, Anskar was set apart as a missionary bishop.[23]

Generously supported by Louis the Pious, Anskar established a monastery, church, library, and schools at Hamburg toward this end of sending missionaries to the North. According to Rimbert, Anskar also employed a new and interesting strategy for recruiting and equipping new missionaries: "He began also to buy Danish and Slav boys and to redeem some from captivity so that he might train them for God's service."[24] Although missionaries had been expelled from Sweden, Anskar set apart his nephew Gautbert as a missionary bishop and sent him along with a team back to Birka to continue the work.[25]

---

20. Rimbert, *Life of Anskar*, 11; also Neill, *History of Christian Missions*, 70; Sawyer, *Kings and Vikings*, 39–40; and Winroth, *Conversion of Scandinavia*, 106.

21. Rimbert, *Life of Anskar*, 12.

22. Ibid., 14.

23. Adam of Bremen, *History of the Archbishops* 1.15; also Sørensen, "Religions Old and New," 202; and Neill, *History of Christian Missions*, 70.

24. Rimbert, *Life of Anskar*, 15.

25. Ibid. 14–15; also Tucker, *From Jerusalem to Irian Jaya*, 52; and Blocher and Blandenier, *Evangelization of the World*, 84.

ANSKAR

Perhaps irritated at the mission work that Anskar was facilitating, a band of Vikings attacked Hamburg in 845. As the church and monastery were razed and Bibles and other books were destroyed, Anskar literally escaped with the clothes on his back; however, his work at Hamburg was brought to a grinding halt. Gautbert was also forced to flee Sweden following an anti-Christian attack from a band of pagan sympathizers.[26]

Despite this major setback, in 848 Bishop Nicolas of Rome made Anskar the archbishop of Bremen, which also included Hamburg as well.[27] According to Rimbert, this new diocese was established to fulfill the Lord's command to "Go and teach all the nations."[28] From Bremen, Anskar relaunched the Danish mission and traveled there at the invitation of King Horic. Given this freedom and opportunity, Anskar's mission included preaching, rebuilding the church at Schleswig and setting apart a pastor there, and also starting a new church in the west-coast trading town of Ribe.[29]

Following this successful work in Denmark, Anskar appealed to the Danish king to send laborers once again to Sweden. According to Rimbert, Anskar experienced new visions in which he understood the prophet Isaiah's words, "Listen to me, you islands; hear this, you distant nations," as a specific reference to Sweden and that God would make Anskar "a light for the Gentiles, that my salvation may reach to the ends of the earth."[30] This dream became a reality in 852 as Anskar traveled back to Sweden and was welcomed by King Olaf. Given the past violence and hostility that Christian missionaries had experienced in Sweden, Anskar made fasting and prayer a priority before attempting any ministry. He also allowed the Swedes to cast lots to decide if churches ought to be built and worship services convened. According to Rimbert, the Swedes were favorable to starting new churches, and Gautbert's nephew Erimebert was set apart to pastor them.[31]

---

26. Rimbert, *Life of Anskar*, 16–17; also Sawyer, *Kings and Vikings*, 135; and Winroth, *Conversion of Scandinavia*, 27–28.

27. For a dissenting view of the traditional acceptance that Anskar served as bishop of Bremen, see Nibbs, *Ansgar, Rimbert and the Forged Foundations*.

28. Rimbert, *Life of Anskar*, 23.

29. Ibid., 24; Adam of Bremen, *History of the Archbishops* 1.27; also Winroth, *Conversion of Scandinavia*, 108; and Neill, *History of Christian Missions*, 70.

30. Isa 49:1, 6 cited in Rimbert, *Life of Anskar*, 25.

31. Rimbert, *Life of Anskar*, 25–26; also Blocher and Blandenier, *Evangelization of the World*, 84.

Anskar continued his mission work in Scandinavia until his death in 865. The scholarly consensus is that during Anskar's lifetime, there was little lasting fruit among the Vikings. Indeed, there was continual resistance to the gospel from Scandinavian pagans, including a strong reaction in Denmark toward the end of Anskar's life. There was also continued violence and pillaging on the part of pirates. Christianity most clearly took hold in Scandinavia in the tenth century with the public conversion and baptism of a number of kings who also began to ban pagan worship and practices in society.[32] That said, Anders Winroth notes that Anskar probably accomplished more in his lifetime than we realize but that the documents for ninth-century Scandinavian church and mission history are very limited.[33]

Approaches to Mission

What values, thoughts, and approaches characterized Anskar's missionary work? At least nine tendencies can be observed; not surprisingly, a number of them relate directly to his monastic vision and calling. First, similar to Patrick of Ireland, Anskar was influenced by dreams and visions at various stages of his ministry, including when he contemplated mission to Sweden on two different occasions and as he prayed about leading the church at Bremen.[34]

Second, Anskar's monastic theology and theology of mission involved embracing suffering. As a young monk, Anskar was apparently convinced that he would earn a martyr's crown, which probably informed his motivation to go and minister among the Vikings in the first place. Rimbert indicated that a willingness to suffer stayed with Anskar throughout his life: "The life that he lived involved toils which were accompanied by constant bodily suffering: in fact his whole life was like a martyrdom. He endured many labors amongst foreigners apart from those within his own diocese, which were caused by the invasions and ravages of barbarians and the opposition of evil men, and in addition the personal suffering which, for the love of Christ, he never ceased to bring upon himself."[35] Rimbert's claim is supported by Anskar's expulsion from Denmark in 827, the hardship

---

32. Rimbert, *Life of Anskar,* 31–34; also Sawyer, *Kings and Vikings,* 9, 138–43; and Winroth, *Conversion of Scandinavia,* 150–52.

33. Winroth, *Conversion of Scandinavia,* 110–12.

34. Rimbert, *Life of Anskar,* 9, 25, 36; cf. Cabaniss, "Motives for Conversion," 379.

35. Rimbert, *Life of Anskar,* 40.

he endured getting to Sweden in 830, and the attack that he and others experienced in Hamburg in 845. Rimbert also likened Anskar's hardships to the apostle Paul's sufferings recorded in 2 Corinthians 11:26–29, which included dangers at sea, from bandits, and betrayal from other believers.[36] In addition to these challenges, Anskar also suffered sickness as well as physical and emotional pain throughout his years in ministry. Anskar never achieved his goal of martyrdom and identifying with Christ in his suffering, however, he did cultivate a sense of patience and endurance that kept him serving in mission among the Vikings for nearly forty years.[37]

Third, and quite related to the last value, Anskar demonstrated a good balance of the contemplative and active lives as he engaged in mission. Rimbert's biography offers a helpful window into Anskar's daily life as a monk, which included practices such as prayer, fasting, simple living, singing the Psalms, copying books, and working with his hands while singing and praying.[38] In fact, Rimbert asserted that Anskar's monastic calling was itself a type of martyrdom: "For day by day, by tears, watchings, fastings, tormenting of the flesh and mortification of his carnal desires, he offered up a sacrifice to God on the altar of his heart and attained to martyrdom as far as was possible in a time of peace."[39]

Rimbert captured Anskar's value for balancing a life of ascetic withdrawal with a commitment to serving others. He wrote:

> In accordance with what he had read in Martin's life, he made a special effort to benefit the common people by preaching to them the word of God. At the same time he loved to be alone in order that he might exercise himself in divine philosophy [monastic discipline and contemplation]. With this end in view he had a special cell built for himself which he called a quiet place and one friendly to grief. Here he dwelt with a few companions and, as often as he could get free from preaching and ecclesiastical duties and the disturbances caused by the heathen, he dwelt here alone, but he never allowed his own convenience, or his love of solitude, to interfere with the interests of the flock that had been entrusted to him.[40]

---

36. Ibid., 29, 42.
37. Ibid., 40; also Neill, *History of Christian Missions*, 70.
38. Rimbert, *Life of Anskar*, 35.
39. Ibid., 42.
40. Ibid., 35.

In this sense, Anskar followed Gregory the Great's thinking that service to others was itself a form of devotion and as such should trump the monks' personal spiritual disciplines. Adam of Bremen supported this by remarking that Anskar was "outwardly an apostle but inwardly a monk" and that he was "never idle."[41] Similarly, Ruth Tucker concludes that Anskar "was an ascetic who regarded prayer and fasting as paramount—though never to be done at the expense of useful activity."[42]

Fourth, Anskar worked in teams throughout his life—a clear reflection of his communal monastic values. While there were colleagues mentioned by name—Autbert who served with him in Denmark and Witmar in Sweden—Rimbert's biography alluded to other unnamed co-laborers who were probably recruited from the monastery at Corvey. In every place that Anskar served, one of his first steps was to establish a monastery that functioned as the base for mission work.

Fifth, Anskar's engagement in ministry was often prompted by the initiative of political leaders. As shown, in the initial mission to Denmark, he responded to King Harald's request for missionaries via the Christian Frankish King Louis the Pious. The Swedish mission began at the request of King Bjorn. In a later trip to Denmark, Anskar was invited to serve there by King Horic. It appears that the later Swedish mission from Denmark was the only work that was purely Anskar's initiative. While Scandinavian kings and leaders invited Anskar and gave him space and freedom to proclaim Christ, we do not see kings being baptized and urging their people to do the same as we observed in the ministries of Augustine of Canterbury, Columba, and possibly Patrick. This, of course, changed in tenth-century Scandinavia as a number of Viking kings embraced Christianity.[43]

Sixth, Anskar's ministry was unique and innovative because he was able to establish a mission base and training center in Hamburg through the generous endowment of the emperor. While Anskar was involved in going to the northern regions on itinerant trips, the bases at Hamburg and later Bremen allowed him to be an equipper and sender of other missionaries as well. As Neill observes, by using established churches as bases for mission, Anskar was "the first of a great succession of bishops who worked outwards from a well-established Christian center into the

---

41. Adam of Bremen, *History of the Archbishops* 1.35.
42. Tucker, *From Jerusalem to Irian Jaya*, 53.
43. Winroth, *Conversion of Scandinavia*, 104.

regions beyond which were still pagan."⁴⁴ Finally, this discussion reminds us that Anskar's ministry was done under the auspices of the church. As we have shown, he was ordained a missionary bishop for the North under the authority of Bishop Gregory IV of Rome and later his colleague Gautbert was also consecrated a missionary bishop. One of the clear outcomes of their work in Denmark and Sweden was establishing new congregations with baptized believers.

Seventh, teaching and establishing schools were key elements of Anskar's missionary strategy. Beginning at the Corvey monastery, teaching was central to his monastic service. As he established monasteries in Denmark, Sweden, and Hamburg, he also began schools in order to teach Scripture and other disciplines.⁴⁵ This emphasis on education probably points back to the similar values of the Columban monks who founded the Corbie monastery where Anskar was raised.

Eighth, social justice was also important to Anskar. As noted, in his initial journey to Sweden, he encountered enslaved Christians, and he successfully lobbied to gain their release. Later, he deliberately purchased the freedom of Danish boys and trained them in the monastery to serve as missionaries among their own people. Finally, Rimbert indicated that Anskar also confronted Christians who were involved in slave trafficking.⁴⁶

A final aspect of Anskar's missionary service was caring for the poor and the sick. Rimbert noted that the monk regularly gave offerings and alms to the poor, washed their feet, and opened the doors of his monastery to offer them hospitality.⁴⁷ Rimbert added that Anskar founded a hospital at Bremen for those who could not afford a doctor "so that those who were poor and sick might be daily sustained and refreshed."⁴⁸

Anskar offered both medical and spiritual care. While providing the sick with medicine, he likewise ministered to them by praying for their healing. Rimbert wrote: "It is impossible to count the number of those who were healed by his prayers and by his anointing. For, according to the statement made by many persons, sick people came eagerly to him, not only from his own diocese, but from a great distance, demanding from him

---

44. Neill, *History of Christian Missions*, 70

45. Cabaniss, "Motives for Conversion," 380–81.

46. Rimbert, *Life of Anskar*, 35, 38; also Cardoza-Orlandi and Gonzalez, *To All Nations from All Nations*, 102.

47. Rimbert, *Life of Anskar*, 35.

48. Ibid.; cf. Adam of Bremen, *History of the Archbishops* 1.32.

healing medicine. He, however, preferred that this should be kept quiet rather than that it should be noised abroad."[49]

Summary

For most of the ninth century, European Christians were understandably fearful of their northern neighbors in Scandinavia and very few were thinking about engaging them missionally. Though King Harald's initiative in 826 was more politically motivated, his initiative toward Louis the Pious and Anskar began a wave of Christian mission toward the Vikings. Hardship, patience, and endurance characterized Anskar's ministry. Though Christianity did not gain broad acceptance in Scandinavia until the tenth century, the faithful ministry of Anskar and his colleagues surely helped pave the way to evangelizing this region.

---

49. Rimbert, *Life of Anskar*, 39; cf. Canaiss, "Motives for Conversion," 383.

CHAPTER 10

Cyril and Methodius

EACH DAY WHEN STUDENTS enter the national library of Bulgaria in Sofia, they pass by a statue of two Greek brothers—Saints Cyril (ca. 826–869) and Methodius (815–885)—for whom the library is named. Also, every year on May 24th, Bulgaria celebrates Slavonic Alphabet Day, which points back to the work of Cyril, who is credited with developing the first Slavic alphabet. In a later form, this alphabet became the medium for advancing Slavic literature and culture for the next eleven hundred years. To this day, Slavic speakers in Eastern Europe and Russia refer to their alphabet as Cyrillic.

While Cyril (known as Constantine until shortly before his death) and Methodius were indeed culture makers to whom Slavic peoples are indebted, what is more significant is that they were missionary monks who were motivated to develop a Slavic alphabet in order to translate liturgy and Scripture into Slavonic. Like the Coptic and Armenian languages, the Slavic alphabet was first developed in order to translate Scripture and facilitate the spread of the gospel and Christian teaching. In this chapter, we will explore the lives of these two brothers, their journey in monasticism and mission, and evaluate the characteristics and innovations in their approach to mission.

Backgrounds

The best sources for examining their lives are two ninth-century sacred biographies—the *Life of Constantine (Cyril)* and the *Life of Methodius* respectively—that were written within a couple decades of each brother's passing. Like other saints' lives or sacred biographies discussed, these works were not intended to stand up to the scrutiny of modern historiography but rather to show concrete models of faith and also to defend the validity of Slavic Christianity. That said, they were authentic works written for a ninth-century Slavic audience that also offer the modern reader a window into their worlds.[1]

Cyril and Methodius were born in Thessalonica and, according to their biographies, their father Leo was a Greek military leader and their family was wealthy.[2] Because of their privileged position, they were educated from a young age by private tutors, and they studied grammar, poetry, rhetoric (communication), and theology. Due to Thessalonica's place as the second leading city in the eastern Roman Empire behind Constantinople, their learning environment was quite rich. Spiritually, Cyril and Methodius were influenced by scholarly bishops such as Leo as well as a number of monastic communities in the area.[3]

Due to Methodius' intellectual abilities, and possibly because of his family's prominence, he was appointed as governor of a Slavic province where he served from 843 to 856. Though probably located in Asia Minor, our sources do not indicate an exact location.[4] What is certain, however, is that "through the constant contact with the Slavs, Methodius was to acquire a profound knowledge of the Slavic world, to learn the Slav's customs and traditions, and above all to become proficient in the Slavonic tongue."[5] This work in government proved foundational for his later work among the Slavs.

From an early age, Cyril showed great academic promise and was already well versed in the writings of the Cappadocian father Gregory of Nazianzus. At the age of fifteen, Cyril received a special imperial invitation to study in Constantinople, where he received a thorough education in grammar, poetry, math, rhetoric, and, most importantly, philosophy. After completing his studies, he was given the title "the philosopher," which stayed

---

1. See Tachioas, *Cyril and Methodius*, 146; also Dvornik, *Byzantine Missions*, 53, 183; and Vlasto, *Entry of the Slavs*, 29–32.

2. *Life of Cyril*, 2; *Life of Methodius*, 2; also Tachioas, *Cyril and Methodius*, 3–4.

3. Tachioas, *Cyril and Methodius*, 5–9; also Wilken, *First Thousands Years*, 344.

4. *Life of Methodius*, 2; also Dvornik, *Byzantine Missions*, 58; and Tachioas, *Cyril and Methodius*, 21–22.

5. Tachioas, *Cyril and Methodius*, 22–23.

with him for the rest of his life.[6] His biographer introduced Cyril's *Life* by calling him, "Constantine the Philosopher, our teacher and enlightener."[7]

Resisting the opportunities that came with his family's connections, Cyril rejected a prominent marriage and made the pursuit of wisdom his first priority. He was, however, ordained as a deacon in the church and initially was given an administrative role in the church at Constantinople. This post was short lived as Cyril retired to a monastery on the Bosporus where he continued to study. After six months in the monastery, he returned to Constantinople where he taught philosophy in a school that most likely operated under the auspices of the church.[8]

Following the Arab-Muslim Caliph al-Mutawakkil's movements toward Byzantine territory around 851, the Byzantine leaders responded by sending a delegation to Samarra (modern Iraq) to renegotiate a treaty with the Arabs and the twenty-four-year-old Cyril was selected to be part of the team. This effectively began his work in cross-cultural ministry as he participated in what was both a diplomatic and Christian mission to the Arabs.[9]

According to his biographer, Cyril's conversations with the Arab delegation included philosophy, science, and theology—particularly the doctrine of the Trinity. Responding to the charge that Christians worship three gods, Cyril reportedly replied:

> Do not disgrace yourselves with blasphemy. We have been well taught by the prophets and the fathers and teachers of the church to praise the Holy Trinity: the Father, the Word, and the Spirit—three persons within a single being. The Word becomes flesh in a virgin, and was born for the sake of our salvation, as your prophet Muhammad himself witnesses, writing, "We sent our spirit unto a maiden and willed that she delivered a child" (Surah 19:17). Here, you see, I am explaining the Holy Trinity by the Qur'an.[10]

---

6. *Life of Cyril*, 3; cf. Dvornik, *Byzantine Missions*, 56–60; and Tachioas, *Cyril and Methodius*, 23–25, 28.

7. *Life of Cyril*, 2 (unless otherwise noted, all English translations are from Duichev, *Kiril and Methodius*).

8. *Life of Cyril*, 3–4; also Dvornik, *Byzantine Missions*, 54–55, 59–60; and Tachioas, *Cyril and Methodius*, 28–29.

9. Dvornik, *Byzantine Missions*, 62–64; 285–94; also Tachioas, *Cyril and Methodius*, 30–32.

10. *Life of Cyril*, 6.

Communicating rather directly to his hosts, Cyril based his claims on historic Christian teaching given through the church fathers and the Nicene Creed. Interestingly, he also appealed to the Muslims' holy book, with which he was apparently acquainted. In addition, Cyril argued that the mystery within the Christian understanding of the godhead was actually more satisfying than Islam's simplicity. On a practical note, Cyril questioned aloud why Muhammad gave no practical commands for moral living. Finally, upon hearing his Arab hosts boast of their caliph's wealth, the ascetically-minded philosopher stated that all wealth and gifts should be received from God with an attitude of praise.[11]

Monastic Journey

Although their respective careers took them in different directions, Cyril and Methodius were reunited by their mutual desire for ascetic lives. Since the fourth century, monasticism had remained an important aspect of Christianity in Asia Minor, reaching a high point in the eighth century as monasteries and hermitages continued to grow. Eastern monasticism was largely influenced by Basil's coenobitic vision that involved group and individual prayer, contemplation, and activism in the way of service and mission. As the church expanded eastward, monastic communities continued to be established and to flourish. According to Cyril's biographer, Cyril and Methodius' parents embraced asceticism in their later years, which probably influenced the brothers in this direction.[12]

After more than a decade of government service, Methodius retired to a monastery on Mt. Olympus in Bithynia. His biographer wrote: "When the opportunity came, he resigned from the *archontia* [province he was governing] and went to Olympus, where holy fathers live, and, having become a monk, donned the black habit and obeyed submissively, fulfilling all the monastic rule; and he applied himself to the study of books."[13] Following the Arab mission, Cyril decided to avoid Constantinople and its political upheaval and joined his brother on Mt. Olympus where they pursued a life of simplicity, prayer, reading, and study.[14] Tachioas notes that "unlike

11. Ibid., 6.

12. *Life of Cyril*, 2; also Tachioas, *Cyril and Methodius*, 35; also Vlasto, *Entry of the Slavs*, 296–98.

13. *Life of Methodius*, 3 cited in Tachioas, *Cyril and Methodius*, 34.

14. *Life of Cyril*, 7; also Tachioas, *Cyril and Methodius*, 33; and Dvornik, *Byzantine*

Methodius, Cyril did not become a monk at this time (he did so only just before his death), but simply led the monastic life and, like his brother, occupied himself with book-reading or writing."[15]

The Mt. Olympus monastery environment served as a launching point for the brothers' further involvement in mission for at least a few reasons. First, as missionary monks were already being sent to serve in Armenia and other places, the monastery's ethos celebrated and encouraged mission. Second, Cyril and Methodius' program of reading and study offered continual preparation for future service that was both academic and literary. Finally, as there were Slavs living in the region of Mt. Olympus, including some who may have joined the monastery, the brothers may have had a spiritual influence on Slavic peoples well before their mission to them.[16]

Khazar Mission

After a number of years of living in the monastery at Mt. Olympus, Cyril and Methodius were summoned by Emperor Michael III for mission work to the Khazar people. A Turkic nomadic people living in the Caucuses region of Russia, the Khazars had followed traditional pagan religions. However, at this point in their history, they were becoming increasingly influenced by Judaism and Islam. Since 750, the Muslim Abbasid Caliphate had been based at nearby Baghdad and this accounted for the Muslim influence. Interestingly though, due to the presence of zealous proselytizing Jewish merchants in the region, Judaism's influence was actually stronger than that of Islam. In this context, the Khazar khan reached out to the Byzantine Emperor, with whom he had enjoyed good diplomatic relations, and inquired of a third faith alternative—Christianity.[17]

Given their previous diplomatic work and Cyril's reputation as a teacher, Michael III responded to the khan's request by setting the brothers apart to go the Khazars.[18] Cyril's biographer recorded the emperor challenging Cyril and framing the mission in these terms: "Go forth, philosopher, to these people, speak to them and explain to them the Holy

---

Missions, 63–65.

15. Tachioas, *Cyril and Methodius*, 34.

16. Ibid., 36; also Vlasto, *Entry of the Slavs*, 37.

17. *Life of Cyril*, 8; also Tachioas, *Cyril and Methodius*, 39; and Dvornik, *Byzantine Missions*, 50–53, 65.

18. Tachioas, *Cyril and Methodius*, 41.

Trinity."[19] While Cyril was the younger brother, both men's biographies indicated that Cyril was the clear leader of the mission and that Methodius seemed happy to serve in this capacity.[20] Finally, since the khan's request was directed toward the emperor, this mission was both a state and church sponsored initiative.

Cyril and Methodius' work among the Khazars involved a variety of approaches. First, it appears that they were committed to language learning and they managed to learn both Khazar and Russian in the course of their ministry. Second, they were probably involved in preaching and communicating biblical ideas. Cyril's discourse was quite philosophically oriented, however, it is interesting to note that one Khazar philosopher criticized him for referring to the Bible too often in their discussions.[21] Finally, their work was characterized by much open dialogue with both Jewish and Muslim contacts.

When asked about his rank and identity by his Jewish hosts, Cyril responded that he was "Adam's grandson"—a rather contextual response that made creation and humanity a common ground element in the conversation. He spent a good deal of his time defending the notion of the Trinity and the Incarnation of Christ. Revealing a profound knowledge of the Bible, Cyril presented the gospel and argued for the centrality and preeminence of Christ by appealing almost entirely to Old Testament texts.[22]

Although his discussions were mostly with Jewish thinkers, Cyril devoted some time to Khazar Muslims. Referencing Daniel 9:24, which indicated that vision and prophecy would be sealed up with the Messiah's coming, Cyril questioned how revelation in Islam could be regarded as valid. Specifically, he questioned whether there could be prophets after Christ, including Muhammad. Similar to his dialogue with the Jews, Cyril's arguments were completely taken from the Old Testament.[23]

Apparently the mission was fruitful as some two hundred Khazars embraced the gospel. In the khan's letter to Michael III, which was preserved in the *Life of Cyril*, the Khazar leader communicated gratitude to the missionaries for their ministry and tolerance to those who accepted Christianity and to those who did not: "You sent us, Lord, a holy man who has

---

19. *Life of Cyril*, 8.
20. *Life of Methodius*, 4.
21. *Life of Cyril*, 8–9; also Tachioas, *Cyril and Methodius*, 50–51.
22. *Life of Cyril*, 9; cf. Dvornik, *Byzantine Missions*, 68.
23. *Life of Cyril*, 9; also Dvornik, *Byzantine Missions*, 69.

shown us the Christian faith by words and deeds. Having established that this is the true faith, we have ordered those who so wish should be baptized, in hope that we too shall follow suit."[24] The work was also successful on the diplomatic side as Cyril successfully intervened against a Khazar attack on a Christian town and was also able to negotiate the release of some two hundred Greek prisoners.[25]

During the return from the Khazar mission, Cyril and Methodius preached through the Tauric Peninsula in what it is now Crimea. Though this region had been previously evangelized, syncretism had prevailed. The brothers preached against mixing Christianity with pagan elements. Reminiscent of Boniface's actions at Geismar, Cyril invited the people to cut down a tree that had served as a place for pagan worship and to restore regular church gatherings.[26]

After arriving home, the brothers once again retreated into a monastery. Vlastos comments that "the two saints and their companions probably lived as a monastic community as far as their work allowed."[27] According to Cyril's biographer, "the philosopher went to Constantinople and after arriving before the emperor went to live in the St. Apostles' Church in silence and prayer."[28] In addition, Cyril was likely involved in teaching theology and philosophy and educating clergy in a theological school based in the church.[29] Possibly a reward for his service to the Khazars, Methodius was appointed by both the emperor and patriarch of Constantinople to serve as the abbot of the Polychroniou monastery on Mt. Olympus—a well-endowed community of some seventy monks.[30]

Mission to the Slavs

In 862, Prince Ratislav of Moravia approached the Byzantine Emperor Michael III with a request to send Christian teachers to his people, the Slavs. Although their origins have been debated, the Slavs were an Indo-European

---

24. *Life of Cyril*, 11 cited in Tachioas, *Cyril and Methodius*, 48.

25. *Life of Cyril*, 8, 11; also Tachioas, *Cyril and Methodius*, 46–48; and Dvornik, *Byzantine Missions*, 67, 69.

26. *Life of Cyril*, 12; also Tachioas, *Cyril and Methodius*, 48

27. Vlasto, *Entry of the Slavs*, 299; cf. Tachioas, *Cyril and Methodius*, 55–56.

28. *Life of Cyril*, 13.

29. Dvornik, *Byzantine Missions*, 70–72.

30. Tachioas, *Cyril and Methodius*, 55–56.

people occupying what is now Eastern Europe and Southern Russia. A cluster of tribes that included Serbs, Croats, and Bulgarians among others, the Slavs generally shared a common language. In terms of social structure, the Slavs were a tribal people organized around the extended family. Their livelihood was based largely on agriculture, raising cattle, hunting, and fishing. Spiritually, they were pagan monotheists who gave homage to a supreme being while venerating other deities. Probably influenced by traditional Persian worship, the Slavs also venerated rivers and made sacred space out of other natural places.[31]

Historically, the Greeks regarded the Slavs as barbarians. In the seventh and eighth centuries, the eastern part of the Roman Empire was forced to defend itself against Slavic military advancements, including an attack in 836 against Thessalonica in which Cyril and Methodius' father Leo was likely involved. By the later ninth century, however, the Slavs and Greeks enjoyed a more peaceful coexistence that included much cultural, economic, and even spiritual interaction. With Slavic merchants conducting daily business in the markets of Thessalonica, many Greeks—including Cyril and Methodius—began to relate to the Slavs and speak their language.[32]

In a letter to Emperor Michael preserved in Cyril's biography, the Moravian prince wrote: "Since our people rejected idolatry and came under Christian law, we have not had a teacher capable of explaining this faith to us in our own tongue, so that other countries, seeing this, might imitate us. Therefore send us, Lord, such a bishop and teacher, for it is from you that the good law ever flows out to all the lands."[33] In another portion of the letter, which was captured in the *Life of Methodius*, Ratislav added: "We Slavs are simple people and have no one to guide us to the truth and teach us knowledge. Therefore, good Lord, send us such a man as can teach us the whole truth."[34] As the letters indicate, the prince was not asking for pioneer missionaries but rather for Christian teachers to help fortify the Slavs in their faith. Initial evangelization work among the Slavs probably began in the early seventh century when the bishop of Rome sent missionaries to the Slavs at the request of the Roman Emperor Heraclius. Despite their pagan heritage, the Slavs were rather tolerant toward Christian teachers and even-

---

31. Dvornik, *Slavs*, 42, 47–51, 53–54, 57–59; also Wilken, *First Thousand Years*, 344.

32. Tachioas, *Cyril and Methodius*, ix–x, 10–13, 16; also Dvornik, *Byzantine Missions*, 1–5, 40–42; *Life of Cyril*, 5.

33. *Life of Cyril*, 14, cited in Tachioas, *Cyril and Methodius*, 57.

34. *Life of Methodius*, 5, cited in Tachioas, *Cyril and Methodius*, 57.

tually embraced Christianity in the seventh and eighth centuries through the work of Frankish, German, and Greek missionaries.[35]

Ratislav's request was apparently twofold. First, as Great Moravia was developing as a nation, the prince apparently wanted a more local and indigenous expression of Christianity for his people. Though Frankish and German missionaries and bishops had been laboring successfully among the Slavs, they brought a western, Latin form of liturgy and worship. Second, through this request for Christian teachers from the Greek East, Ratislav seemed interested in establishing deeper political ties with Byzantium and Michael III.[36]

In response to Ratislav's request, the emperor again summoned Cyril and Methodius for the task. Not only were they deemed suitable for the mission because of their intellectual abilities and previous diplomatic experience in the Khazar mission, but they were already fluent in Slavic. According to Methodius' biographer, the emperor commanded Cyril: "Take with you your brother, Abbot Methodius, and go, for you are Thessalonians, and all Thessalonians converse correctly in Slavic."[37]

The first step in the mission, which began before the brothers even left for Moravia, was to develop a Slavic alphabet in order to translate liturgy and Scripture. Cyril's biographer indicated that he single handedly created a script for Slavonic; however, in reality he was more likely the leader of a team of scholars and linguists who worked on the project. Given the possibility of their existing relationships with Slavic monks and due to the bookish nature of their monastic program, it is likely that the Mt. Olympus monastery served as Cyril and Methodius' base of operations for the Slavic language project. The team probably started with a rough version of the Slavonic alphabet and produced a script known as Glagolithic or Old Slavonic that was derived from Hebrew, Syriac, Georgian, and other alphabets.[38]

Beyond developing the alphabet, Cyril and the team labored to develop a spiritual and scholarly vocabulary in Slavonic as well. Tachioas notes, "In order to render the gospel in Slavic, it was necessary to build up an enormous stock of abstract nouns and adjectives and even compound words,

---

35. Dvornik, *Byzantine Missions*, 5–6, 9–11, 13–48, 78–79; also Vlasto, *Entry of the Slavs*, 24–26.

36. Tachioas, *Cyril and Methodius*, 67; also Dvornik, *Byzantine Missions*, 88–89.

37. *Life of Methodius*, 5, cited in Tachioas, *Cyril and Methodius*, 19.

38. *Life of Cyril*, 14; *Life of Methodius*, 6; also Tachioas, *Cyril and Methodius*, 68–72; Dvornik, *Byzantine Missions*, 103; Vlasto, *Entry of the Slavs*, 38–45; and Obolensky, *Byzantium and the Slavs*, 206–7.

none of which existed in Slavic."[39] In some cases, the team was forced to import some Greek words and ideas into the new language. Commenting on the process, Cyril stated: "The words were not rendered blindly with their Slavic equivalents; for it was not the words that we required but their meaning. For this reason, wherever the meaning in both Greek and Slavic chanced to coincide, we used the same word to translate it; but where the expression was longer or caused the meaning to be lost, we did not forsake the meaning, but rendered it with another word."[40] While the goal was to develop liturgy and Scripture for an authentic Slavic worship experience, Cyril's words reveal how difficult that task would be and how there would be influences of Byzantine Christianity on the Slavs. With an alphabet and spiritual vocabulary in place, the next stage of the project was to translate portions of the four Gospels that would be used in the Slavonic liturgy.[41]

Following this year of preparation, Cyril and the team left for Moravia in 863. Based on the number of gifts that were offered to Ratislav, the team was probably quite large. Cyril's primary task was translating the Byzantine liturgy (the mass, daily office, and Psalter) so that Slavic worship assemblies could begin to take place. Next, the team turned their focus to translating the four Gospels into Slavic. While these projects were going on, Cyril also began training a group of students who had been selected by Ratislav to learn the Slavic script and religious language and could begin to serve as national teachers—a "Slavo-Moravian clergy."[42] Though they were training local clergy, Cyril and the Byzantine delegation resisted setting apart bishops and introducing a Byzantine church hierarchy, actions that would have surely slowed down the translation work and created unnecessary conflict with the Frankish and German bishops already in Moravia.[43]

Trilingualist Controversy

Despite their best efforts to stay focused on translation work and to avoid ecclesiastical conflict, Cyril, Methodius, and the team encountered great

---

39. Tachioas, *Cyril and Methodius*, 73.

40. *Life of Cyril*, 14, cited in Tachioas, *Cyril and Methodius*, 75; cf. Vlasto, *Entry of the Slavs*, 58–59.

41. Tachioas, *Cyril and Methodius*, 73.

42. Ibid., 79.

43. Dvornik, *Byzantine Missions*, 104–9, 117; also Vlasto, *Entry of the Slavs*, 59–65; Tachioas, *Cyril and Methodius*, 77; and *Life of Methodius*, 15.

opposition from the German clergy in Moravia. The source of the conflict was the focus of Cyril's work—rendering liturgy and Scripture in Slavonic toward realizing an indigenous Slavic Christianity. The Germans propagated Trilingualism—the belief that the only acceptable languages for Christian worship in the world were Latin, Greek, and Hebrew. Following a curious logic and hermeneutic, they argued that since Jesus' title "King of the Jews" had been affixed to the cross in these three languages, only these languages could be used in worship.[44]

After three years in Moravia, the team left and stopped over in Venice in hopes of securing the ordination of their Slavic disciples, which brought the conflict with the Germanic clergy to a head. Cyril appeared before a local church council in Venice to defend their work against the Trilingualists. According to Cyril's biographer, they challenged him: "Tell us, man, how is it that you now invent books for the Slavs and teach them? . . . We only know of three languages in which it is becoming to praise God with books: Hebrew, Greek, and Latin."[45] Cyril famously responded:

> But does rain not fall equally upon all people, does the sun not shine for all, and do we not all breathe the air in equal measure? Wherefore, then, are you not ashamed to recognize but three tongues and command other nations to be blind and deaf? Say, will you have God weak, as though unable to bestow this [script], or jealous, that He does not wish to? For we know many peoples who have a script and give glory to God, each in its own tongue. It is known that such as Armenians, Persians, Abasgians, Iberians, Sogdi, Goths, Avars, Turks, Khazars, Arabs, Egyptians, Syrians, and many others besides.[46]

Rejecting the idea that his own Greek language held any place of prominence, Cyril cited a litany of fourteen different passages of Scripture to make a biblical claim that the gospel should go out to all ethno-linguistic peoples in their heart languages.[47]

---

44. Blocher and Blandenier, *Evangelization of the World*, 92.

45. *Life of Cyril*, 16; cf. Vlasto, *Entry of the Slavs*, 48; and Tachioas, *Cyril and Methodius*, 83.

46. *Life of Cyril*, 16, cited in Tachioas, *Cyril and Methodius*, 83

47. Dvornik, *Byzantine Missions*, 129–30. His apologetic captured in *Life of Cyril* 16 would be adopted and used by Popes Hadrian II and John VIII to stand by ongoing Slavic mission work.

Roman Affirmation

As a result of the local church council in Venice, Pope Nicholas summoned Cyril and Methodius to Rome where he would hear the case personally. Despite Nicholas' death before the brothers arrived, his successor, Pope Hadrian II, received the team favorably and even took a copy of the Slavonic Scriptures and blessed them in a worship assembly in Rome. Further, Hadrian personally participated in a Slavic liturgical assembly that took place in the famous St. Peter's basilica. Through this show of support, the pope joined the eastern Byzantine church, which had initiated the mission, in encouraging the development of an indigenous Slavic Christianity. In a final act of affirmation, Hadrian ordained Abbot Methodius as a priest.[48]

This victory in Rome was coupled with hardship as Cyril, worn out from years of work and travel, died at the age of forty-two. In the last fifty days of his life, he requested the tonsure (shaving of the scalp) and officially became a monk and his name was changed from Constantine to Cyril. Although Cyril's status as a monk did not become official until the end of his life and though he labored as a philosopher, linguist, and apologist, his life was very much characterized by monastic values, which shaped his mission efforts. His prayer in death was that the baseless teaching of Trilingualism would be destroyed and that the Slavs would worship freely in their own language. He begged Methodius to return to the Slavs and continue the work.[49]

Later Work among the Slavs

Following Cyril's death, Methodius, who had largely assisted his younger brother, returned once again to minister among the Slavic peoples. Prince Kocel of Pannonia requested that Pope Hadrian set apart Methodius as bishop for Pannonia; however, the pope appointed Methodius as a papal legate and bishop for the Slavic regions instead. While Hadrian celebrated the Slavic work and encouraged the ongoing training of Slavic ministers

---

48. *Life of Cyril*, 17; *Life of Methodius*, 6; also Dvornik, *Byzantine Missions*, 131; and Tachioas, *Cyril and Methodius*, 84–86.

49. *Life of Cyril*, 18; also Dvornik, *Byzantine Missions*, 142–44; and Tachioas, *Cyril and Methodius*, 89–90.

and teachers, it was clear that he considered the Slavic church and mission to be under his authority and subject to Rome.[50]

Despite this support from Rome, this event marked the beginning of many problems for Methodius and the Slavic work. The Germans captured Ratislav, who had initiated the Moravian mission, and blinded him. The Germans then brought accusations against Methodius and exiled him to a monastery in Swabia for two years. During this time, Pope Hadrian also died and it was a long time before his successor, John VIII, even learned of Methodius' banishment. The pope was able to secure Methodius' release, which allowed him to return to the work in Moravia. Despite the previous papal support for Slavic liturgy, the Trilingualist controversy reared its head again and John VIII waffled on his position while later popes completely withdrew their support.[51] Finally, as the Filioque controversy[52] was brewing between the eastern and western churches, Methodius got caught in the middle and was accused by the German bishops of heresy. However, Pope John VIII reviewed Methodius' teaching and declared that he was within the bounds of orthodoxy.[53]

Faced with these significant challenges, Methodius persevered in the Slavic ministry and labored furiously in the final years of his life to finish the Slavic Scriptures while also composing other theological works. Though Cyril had been the clear leader of the Slavic mission team, Methodius demonstrated both the skill and resolve to bring it to completion. It should be noted that Methodius' grasp of Slavic language and culture was actually superior to his brother's, given the many years that he had lived and worked among Slavs as a governor.[54]

The legacy of Cyril and Methodius' work among the Slavs is both tragic and heartening. On one hand, following their deaths, some two

---

50. *Life of Methodius*, 8; also Dvornik, *Byzantine Missions*, 145–51; Tachioas, *Cyril and Methodius*, 92–94; and Wilken, *First Thousand Years*, 349–50.

51. Blocher and Blandenier, *Evangelization of the World*, 93.

52. *Filioque* (literally "and the Son") was a phrase added to the Nicene Creed by the western churches in the sixth century indicating that the Holy Spirit proceeds from the Father *and the Son*. The eastern, Byzantine church rejected this phrase and there was controversy between eastern and western churches beginning in the seventh century.

53. *Life of Methodius*, 9; also Dvornik, *Byzantine Missions*, 153–54, 162–66; Tachioas, *Cyril and Methodius*, 96, 100; Vlasto, *Entry of the Slavs*, 72–73; and Obolensky, *Byzantium and the Slavs*, 210.

54. *Life of Methodius*, 15; also Dvornik, *Byzantine Missions*, 174–76; Tachioas, *Cyril and Methodius*, 97–98, 104; and Vlasto, *Entry of the Slavs*, 78–79.

hundred of the brothers' disciples were captured by the Germans and sold into slavery. Upon learning of this, the Emperor Basil redeemed them and brought them back to Constantinople, which effectively ended their work in Moravia. On the other hand, because many of Cyril and Methodius' followers were monks and continually organized themselves in ascetic communities, they had a lasting impact in the Slavic world outside of Moravia, including Poland, Bohemia, Croatia, and Russia.[55] Following the baptism of Prince Boris of Bulgaria, his country became increasingly Slavicized and aligned with Constantinople politically. Cyril and Methodius' followers were welcomed into this expanding state. Dvornik writes: "The work of Constantine-Cyril and Methodius, rejected by the West, was saved by the Bulgarians, and became a medium by which Byzantium was to tie the majority of the Slavic nations to its culture and church." Of course, with a Slavic alphabet, liturgy, Christian Scriptures, and a growing body of Christian literature, Slavic Christianity was kept alive and Cyril and Methodius' legacy remained intact.[56]

Approaches to Mission

Cyril and Methodius probably did not grow up thinking they would be Bible translators and missionaries, however, their cross-cultural ministry among the Arabs, Khazars, and Slavs demonstrated a burden for those beyond reach of the gospel. In the biographies of both men, the biblical text most often cited to describe their work was 1 Timothy 2:4: "[God] who wants all people to be saved and to come to a knowledge of the truth."[57] With this in mind, let us consider their approaches to and values in mission.

First, like other missionary monks we have surveyed, the brothers were in touch with political leaders before launching any work. Similar to Anskar, every mission that Cyril and Methodius were involved in came at the request of the host nation's leader. Within a context of fully developed-Christendom, political leaders such as the Khazar khan and Prince Ratislav did not contact the missionaries directly or even reach out to the patriarch of Constantinople. Instead, they communicated their request to

---

55. Dvornik, *Byzantine Missions*, 193–244, 272–82; also Vlasto, *Entry of the Slavs*, 299–300; and Wilken, *First Thousand Years*, 350–54.

56. Dvornik, *Byzantine Missions*, 244–45; also Tachioas, *Cyril and Methodius*, 108–16; Obolensky, *Byzantium and the Slavs*, 210–11; and Wilken, *First Thousand Years*, 346.

57. *Life of Cyril*, 1; *Life of Methodius*, 2.

the Byzantine emperor who, in consultation with the patriarch, set apart the brothers for these missions. Given their family and educational backgrounds as well as Methodius' prior service as a governor, Cyril and Methodius were comfortable relating to political leaders, and they functioned in a sense as missionary diplomats.[58] This relationship to political leaders was, of course, a double-edged sword: they had favor in Moravia when Ratislav was in power, but Methodius suffered and was exiled following the Moravian prince's demise.

Second, the brothers' missionary work was quite itinerant and short-term in nature. As discussed, they spent no more than two years among the Khazars, about three years and four months during the initial trip to Moravia, and a few months in Pannonia following their time in Moravia. Methodius spent the last several years of his life back in Moravia. As monks, they used the monasteries in Constantinople and Mt. Olympus as their launching and regrouping bases for itinerant ministry.

Third, Cyril and Methodius were intellectuals engaged in mission. Of all the missionary monks we have studied to this point, they were perhaps the best educated. Cyril was a philosopher and capable of having significant philosophical discussions about the meaning of the Trinity and the Incarnation with Jewish and Muslim conversation partners. Methodius proved himself capable of articulating his theology when interrogated by western church leaders during the Filioque controversy. Not only were both men gifted linguists, but Cyril also crafted a compelling apologetic for the legitimacy of an indigenous Slavic Christianity. Their life-long monastic commitment to reading and study only served to strengthen their intellectual abilities. In addition to putting these gifts of the mind to work in mission, Cyril and Methodius ultimately inspired a Byzantine renaissance of learning during the medieval period.[59]

Fourth, facilitated by their intellectual abilities, Cyril and Methodius were quite committed to learning new languages in the task of mission. In addition to their native Greek language, both men probably learned Slavic growing up in Thessalonica and Methodius, of course, mastered the language while serving as a governor. During the Khazar mission, they gained proficiency in Russian and Hebrew in order to speak with their hosts and make arguments from the Old Testament.[60] A commitment to and excel-

58. Obolensky, *Byzantium and the Slavs*, 244–46.

59. Ibid., 212–13.

60. Dvornik, *Byzantine Missions*, 66.

lence with language certainly characterized the brothers' mission to the Slavs. As discussed, Cyril and his team are credited with finalizing the first Slavonic alphabet in the Glagolithic script. Under the supervision of Bishop Constantine of Preslav (Bulgaria), the alphabet underwent a revision toward the end of the ninth century and it was named "Cyrillic" in honor of the Greek missionary. Fresh translations of Scripture and other works in Cyrillic were also completed in Bulgaria in the late ninth century. The fact that these revisions occurred should not suggest that Cyril's initial work was insufficient. On the contrary, Dvornik notes that "Slavic philologists [today] recognize the excellent qualities of his translation, which reveals a very deep knowledge of the Greek and Slavic languages and their character."[61] Later, Cyrillic would be the key vehicle for spreading Christianity into the Slavic regions of Eastern Europe and Russia and also for being the primary means of expressing Eastern Orthodox Christianity.[62]

Fifth, through their work in language learning and translating liturgy and Scripture into Slavic, Cyril and Methodius were early champions of what historian Lamin Sanneh calls the "vernacular principle." Building from the Incarnation of Christ—the Word made flesh bringing God's message to people where they are—Christianity is a missionary faith that is accomplished in part through translation of Scripture.[63] Sanneh adds, "Mission as translation affirms the *missio Dei* [mission of God] as the hidden force for its work. It is the *missio Dei* that allowed translation to enlarge the boundaries of the proclamation."[64] Further, the gospel finds a rightful home wherever Scripture is translated into the heart languages of the world's cultures. Sanneh summarizes, "Scriptural translation rested on the assumption that the vernacular has a primary affinity with the gospel, the point being conceded by the adoption of indigenous terms and concepts for the central categories of the Bible."[65]

While translating Scripture had been common in the first six centuries of the church,[66] by the ninth century, Greek and Latin had become

---

61. Ibid., 117.

62. Dvornik, *Byzantine Missions*, 250–51, 255; also Tachioas, *Cyril and Methodius*, 120–21; Obolensky, *Byzantium and the Slavs*, 249; and Wilken, *First Thousand Years*, 345–46.

63. Sanneh, *Translating the Message*, 7, 29.

64. Ibid., 31, 82.

65. Ibid., 166.

66. Smither, *Mission in the Early Church*, 91–108.

unduly exalted as the acceptable languages for worship in the global church, which made Cyril and Methodius' work ground breaking. As we have shown, western church leaders in the region greatly resisted the brothers' Slavic translation. Had it not been for their equally strong conviction that Trilingualism was a false teaching, they might not have persevered with the project. Though at times Greek and Byzantine words and ideas were imported into Slavonic and an indigenous Slavic Christianity was a work in progress, Cyril and Methodius were catalysts for local expressions of Christianity within the broader catholic church. In short, they labored to bring to fruition Emperor Michael's visionary words to Ratislav: "that you, too, may be numbered among the great nations who praise God in their own language."[67]

A sixth characteristic of Cyril and Methodius' mission work was captured well by Dvornik, who wrote: "the main object of the Byzantine mission was not conversion but instruction."[68] German, Frankish, and other missionaries had been laboring among the Slavs since the seventh century; so Ratislav's request was for Christian teachers more than pioneer missionaries.[69] This does not mean that the brothers and their team did not evangelize or preach to non-believers; however, their primary focus was developing resources (Scripture, liturgy, literature) as well as leaders to aid in the discipleship and spiritual growth of the Slavic church. In short, theirs was a mission focused on teaching.

Seventh, quite related to their monastic calling and commitment to living in community with others, Cyril and Methodius valued having a missionary team, and they invested much in developing new leaders. Beginning with the Khazar mission, Cyril served as the team leader and his older, ex-governor brother served as his assistant. Methodius' posture of service and humility probably contributed much to the health of the team. As shown, the team that went to the Slavs was quite large in number and probably consisted largely of monks from the Mt. Olympus monastery.[70]

An integral part of the mission of teaching was involving Slavs in the work of translation and also raising up new Moravian Slavic clergy.

---

67. *Life of Cyril*, 15, cited in Obolensky, *Byzantium and the Slavs*, 215; cf. Tachioas, *Cyril and Methodius*, 127–43.

68. Dvornik, *Byzantine Missions*, 105; cf. Vlasto, *Entry of the Slavs*, 47.

69. *Life of Methodius* 5; also Vlasto, *Entry of the Slavs*, 24–26; and Wilken, *First Thousand Years*, 345.

70. Dvornik, "Significance of the Missions of Cyril and Methodius," 200.

Dvornik writes: "Having laid the foundation for a Moravian church with its own Slavic liturgy and religious literature, and having formed a new school of disciples, the brothers could plan to the fulfillment of the second stage of their missionary operations, which was the ordination of their disciples to the priesthood and the establishment of a hierarchy."[71] It is interesting to note that during Methodius' exile in Swabia, his disciples stepped up to lead the church in Pannonia. Despite facing a great deal of opposition from German church leaders, Methodius' disciple Gorazd also carried on the vision for a Slavic church. Again, Slavic Christianity grew eastward because of the missionary commitment of monks from Mt. Olympus and elsewhere who were disciples of Cyril and Methodius.[72]

A final aspect of Cyril and Methodius' mission work, related to the diplomatic nature of their ministry, was confronting social problems. On at least two occasions—during the Khazar mission and ministry in Pannonia following the Moravian mission—the brothers successfully negotiated the release of large numbers of prisoners. Also, during the Moravian mission they defended the sanctity of marriage, and confronted pagan customs in the region. Although their work was primarily focused on Scripture and teaching, an element of social action pervaded their ministry as well.[73]

Summary

Cyril and Methodius' mission to the Slavs was a ministry from both the East and the West. The brothers were recruited for the Slavic mission by Emperor Michael III and were later affirmed and supported in the work by Pope Hadrian II of Rome. Commenting on the bridge-building nature of their work, Obolensky notes: "In a Christendom that was beginning to feel the growing tension between East and West, they sought to reconcile and to unite three important elements in the civilization of medieval Europe: the Byzantine, the Roman, and the Slavonic."[74]

Although Methodius was the only official monk for most of the brothers' adult lives, both brothers spent a great deal of their lives together in a monastic community and their work in mission was clearly framed

---

71. Dvornik, *Byzantine Missions*, 128.

72. Ibid., 154, 186–87; also Obsolensky, *Byzantium and the Slavs*, 213; and Wilken, *First Thousand Years*, 350.

73. Dvornik, *Byzantine Missions*, 118–19.

74. Obsolensky, *Byzantium and the Slavs*, 212.

by monastic convictions. Cyril's scholarship and ability to relate to intellectuals was cultivated in a monastic environment of study. Their commitment to the study, translation, and teaching of Scripture—the heart of their ministry among the Slavs—also reflected a monastic devotion to Scripture. The value that they placed on being a team and in raising up other leaders was also quite compatible with discipleship in a monastic setting. Finally, their ascetic lifestyle prepared them to endure hardship in mission, which included declining health for Cyril and accusations of heresy and exile for Methodius.

In short, both Slavic culture in general and Eastern Orthodox Christianity specifically are indebted to these two missionary monk brothers from Thessalonica. Evaluating their legacy, Obolensky writes: "A mission, whose original purpose was preaching Christianity in the idiom of the Moravians, led to the rise of the whole Slavonic culture. A liturgy, in a language, rich, supple and intelligible; the Christian Scriptures, translated into the same vernacular tongue; access to the treasury of Greek patristic literature and Byzantine secular learning: truly a new world was opened to the Slavs by the work of Cyril and Methodius."[75]

---

75. Ibid., 214.

CHAPTER 11

Church of the East

AN OFTEN-OVERLOOKED FACT IN Christian history is that during the medieval period, the Christian message traveled much farther east than it ever did west. Our understanding of the eastern church's story was greatly enhanced in 1623 with the discovery of the so-called Nestorian monument in X'ian in Central China—a large black stone monument measuring three meters tall and one meter wide that had been erected in 781. The writing on the monument claimed that, among other things, in 635 a certain missionary monk named Alopen arrived in the region and was welcomed by the Emperor T'ai Tsung to preach *Jiang Jiao* or the "luminous religion of Syria."[1] Alopen's mission captures a part of the story of the Church of the East and a movement of missionary monks who spread the gospel from Syria and Persia eastward through Central Asia and into China by the mid-seventh century. What was the Church of the East? How did it emerge and develop, and how did monastic elements influence the life of the church? Finally, how did missionary monks from the Church of the East approach mission?

Origins of the Church of the East

Three main groups comprise the ancient Christian communities of Syria and the Middle East: the Melkites, who followed the Byzantine liturgy and accepted the Formula of Chalcedon of 451; the Syrian Orthodox or Jacobites, comprised of believers from western Syria; and the Church of the

---

1. Neill, *History of Christian Missions*, 82; cf. Irvin and Sunquist, *History of the World Christian Movement*, 316; and Lieu and Parry, "Deep into Asia," 159–64.

East. The latter group, the focus of our study, has often been incorrectly referred to in history as Nestorians because of a supposed connection to the embattled fifth-century bishop, Nestorius of Constantinople, who was condemned as a heretic for his Christological views. However, as Lieu and Parry correctly assert, this title is certainly a misnomer: "So-called Nestorianism is an erroneous Byzantine construct resulting from the Christological debates and ecclesiastical politics centered on Constantinople in the fifth century. It has little bearing on the Christian communities in Central Asia, China, and India."[2] For our purposes, the Church of the East refers to Syrian and Persian Christians who lived between Edessa and Nisibis in the border region between the Roman and Persian Empires and who related to the Patriarch of Seleucia-Ctesiphon.[3]

The Church of the East was birthed as the gospel spread eastward from Antioch to Edessa—a city on the Old Silk Road connecting travelling merchants between Rome, Persia, Armenia, and Arabia. As the church grew in the second century in this Syriac-speaking region, the Scriptures were translated into Syriac around 170 by the eastern church father Tatian of Mesopotamia. In the early third century, a bishop was set apart for the church at Edessa.[4] Because of Edessa's position on the Silk Road, the gospel quickly moved east toward the Persian regions largely through the witness of business people. Stewart writes: "[merchants] came to Mesopotamia with the arts and crafts of life—carpenters, smiths, weavers, the best of the artisan class. They came to start industries and lay the foundations of manufacturing prosperity in the land of their adoption."[5] Between the third and sixth century, displaced and deported Christians were also entering Persia from Antioch, Syria, Cilicia, and Cappadocia.[6]

Following the emergence of the Sassanid Empire in Persia in 225, the Church of the East took on much more of a Persian identity. The church was based at the Persian capital of Seleucia-Ctesiphon and its theological school was located at Nisibis. This did not mean, however, that Christianity gained official acceptance in Persia. Despite enjoying a brief period

---

2. Lieu and Parry, "Deep into Asia," 147; cf. Moffett, *A History of Christianity in Asia*, xiv; Atiya, *History of Eastern Christianity*, 241–42; also Baum and Winkler, *Church of the East*, 3–5.

3. Irvin and Sunquist, *History of the World Christian Movement*, 197; also Baum and Winkler, *Church of the East*, 7–9.

4. Moffett, *History of Christianity in Asia*, 46, 72–77.

5. Stewart, *Nestorian Missionary Enterprise*, 9.

6. Baum and Winkler, *Church of the East*, 9–12.

of toleration in 409, for much of the fourth, fifth, and sixth centuries, the church was discriminated against and at times persecuted by the Zoroastrian-dominated government. Persian Christians were often associated with the hated Romans who had, of course, tolerated and then embraced Christianity as an imperial religion in the fourth century. In response to a letter from the Emperor Constantine in 315 requesting that Persian Christians be protected, Shah Shapur II did the opposite and launched a brutal persecution against the Persian believers. Over time, such discrimination and pressure led many Persian believers to leave their homeland and immigrate to places like Arabia.[7]

In addition to producing one of the earliest translations of Scripture in early Christianity, the Church of the East eventually developed its own rich theological tradition. With theological schools at Edessa and later Nisibis, the church was known for thinkers such as Ephraem of Syria (306–373), who articulated theology in the form of hymns and poetry. While the Church of the East began to be more identified with Nestorian theology in the fifth century, they never actually affirmed Nestorius' Christological ideas. Instead, they were guilty by association because they were proponents of the theological tradition of Antioch and were students of its greatest thinker, Theodore of Mopsuestia (350–428). The Church of the East also rejected the Formula of Chalcedon of 451—not out of allegiance to Nestorius, but in opposition to the very Greek manner that it was articulated, which seemed to alienate the Semitic-minded Syrians. As shown, the Church of the East did separate from the other Syrian churches; however, this was more due to political division than theological differences.[8]

Monasticism and Mission

From very early on, the Church of the East was known for its strong ascetic tendencies and a related commitment to mission. Moffett writes, "In the earliest Christian documents of the East, the call to ascetic self-denial

---

7. Moffett, *History of Christianity in Asia*, 92, 112, 117, 137–45, 157–61; also Irvin and Sunquist, *History of the World Christian Movement*, 199–203; and Stewart, *Nestorian Missionary Enterprise*, 16–35, 50–51.

8. Irvin and Sunquist, *History of the World Christian Movement*, 197–201; also Moffett, *History of Christianity in Asia*, 154, 169–80, 200–205; Baum and Winkler, *Church of the East*, 7, 11, 19–32; and Lieu and Parry, "Deep into Asia," 148.

is almost always associated with the call to go and preach and serve."[9] While Syrian and Egyptian monastic movements developed around the same time, the Syrians had more of an emphasis on mobility, outreach, and ministry, including the work of wandering preachers, healers, and those caring for the poor. In early church tradition, Addai is remembered for being a pioneer missionary who planted churches in Edessa, Nisibis, Arabia, and on the border of Mesopotamia, while his disciple Aggai ministered and began new works in Persia, Mesopotamia, Armenia, and toward the borders of India. By 225 and the rise of the Sassanid Empire, Christians had spread as far east as modern Afghanistan.[10]

In fourth-century Persia, monasticism seems to have developed in part as a means for Christians to pursue safe communities given the discrimination they experienced from the Zoroastrian majority and leaders such Shapur II. Irvin and Sunquist add: "Christians were generally found on the margins of Persian life. . . . By the fourth and fifth centuries, monasteries had become the most important centers for preserving Christian life and thought. Many of these had grown into full-fledged educational institutions that provided churches with important resources beyond what might be considered strictly spiritual or theological concerns."[11] In addition to training monks and others in theology and pastoral ministry, Persian monasteries also gave instruction in medicine and often integrated the study of theology and medicine.

Jacob of Nisibis (d. 338) was a fourth-century innovator of Persian coenobitic monasticism. Like other monks that we have studied, Jacob combined the vocations of monk and bishop when he accepted ordination as bishop of the church at Nisibis. Aphratat (270–335), another monk bishop, further united the Persian church and monastery through the community he led at Mar Mattai near Mosul. Through serving the monastery, church, and community, Jacob and Aphratat demonstrated a monastic theology that gave priority to serving others over personal ascetic devotion. In this sense, they modeled a theology in the fourth century that Gregory the Great would articulate in the sixth and seventh century. According to

---

9. Moffett, *History of Christianity in Asia*, 77.

10. Ibid., 77–78.

11. Irvin and Sunquist, *History of the World Christian Movement*, 201; cf. Baum and Winkler, *Church of the East*, 36–39; Moffett, *History of Christianity in Asia*, 225–28; and Stewart, *Nestorian Missionary Enterprise*, 36–48.

Moffett, this ministry included the "greater challenge of service to the poor and evangelism to the unconverted."[12]

As Seleucia-Ctesiphon was located on a crossroads to the East, "the expansion of the Christian movement east of Persia after the year 600 was primarily the work of East Syrian monks, priests, and merchants who traveled the trade routes across Asia."[13] Lieu and Parry add that these Church of the East believers "took Christianity to the oasis towns of Central Asia and, eventually, by the seventh century, to China" and that they "were the most evangelical of the Christians trading on the overland Silk Road."[14] Living, working, and witnessing among Zoroastrian, Manichean, Buddhist, and Muslim peoples, "The 'Church of the East' achieved the greatest geographical scope of any Christian church until the Middle Ages."[15] With over 150 monasteries built in the major cities along the Silk Road route, these eastern believers represented the most vital expression of Christianity east of Antioch following the rise of Islam.[16]

China

As we continue to trace the narrative of Church of the East missions, let us examine briefly the work of missionary monks in China beginning in the seventh century. In addition to the data gleaned from the famous Nestorian monument in X'ian, other ancient Christian texts discovered in the early twentieth century have provided further insight into early Chinese Christianity.[17] In the late seventh century, China came under control of the powerful T'ang dynasty, which brought more stability in the region and encouraged traders, merchants, and others to visit the Far East. While Confucianism was the state religion, around 631 Emperor T'ai Tsung began

---

12. Moffett, *History of Christianity in Asia*, 124.

13. Irvin and Sunquist, *History of the World Christian Movement*, 305; cf. Atiya, *History of Eastern Christianity*, 257.

14. Lieu and Parry, "Deep into Asia," 149.

15. Baum and Winkler, *Church of the East*, 1.

16. Lieu and Parry, "Deep into Asia," 150–59, 175–77; Baum and Winker, *Church of the East*, 51–58; Moffett, *History of Christianity in Asia*, 297; and Every, *Understanding Eastern Christianity*, 28–29.

17. Lieu and Parry, "Deep into Asia," 164.

to show religious tolerance and welcomed Manichean and Buddhist missionaries into China.[18]

In the context of this openness to spiritual ideas, the Church of the East missionary bishop Alopen arrived in 635 preaching the "luminous religion of Syria" and a faith in the "Triune mysterious Person, the unbegotten and true Lord."[19] Alopen and his team of largely Persian monks had been set apart for the mission by Bishop Ishoyahb II of Balad (modern Iraq).[20] The Chinese emperor welcomed the monks and apparently began to study the Christian faith himself. As T'ai Tsung was an educated man with an interest in learning, he seemed especially interested in the fact that the missionaries had Scriptures, which he invited the monks to translate into Chinese. After three years, the emperor issued an edict giving Alopen and his team freedom to proclaim the gospel in China while effectively sponsoring their work by giving them land in the imperial capital, on which to build a monastery.[21]

For about a century, the monks enjoyed much freedom to continue their ministry, although they experienced some backlash from their Buddhist counterparts. In 823, a certain David was consecrated by Timothy of Baghdad as the first bishop overseeing the church in all of China. However, in 845 the Emperor Wu Tsung, a committed Taoist, led a campaign to suppress Buddhism and Buddhist monasticism throughout the country. Though Christian monks, the Church of the East missionaries were also implicated in these measures and the emperor ordered their monasteries closed. Over three thousand monks were ordered to renounce their monastic callings and ministries.[22]

When a monastic envoy visited China in 987, he reported that he found no visible evidence of Christianity being practiced in the country. While the church probably did not completely die out, the ecclesiastical

---

18. Irvin and Sunquist, *History of the World Christian Movement*, 314–15; also Moffett, *History of Christianity in Asia*, 290–91.

19. Irvin and Sunquist, *History of the World Christian Movement*, 316.

20. Baum and Winkler, *Church of the East*, 40–41; also Moffett, *History of Christianity in Asia*, 298.

21. Lieu and Parry, "Deep into Asia," 164; also Baum and Winkler, *Church of the East*, 47; Moffett, *History of Christianity in Asia*, 293; and Irvin and Sunquist, *History of the World Christian Movement*, 317.

22. Baum and Winkler, *Church of the East*, 47, 50; also Moffett, *History of Christianity in Asia*, 294; Lieu and Parry, "Deep into Asia," 151; and Irvin and Sunquist, *History of the World Christian Movement*, 320–21.

and monastic structures, which had been disbanded, failed to recover and sustain a viable Christian movement. Church of the East missionaries likely continued to minister in port towns along the Chinese coast and they certainly continued their ministry farther west in Central Asia.[23]

Approaches to Mission

In light of the narrative presented, how did the Church of the East missionary monks approach mission along the Silk Road between Persia and China? The first obvious strategy was the establishment of monasteries along the route, which allowed the monks to have a witness in many towns and cities. While the Silk Road environment could at times be dangerous and was populated with merchants and traders intent on making money, the eastern monks lived very simply and their possessions included only coats, sacred books, and walking sticks. Once they had established a new monastery, the monks invited local people in the surrounding area to take part in the physical work of the monastery. Through these connections, the monks proclaimed the gospel. In some cases, members of the community joined the monastery as monks themselves.[24]

Quite related, the Church of the East monasteries were engaged in holistic ministry, which included hospitality, setting up schools, and offering medical care. Many monasteries became small hospitals and were known to the local populations as places to receive medical care. Other monasteries, particularly those established in western China, contained significant libraries with medical and philosophy books, biblical commentaries, sacred biographies of saints and martyrs, and copies of Scripture itself.[25]

Missionary monasticism was especially important in China because the eastern Christians were able to connect with Buddhist adherents and monks because of the shared ascetic values and practices in both faiths. In the western world and along the Silk Road, the monks were often the most educated people in society and developed schools and libraries; however, in China, the Buddhist monks were also significantly educated. While the eastern monks did not serve the Chinese so much with education or

---

23. Neill, *History of Christian Missions*, 83–84; also Lieu and Parry, "Deep into Asia," 146, 171; and Irvin and Sunquist, *History of the World Christian Movement*, 321.

24. Irvin and Sunquist, *History of the World Christian Movement*, 305–7.

25. Ibid., 305, 312–13; also Atiya, *History of Eastern Christianity*, 237–38; and Stewart, *Nestorian Missionary Enterprise*, 77.

libraries, their level of education and literacy certainly gave them common ground to relate to and converse with the Buddhist monks.[26]

Finally, the Church of the East monasteries along the Silk Road served as training centers that cultivated more missionaries and church leaders. For example, the monastery at Beth Abe near Ninevah (modern Iraq) trained and sent out a number of bishops and church leaders for churches as far away as Yemen and China. The monastery gained a reputation for being the "mother of patriarchs and bishops."[27]

A second aspect of Church of the East mission strategy was that they were quite church-centered. As shown, Bishop Ishoyahb II of Balad set apart Alopen and his team for the Chinese mission. This Persian bishop was also responsible for sending missionaries and setting apart new church leaders in Hulwan (modern Iran), Herat (Afghanistan), Samarkand (Uzbekistan), India, and other regions of China. Timothy of Baghdad, who ministered in a city that was also the base for the Muslim Abbassid Caliphate, sent over one hundred missionaries to other parts of Asia. In one case, he responded to the request of a Turkish king for Christian missionaries to come to his territory. Timothy also set apart leaders for new churches in China, Tibet, and among the Turks. In short, the Church of the East missionary monks remained accountable to the bishops that sent them out in mission, and they regularly sent back letters and updates to their sending churches. At the same time, some eastern bishops sent emissaries every few years to visit deployed missionaries.[28]

While Church of the East missionaries valued the church as their sending structure, they also prioritized church planting and it was an evident outcome of their ministries. As monasteries were started along the Silk Road between Sogdiana (Persia) and China, new churches were also started and these two structures were organically integrated. Alopen himself was set apart as a bishop so he could give leadership to Chinese churches once they were planted. This custom of setting apart new bishops—both Persian and Chinese—continued as new Chinese churches were started.[29]

---

26. Neill, *History of Christian Missions*, 82; also Lieu and Parry, "Deep into Asia," 168.

27. Baum and Winkler, *Church of the East*, 44–45.

28. Irvin and Sunquist, *History of the World Christian Movement*, 307, 313; also Baum and Winkler, *Church of the East*, 40–41, 53, 61–62; Lieu and Parry, "Deep into Asia," 149, 151, 153; and Stewart, *Nestorian Missionary Enterprise*, 82–84.

29. Irvin and Sunquist, *History of the World Christian Movement*, 307, 319–20.

A third value of the Church of the East was that its missionaries were ministering in the local languages. Lieu and Parry assert that the eastern monks' "knowledge of international languages added to their ability to spread the Christian faith across a vast expanse of steppe and desert."[30] In China, the missionary monk bishop Adam learned Chinese so well that Buddhist missionaries would actually come to him for help in translating their sacred texts into Chinese.[31] In addition to speaking the language, Church of the East monks translated texts into Chinese, including the entire New Testament, some of the Old Testament, and some liturgical manuals. They also labored to produce a Chinese Christian literature that seemed to connect well with the educated Chinese.[32]

Though there were around five hundred Chinese Christian texts available by the year 1000, let us briefly survey several examples of earlier seventh- and eighth-century works. In the *Jesus-Messiah Sutra*, the authors discussed monotheism, attacked idolatry, expounded upon the Ten Commandments, surveyed some teachings from the Sermon on the Mount, and probed Christ's incarnation, life, and suffering. Another work, *Discourses on Monotheism*, was a philosophical treatise that argued for the supremacy of a monotheistic worldview. In *Sutra of Mysterious Peace and Joy*, a master and disciple engaged in theological dialogue that made use of Buddhist language. Similarly, *Sutra on the Roman Luminous Religion* dealt with law and the new way (*Tao*) of Christ. Finally, these early writings included some hymns such as *Hymn of the Luminous Religion*, a Chinese version of the Latin hymn "Glory to God in the Highest," and *Praise in Adoration of the Great Sage Penetrating the Truth and Returning to the Law of the Luminous Roman Religion*.[33]

A final facet of Church of the East missions was that its missionaries contextualized the gospel through using local forms and ideas. In developing Chinese Christian literature, the monks purposefully used the Buddhist genre of sutras for some of the works. In these works and in their religious vocabulary, they used the term "Buddha" to describe divinity, "pure wind" to describe the Holy Spirit, and they chose a very local Chinese term when

---

30. Lieu and Parry, "Deep into Asia," 149.

31. Moffett, *History of Christianity in Asia*, 300.

32. Neill, *History of Christian Missions*, 82; Baum and Winkler, *Church of the East*, 49; and Irvin and Sunquist, *History of the World Christian Movement*, 315, 320.

33. Lieu and Parry, "Deep into Asia," 165–67; and Moffett, *History of Christianity in Asia*, 305–9.

speaking of God in general. The monks also constructed crosses that connected with their Buddhist context. Philip Jenkins comments, "one moving visual token of the [Church of the East's] effort to make their faith intelligible is the combined lotus-cross symbol that appears widely . . . on tombstones from China's Fujian Province."[34]

Despite these clear efforts to contextualize the gospel, the Church of the East monks probably identified too much with Chinese Buddhism. When China later came under Taoist leadership, Christianity came to be regarded as a foreign religion and was ultimately suppressed along with Buddhism in the ninth century.[35]

Summary

This chapter has shown that from the seventh to tenth centuries, Christianity traveled much farther east than it did west and that the Church of the East missionary monks were a key means for facilitating this growth and expansion. Amazingly, the church continued to exist and grow even as a minority religion under Zoroastrian and later Muslim kingdoms. The Church of the East was also a diaspora church that flourished along the Silk Road between Persia and China. Led by mission-minded bishops like Timothy of Baghdad, the church was strategic to establish monasteries and churches that ministered in a holistic manner to local communities along the Asian trade routes. As they learned local languages and cultures and wrestled to communicate the gospel using local ideas and forms, the Church of the East missionary monks offer a fascinating model of mission to the ends of the earth during this period.

---

34. Jenkins, *Lost History of Christianity*, 92.

35. Irvin and Sundquist, *History of the World Christian Movement*, 317–22; also Jenkins, *Lost History of Christianity*, 15–16, 64; Lieu and Parry, "Deep into Asia," 168; and Moffett, *History of Christianity in Asia*, 310–12.

CHAPTER 12

The Mendicants

THE MOST SIGNIFICANT MISSIONARY monastic orders of the Middle Ages—the mendicants—emerged in the thirteenth century as a direct response to the changing economic landscape of Europe. Prior to the eleventh century, Europe had subsisted on a gift economy of bartering and the exchange of goods; however, in the twelfth century this was replaced by a money economy where goods began to be sold for a profit. This new economy led to an increase in the number of towns and cities across the continent; a medieval urbanization that also gave rise to new religious ideas and dissent against the Roman Catholic Church.[1] Greg Peters notes that "the response to this shift gave rise to the mendicant monastic movement," which rejected riches and greed and embraced poverty.[2] Peters adds, "This poverty was not just a poverty of material possessions but a poverty of power, authority, influence, and thinking of oneself as higher than others."[3]

More than simply being a response to greed and materialism, the mendicant movements or friars ("brothers") also experienced a renewed apostolic vision and a commitment to Christian mission. C. H. Lawrence writes: "The authentic apostolic life was seen to be modeled upon the earthly life of Jesus.... [T]his involved voluntary poverty, the renunciation of wealth and a mission to the unconverted; for all would-be disciples it meant a life devoted to prayer, penance, and service to their neighbors."[4] Around 1255, the Dominican friar Humbert of Romans captured this men-

1. Lawrence, *The Friars*, 2–4; also Peters, *Story of Monasticism*, 171–72.
2. Peters, *Story of Monasticism*, 172.
3. Ibid., 183.
4. Lawrence, *The Friars*, 17.

dicant missionary spirit when he wrote: "through the ministry of our order, schismatic Christians should be recalled to ecclesiastical unity, and the name of Jesus Christ should be taken to the faithless Jews, to the Saracens [Muslims], . . . to the pagan idolaters, barbarians, and all peoples, so that we are His witnesses to bring salvation to all peoples to the ends of the earth."[5]

In this chapter, we will focus on the mendicant missionary orders; those committed to voluntary poverty and who supported themselves by begging for alms. A number of mendicant groups could be studied;[6] however, we will look at two of the earliest and most well-known orders—the Franciscans and Dominicans—and discuss their early leaders and innovators as well as their approaches to mission in the thirteenth and fourteenth centuries.

Franciscans

The Franciscans or Friars Minor ("little brothers") were founded as a direct result of the conversion, vision, and ministry of Francis of Assisi (1182-1226).[7] Like others we have surveyed in this book, the legends associated with Francis pose a bit of a challenge toward getting an accurate sense of his life and work. The earliest sacred biography on his life was written by the Franciscan friar Thomas of Celano just two years after Francis' death. Thomas followed up with a more expanded account sixteen years later. In 1260, Bonaventure (1221-1274), a theologian and leader of the Friars Minor, contributed his own *Life of St. Francis*. Despite being more hagiographical in nature and largely dependent on Thomas' previous works, Bonaventure's biography became the officially accepted account among Franciscans. Though these works must be evaluated carefully, the Franciscans have been good historians of their order, which allows the modern reader to have a useful picture of the origins and early ministries of the Friars Minor.[8]

Francis Bernardorne was born in 1181. His father was a wealthy Italian cloth merchant and his mother was French. As a young man, Francis' greatest dreams were to be a knight and warrior and he engaged in the

---

5. Cited in Lawrence, *The Friars*, 202.

6. For other mendicant groups, see Andrews, *The Other Friars*.

7. Francis, *The Rule* 6.4; also Lawrence, *The Friars*, 34.

8. Lawrence, *The Friars*, 26-28; also Moorman, *History of the Franciscan Order*, 278-91; Blastic, "Francis and his Hagiographic Tradition," 68-83.

clan warfare going on in his home region of Perugia in central Italy. While his hometown of Assisi was embroiled in civil war in 1202, Francis was captured and taken prisoner for an extended period of time, which led him to rethink his life and ultimately embrace the gospel. By 1205, Francis had renounced his family's wealth and his own aspirations for glory in battle, and he withdrew and became a monk.

Francis' conversion and call to monastic living and service, which unfolded between 1205 and 1208, contained three distinct elements. First, he reportedly heard a voice calling him to repair the dilapidated church at San Damiano, which also served as a call to bring spiritual renewal to the universal church. Second, having encountered a leper, Francis embraced the man and committed his life to actively serving the poor. Third, Francis' vision was to imitate Christ in complete simplicity and voluntary poverty, which included wearing a single tunic and walking around barefooted.[9] Francis' active ministry was launched in full force in 1208 when he heard Jesus' words read in church: "As you go, proclaim this message: 'The kingdom of heaven has come near.' Heal the sick, raise the dead, cleanse those who have leprosy, drive out demons. Freely you have received; freely give. Do not get any gold or silver or copper to take with you in your belts—no bag for the journey or extra shirt or sandals or a staff, for the worker is worth his keep" (Matt 10:7–10). Armstrong and Brady note that when Francis "heard the missionary discourse of Matthew's Gospel . . . he responded immediately and embarked on the life of a poor, itinerant preacher, proclaiming a message of penance and peace."[10]

By 1210, Francis had attracted a small band of followers who joined him in both service and preaching. Informed by the way of Christ—his incarnation, life of poverty, and passion—the Friars Minor valued poverty, simplicity, and humility. They were unmatched among the other medieval mendicant orders in their commitment to radical poverty. Though Francis did advocate periods of withdrawal for the purpose of prayer and meditation, the Friars Minor were deliberately coenobitic in their monastic vision, which facilitated one of their core values and activities—itinerant preaching. The brothers were expected to obey their monastic leaders; however, the Franciscans resisted a hierarchical structure that emphasized power.

---

9. Moorman, *History of the Franciscan Order*, 4–6; also Peters, *Story of Monasticism*, 179–80; Lawrence, *The Friars*, 32; Robson, "Introduction," 1–3; and Robson, "Writings of St. Francis," 35–38.

10. Armstrong and Brady, *Francis and Clare*, 4.

Instead, leaders were to wash the feet of others and maintain the posture of a servant. Interestingly, Francis resigned as the leader of the Friars Minor in 1219 so he could focus on being a missionary among Muslims.[11]

Beginning in 1209, Francis sought the bishop of Rome's approval to have the Friar Minors officially recognized as an order. The Franciscans did not follow an existing monastic rule (e.g., Augustinian, Benedictine); however, they were given official status through a papal bull in 1216. In keeping with their value of voluntary poverty, the brothers accepted the run down church at Portiuncula (a gift from the Benedictines) where they constructed a simple mud dwelling that became the base for their community and mission outreach.[12] By 1221, the Friars Minor had grown to include more than three thousand monks. While individuals from all classes of society followed his vision, Francis seemed to especially enjoy recruiting the rich to renounce all material possessions and join the community. The growth of the Franciscan order also included women as a community of sisters led by Clare of Assisi emerged.[13]

The Franciscan way of life was largely articulated in two rules—the *Earlier Rule* (*regula non bullata*), which was drafted and approved by the pope in 1221, and the *Rule* (*regula bullata*) that was developed and approved by Rome in 1223. Interestingly, the *Earlier Rule* was longer and provided more detail on Francis' monastic values and practice, while the latter *Rule* was more concise and is still accepted by the Franciscans to this day.[14] Francis set the tone for the *Rule* and his monastic vision by asserting: "The *Rule* and life of the Friars Minor is this: to observe the holy gospel of

---

11. Francis, *Earlier Rule*, 1-2, 5, 7, 11; Francis, *Admonitions*, 4-5; also Peters, *Story of Monasticism*, 180; Moorman, *History of the Franciscan Order*, 10-12, 25; Lawrence, *The Friars*, 31; Robson, "Introduction," 3; Cusato, "Francis and the Franciscan Movement," 20-21, 26-29; Robson, "Writings of St. Francis," 39-41.

12. As the movement expanded in the generations after Francis' death and as different leaders emerged, there was a developing array of thought on what constituted simple living. Consequently, the Friar Minors would not always stay in such simple dwellings at the church at Portiuncula. Cf. Lawrence, *The Friars*, 48-60, 108-12; also Moorman, *History of the Franciscan Order*, 184-87.

13. Lawrence, *The Friars*, 34, 37, 41; also Moorman, *History of the Franciscan Order*, 20-23, 32-39; Cusato, "Francis and the Franciscan Movement," 21-23; and Godet-Calogeras, "Francis and Clare," 115-26.

14. Short, "The *Rule* and the Life," 50-51, 54-59; also Moorman, *History of the Franciscan Order*, 14-15, 18-19; and Armstrong and Brady, *Francis and Clare*, 107-8.

our Lord Jesus Christ by living in obedience, without anything of one's own, and in chastity."[15]

For Francis and his brothers, living out the gospel included a daily observance of prayer, meditation on Scripture, and liturgy following the daily office. They also fasted on a regular basis. The community was also occupied with manual labor—both as a strategy for staying focused in prayer and as a means for earning a living. Francis and the brothers often worked in exchange for food and avoided the temptation of having money by not accepting actual coins. In many respects, this attitude and approach toward money exemplified the heart of the mendicant movement and served as a prophetic example toward the growing merchant economy in Europe, which Francis had, of course, personally abandoned. The friars also survived materially by begging for alms. Finally, in addition to prayer, worship, and work, the Franciscans occupied themselves largely with itinerant, evangelistic preaching.[16]

Francis and the Friars Minor took the Lord's words in Matthew 10 seriously and began to engage in cross-cultural mission work from a very early point in their history. Particularly burdened to "preach the Christian faith and penance to the Saracens [Muslims]," Francis set sail for the Holy Land in 1212 but never made it because of a shipwreck.[17] Later, he attempted to go to Spain and meet with the Muslim leader of Morocco but was unable to because of illness. In 1217, as the order expanded, their mission efforts also grew as brothers were sent to other Italian provinces, Switzerland, Germany, France,[18] Spain (to work with Muslims), Morocco, and Tunisia. A certain Brother Giles was deployed to work with Muslims, journeying to Spain in 1209, Palestine in 1215, and Tunisia in 1219. Francis's dream of preaching the gospel to Muslims was finally realized in 1219 when he took advantage of the Fifth Crusade and travelled with the so-called Christian armies to Egypt. There, he walked across enemy lines and

---

15. Francis, *Rule* 1 cited in Short, "The *Rule* and the Life," 50.

16. Francis, *Earlier Rule*, 3, 7.3–12, 8, 9.1–12, 14–15; *Rule* 3.1–9, 4–5, 6.1–6; also Robson, "Introduction," 5; Robson, "Writings of St. Francis," 40, 42; Cusato, "Francis and the Franciscan Movement," 19; and Moorman, *History of the Franciscan Order*, 17.

17. Thomas of Celano, *Life of Francis* 20.55 cited in Cusato, "Francis and the Franciscan Movement," 24. Cf. Daniel, "Franciscan Missions," 241–42; and Moorman, *History of the Franciscan Order*, 24–25.

18. While Francis is largely remembered for his ministry to Muslims, he also had a great burden for France, the homeland of his mother. Cf. Moorman, *History of the Franciscan Order*, 46; also Armstrong and Brady, *Francis and Clare*, 3.

met with the Egyptian Sultan Malik al-Kamil, proclaiming the Christian message to him. In the following year, Francis continued his ministry to Muslims in Syria, while also reaching out to the Muslim diaspora in cities such as Jerusalem, Antioch, and Acre. This first decade of Franciscan mission activity was marked by vision and courage, but the brothers also encountered much hardship as they often had no contacts in these regions and they did not speak the local languages. Over time, the friars overcame these mistakes and became effective students of language and culture.[19]

Dominicans

The second major mendicant order was the Dominican order, also known as the Friars Preachers or the Black Friars. They received this latter distinction because the members wore a black coat over a white habit. They were founded in the early thirteenth century by the Castilian priest Dominic de Guzman (ca. 1170–1221) who was a member of a monastic community in Spain that followed the Rule of St. Augustine. Around 1203, while accompanying his bishop on a trip to Denmark, Dominic was given hospitality by a deacon in the Cathar or Albigensian church in France. The Cathars were rather Manichean in their thinking and held to a dualistic view of God (i.e., that God has a good spiritual side but also an evil material one), condemned marriage and sexual relations, and also opposed water baptism and the Eucharist. The Cathars believed that they were purified through the laying on of hands and receiving the Holy Spirit. In the early thirteenth century, Pope Innocent III had dispatched Cistercian monks to try to convert the Cathars back to the Catholic Church, but they were unsuccessful. Dominic, on the other hand, was able to reach this Cathar deacon and lead him back to Christian orthodoxy, which led to Dominic's vision for the new order. Peters asserts: "The immediate context for the genesis of the Order of Preachers . . . was the proliferation of heresy, especially the Cathar (or Albigensian) heresy."[20]

In 1206, Dominic established an initial monastic and mission base at Prouille (modern France). It served as a place of rest and renewal for

---

19. Lawrence, *The Friars*, 37–38, 43–46; also Moorman, *History of the Franciscan Order*, 30–31, 62–74, 166–69, 227–29; Cusato, "Francis and the Franciscan Movement," 25–27; and McMichael, "Francis and the Encounter with the Sultan," 128.

20. Peters, *Story of Monasticism*, 172–73; cf. Tugwell, *Early Dominicans*, 9–11; also Lawrence, *The Friars*, 8, 65–67.

itinerant ministers who were preaching against heresy and also as a refuge for Cathar women who had turned to the Catholic Church and were rejected by their families. By 1214, this developed into an order for Dominican sisters.

In 1214, Dominic was invited by the bishop of Toulouse to establish a base for training preachers. The friars were given a house to live in and were supported by tithes from the church. At this time, Dominic began to send many of his monks to study theology at the cathedral school to be trained to combat the Cathar heresy. Increasingly, the men joining the Friar Preachers tended to be more educated, although illiterate monks who focused on manual labor were still welcomed into the community. Like the Franciscans, the Dominicans did not have a social hierarchy in their order.[21]

Dominic attended the Fourth Lateran Council at Rome in 1215, a gathering that had significant implications for the life of the Dominican order. The council gave the Friar Preachers official permission to preach; however, the brothers were to live on tithes from the church instead of begging. The church also required that the Dominicans adhere to a recognized monastic rule to keep from drifting into heresy. The friars adopted the Augustinian rule, which Dominic had already been following. Finally, in 1216, the Dominicans were officially recognized through a papal bull that was sent to all Latin-speaking bishops, who were ordered to accept the work of the preachers.[22]

Though both men led coenobitic monastic orders, Dominic was probably more gifted at organizational leadership than Francis. By using the Augustinian rule, which said little about monastic structure, Dominic was able to determine the organizational shape of his order. The rhythm in the monastery included the daily office for prayer and liturgy, confession, the keeping of regular fasts, and also the practice of keeping silence within the house. There was also a good bit of flexibility within this schedule so that monks could leave the monastery and study at the university or engage in itinerant preaching.[23]

Dominic's vision for global mission apparently developed early and was probably first influenced by the missionary zeal that he encountered

---

21. Peters, *Story of Monasticism*, 174; also Lawrence, *The Friars*, 69–70, 74–79; and Tugwell, *Early Dominicans*, 26–31.

22. Peters, *Story of Monasticism*, 174–75; also Lawrence, *The Friars*, 70–71.

23. Lawrence, *The Friars*, 74, 81–83.

in the church at Lund (Sweden) while traveling there with his bishop. It also seems that his participation at the Fourth Lateran Council further fueled this passion. Shortly after the council, Dominican chapters—monastic mission bases—were established in France, Italy, and Spain and then later in England, Germany, Denmark, Hungary, Poland, Greece, and Jerusalem. Dominic himself set up his base at Bologna and from there he regularly traveled and visited his preachers in the field. His burden for evangelizing heretics and unbelievers was so great that at times he recruited non-Dominicans to participate in preaching missions.[24]

Approaches to Mission

Because the Franciscan and Dominican orders emerged at about the same time and had quite a number of shared values in mission, it seems best to evaluate their approaches to mission together. This does not discount, however, the distinctiveness of each movement and their respective strengths in the areas discussed. Seven key aspects of mendicant mission will be discussed in this section: preaching, academic study, ministry to the poor and through poverty, urban ministry, ministry to Muslims, diplomatic missions, and a church-centered focus.

Preaching

Francis' *Earlier Rule* of 1221 indicated that preaching was vital to the work of the Friars Minor. Following the model given by Jesus in Luke 10, the brothers were sent out two-by-two, with no possessions, and barefooted. For Francis, the ministry of preaching was characterized by humility and peace. Describing his preaching brothers in the *Rule*, Francis wrote: "when they go about the world, they do not quarrel or fight with words (cf. 2 Tim 2:14) or judge others; rather, let them be meek, peaceful, and unassuming, gentle and humble, speaking courteously to everyone, as is becoming."[25] Further, Francis taught that gospel preaching should be in both word (proclaiming the death, burial, and resurrection of Christ) and deed (caring for real human needs). According to his *Earlier Rule*, deed ministry at

---

24. Tugwell, *Early Dominicans*, 11–12, 14–16; also Lawrence, *The Friars*, 71–72, 79–80.

25. Francis, *Rule* 3.10–11 cited in Armstrong and Brady, *Francis and Clare*, 139. Cf. Francis, *Earlier Rule* 17.5.

times included praying for healing and the working of miracles. In terms of doctrinal content, Francis insisted that the friars' preaching should not contradict the historic teaching of the church. Finally, repentance and penance were key themes in Franciscan preaching and sometimes the friars heard confessions at the end of their messages.[26]

Pope Gregory IX observed that Francis brought renewal to the church through "preaching in simple words, just as Samson destroyed the Philistines with the jawbone of an ass."[27] Moorman adds: "it was in the simple sermons to village congregations that the friars really excelled. Such sermons, being extemporary and delivered in the vernacular, were far more ephemeral than the Latin sermons of the great doctors."[28] Delivered in a conversational manner that engaged the imagination and emotions of the audience, the friars' sermons were filled with references to Scripture and exemplary Bible characters and made connections to daily life.[29]

Highlighting the foundational place of preaching for the Dominicans, Peters asserts: "the history of the Dominican order demonstrates it was founded for one primary purpose: preaching (whether to bring heretics back into the church or to edify the laity)."[30] In his memorial "Sermon on St. Dominic," Thomas Agni of Lentini remarked that Dominic "became a preacher and then he 'did the work of an evangelist,' renouncing everything, refuting the claims of heretics, and preaching the gospel."[31] Preaching was such an important part of the apostolic life (*vita apostolica*) for Dominic and his followers that the friars eventually abandoned manual labor altogether to focus entirely on it. In order to train and equip Dominican preachers, a number of preaching manuals and resources were developed in the thirteenth and fourteenth centuries, including Humbert of Romans' *The Instruction of Preachers,* Thomas Waleys' *The Art of Preaching,* some Bible concordances, as well as books containing collections of saints' lives. In addition to studying Scripture and theology, Dominican preachers were

---

26. Francis, *Earlier Rule,* 17.1–3; 21.3–9; also Peters, *Story of Monasticism,* 181; Moorman, *History of the Franciscan Order,* 12–14; Lawrence, *The Friars,* 126; Robson, "Writings of St. Francis," 37; and Blastic, "Francis and His Hagiographic Tradition," 73–74.

27. Cited in Blastic, "Francis and His Hagiographic Tradition," 69.

28. Moorman, *History of the Franciscan Order,* 275.

29. Lawrence, *The Friars,* 126; also Moorman, *History of the Franciscan Order,* 275–77.

30. Peters, *Story of Monasticism,* 179.

31. Cited in Tugwell, *Early Dominicans,* 62.

also trained in the art of speaking in order to inspire, compel, and even entertain their audiences.[32]

Academic Study

Francis' writings reveal that he was a simple man and not a scholar. In fact, because of his commitment to humility and simplicity, he did not want books in the monastery. However, following Francis' death, the Friars Minor increasingly valued education and academics as part of their monastic discipline and missionary experience. During the thirteenth century in Europe, literacy, schooling, and even university education were on the rise among the laity and the Franciscans valued being prepared to preach and minister in this context. Members of the order began receiving advanced theological degrees from the European universities and competent theologians such as Bonaventure were emerging. Some members of the Friars Minor were even being appointed as theology professors. While Franciscans were entering the universities as students, the order also set up bases in university cities to recruit new monks who were already trained in theology.[33]

Unlike Francis, Dominic was a proponent of his friars pursuing education. Founded for the purpose of answering heresy, the Dominicans regarded academic theological studies as a vital strategy for training monks for ministry. The thirteenth-century friar Hugh of Saint-Cher probably best expressed this when he wrote, "First the bow is bent in study, then the arrow is released in preaching."[34]

Like the Franciscans, Dominic began to send his preachers to university towns such as Paris, Bologna, and Oxford so they could enroll as theology students. Also, as the order expanded around Europe, new Dominican houses emerged with their own internal theological schools, all equipped with professors who taught Scripture, theology, and philosophy. Arguably, these schools were becoming superior to the university theology

---

32. Lawrence, *The Friars*, 68–69, 120–22; also Tugwell, *Early Dominicans*, 16, 20.

33. Peters, *Story of Monasticism*, 181; also Lawrence, *The Friars*, 8–15, 35, 39, 52–53; Moorman, *History of the Franciscan Order*, 54, 91, 123–39, 140–54; and Şenocak, "Voluntary Simplicity," 84–85.

34. Peters, *Story of Monasticism*, 178; cf. Lawrence, *The Friars*, 69; and Tugwell, *Early Dominicans*, 24–26.

departments and in some cases Dominican houses became affiliated with existing universities.[35]

Like the Franciscans, the Dominicans saw the universities as fertile recruiting grounds for new members and, therefore, vital to the growth of the order. Dominic established his headquarters in the university town of Bologna in part for this reason. The Dominican leader Jordan of Saxony (1190–1237) later engaged in aggressive preaching and recruiting trips in Paris, Oxford, and Vercelli in search of new friars. In addition to recruiting from the universities, the Dominicans also wanted to influence the universities by placing professors in them who could influence theological conversations and even invite students to consider a mendicant lifestyle. Lawrence notes that Dominic's "friars not only sought to provide for the theological education of the preachers; they made it their aim to capture the leading intellectual centers of their time."[36] Over time, the Dominican professors became so numerous and influential that schools began to purposefully limit the number of teaching chairs available to them.[37]

The most famous Dominican friar, who exemplified academic study in theology and philosophy for the purpose of combatting heresy, was Thomas Aquinas (1226–1274). Having grown up among the Benedictine monks at Monte Cassino, Aquinas was attracted to the Dominicans during his university studies at Naples. He pursued advanced theological studies in Paris and later taught in the universities in Paris, Cologne, and Rome. He wrote his greatest work, *Summa Theologica*, as a theological resource for his Dominican colleagues as well as the greater church.[38]

Ministry to the Poor and through Poverty

While the mendicants could relate to educated theologians and heretics in university towns, they also connected well with the poor. Through their commitment to voluntary poverty and simplicity, the mendicants' lifestyle naturally identified with the poor. As shown, Francis' calling to the ascetic life came in part through encountering a man with leprosy whom he loved

---

35. Peters, *Story of Monasticism*, 175; also Moorman, *History of the Franciscan Order*, 135; and Lawrence, *The Friars*, 84–88, 127–51.

36. Lawrence, *The Friars*, 72.

37. Peters, *Story of Monasticism*, 175–76; also Lawrence, *The Friars*, 72–74, 79; and Moorman, *History of the Franciscan Order*, 125–28.

38. Peters, *Story of Monasticism*, 176–77; also Tugwell, *Early Dominicans*, 25.

and embraced, which prompted him to spend the rest of his life caring for the poor, weak, and sick. Lawrence argues that ministering to the poor through preaching and practical care was the most important element of the Friar Minors' work.[39] For Francis, this ministry emphasis flowed directly from his Christology: Christ was a pilgrim, the Suffering Servant, the Good Shepherd who laid down his life for the sheep, and a servant who washed his disciples' feet. Francis' ministry included praying for healing for the sick, which was likely the primary ministry of Clare of the poor sisters at the convent of San Damiano as well.[40]

Though the Dominicans did not pursue voluntary poverty to the extent that the Franciscans did, and though following the directive of the Fourth Lateran Council of 1215 they began to live off of church tithes instead of begging for alms, they still strongly emphasized simple living. For Dominic, embracing poverty was not so much a means for reaching the poor but for evangelizing heretics. When asked by the Cistercians for tips on ministering to the Cathars, he replied, "the message is only as believable as the messenger" and that they should approach them "in humility—barefoot and without gold or silver in imitation of the apostles."[41] Ironically, some Dominican friars later entered the royal courts in Europe to serve as preachers and confessors. While these surroundings certainly presented temptations to abandon the mendicant values of poverty, the Dominicans apparently maintained a good reputation among Europe's elite because of their conviction for simplicity. In short, though the Friar Preachers did not always minister directly to the poor as the Friar Minors did, they clearly ministered through their poverty and testimony of simple living.[42]

Urban Ministry

Similar to the fourth-century mission work of Basil of Caesarea, the mendicants focused much of their ministry on urban centers. Describing the Franciscans, Robson writes: "While Francis and his first companions continued to live outside the walls of Assisi, deriving their inspiration from

---

39. Lawrence, *The Friars*, 36.

40. Francis, *Admonitions* 6; also Peters, *Story of Monasticism*, 179–80; Moorman, *History of the Franciscan Order*, 125–28; Cusato, "Francis and the Franciscan Movement," 22; and McMichael, "Francis and the Encounter with the Sultan," 130.

41. Cited in Peters, *Story of Monasticism*, 174.

42. Lawrence, *The Friars*, 166–73, 179; also Tugwell, *Early Dominicans*, 12, 18–19.

the teaching of Jesus, their mandate to communicate the gospel by word and example took them back to the city."[43] Lawrence adds, "Everywhere they [Franciscans] made for the cities. The urban populations were their chosen mission field."[44] Part of their urban strategy included setting up a monastery as a mission base, which would facilitate ministry to that city as well as the surrounding towns and villages.

In addition to preaching in word and deed, the Franciscans made disciples by inviting men to embrace a mendicant calling and join them in the monastery.[45]

Given their emphasis on connecting with the European universities and also engaging in mission to heresy, the Dominicans also prioritized urban ministry. Lawrence summarizes: "The cities were the chosen objective of the [Dominican] preachers because the urban populations were the most fertile seed-bed of heresy and skepticism; it was there that the largest and most responsive audiences were to be found; and it was there that the struggle for religious orthodoxy was to be won or lost."[46]

Muslim Ministry

During the thirteenth century, the Roman Catholic popes demonstrated an ambiguous and often contradictory approach to Muslims. On one hand, they continued to bless the Crusades, which had been initiated by Pope Urban IV in 1095. On the other hand, some popes sent monks to engage missionally with Muslims. For instance, in 1233, Pope Gregory IX sent Franciscans on mission to Baghdad, Damascus, Aleppo, and Cairo.[47] In this section, we will focus on Francis and the friars' approach to Muslim ministry.

In his *Earlier Rule*, Francis specifically discussed ministry to Muslims. Praising those who felt called to Muslim and offering insights on reaching them, he wrote:

> Therefore, any brother, who by divine inspiration, desires to go among the Saracens and other non-believers should go with the permission of his minister and servant. And the minister should give [these brothers] permission and not oppose them, if he shall

43. Robson, "The Writings of St. Francis," 41.
44. Lawrence, *The Friars*, 46.
45. Ibid., 46, 105.
46. Ibid., 80.
47. Ibid., 204.

see that they are fit to be sent. . . . As for the brothers who go, they can live spiritually among [the Saracens and non-believers] in two ways. One way is not to engage in arguments or disputes, but to be subject to every creature for God's sake (1 Pet 2:13) and to acknowledge that they are Christians. Another way is to proclaim the word of God when they see that it pleases the Lord, so that they believe in the all-powerful God—Father, and Son, and Holy Spirit—the Creator of all, the Son who is the Redeemer and Savior, and that they be baptized and become Christians.[48]

In Francis' visit to the Egyptian Sultan Malik al-Kamil in 1219, he also illustrated some principles for ministering to Muslims that compliment his writings. Jacques de Vitry, a thirteenth-century monk bishop, wrote: "For several days he preached the Word of God to the Saracens and made little progress. The sultan, the ruler of Egypt, privately asked him to pray to the Lord for him, so that he might be inspired by God to adhere to that religion which most pleased God."[49]

What do Francis' writings and these historic accounts reveal about Francis' approach to Muslims? First, while Francis was very eager for members of the order to go and minister to Muslims, he put in place a vetting process to evaluate the readiness of missionary candidates. Second, Francis' initiative toward Muslims seemed to fulfill a longing that he had for martyrdom. This was his motivation in the initial attempt to sail to the Holy Land in 1212 and also to the Egyptian sultan in 1219. Upon learning of the death of five Friar Minors who had been sent to Morocco to preach to Muslims, Francis praised their memories and declared that he truly had five brothers.[50]

Third, while Francis longed for martyrdom, his posture toward Muslims and non-believers was one of peace. In this section of the *Earlier Rule*, arguably written after Francis' visit to the sultan, he wrote:

> All my brothers: Let us pay attention to what the Lord says: Love your enemies and do good to those who hate you, for our Lord Jesus Christ, whose footprints we must follow, called his betrayer a friend and willingly offered himself to his executioners. Our friends, therefore, are all those who unjustly inflict upon us

---

48. Francis, *Earlier Rule* 16.3–7 cited in Armstrong and Brady, *Francis and Clare*, 121–22. Cf. Francis, *Rule* 2.1–2.

49. Cited in McMichael, "Francis and the Encounter with the Sultan," 127.

50. Robson, "Writings of St. Francis," 46–47; also Daniel, "Franciscan Missions," 244; and Lawrence, *The Friars*, 204.

distress and anguish, shame and injury, sorrow and punishment, martyrdom and death. We must love them greatly, for we shall possess eternal life because of what they bring us.[51]

Francis instructed the brothers to serve among Muslims with peace and humility and to avoid arguments and disputes while preaching the gospel. Clearly, Francis illustrated these values through his encounter with the sultan as he refrained from attacking Islam or the prophet Muhammad and focused on proclaiming the gospel and praying for the sultan. Interestingly, Francis received safe passage to the sultan's camp and was returned safely at the conclusion of their discussions. Francis' value for peace in mission contrasted greatly with the environment of the Crusades, but also his own background in Italy, which was marred by warfare and violence.[52]

Finally, while Francis was quite committed to peaceful encounters with Muslims, it would be a mistake to describe his communications with the sultan or others as interfaith dialogue. Instead, he presented a Trinitarian God; an incarnate Christ who was crucified, buried, and risen; and a Holy Spirit that made the virgin birth of Christ possible. Beyond mere dialogue, he called his Muslim listeners to repent and believe this message.[53]

In the generation following Francis' death, Franciscan monks continued to reach out to Muslims and some adopted more polemical approaches. The most famous of these was Raymund Lull (1232–1315), a Castilian Franciscan from the island of Majorca. Lull spent nine years learning Arabic, established Franciscan houses as missionary training centers for the Muslim world, and also convinced the pope to make Arabic and Oriental studies part of the curriculum in European universities. After a career in training and mobilization, Lull himself engaged in three short-term preaching trips to Algeria and Tunisia in North Africa. Lull's approach was to enter a city and invite Muslim leaders to a public debate over the virtues of Islam and Christianity. A polemicist, Lull did not hesitate to criticize Muhammad in his presentation of the gospel. His first two preaching trips ended abruptly as he was expelled from North Africa. During the third trip, the

---

51. Francis, *Earlier Rule* 22 cited in McMichael "Francis and the Encounter with the Sultan," 134; cf. Francis, *Admonitions,* 9.

52. Francis, *Rule* 3; Francis, *Admonitions,* 15; also McMichael, "Francis and the Encounter with the Sultan," 128–29, 135; Daniel, "Franciscan Missions," 242; Robson, "Writings of St. Francis," 47; and Short, "The *Rule* and the Life," 61.

53. Francis, *Rule* 11–12; Francis, *Admonitions,* 1; also Daniel, "Franciscan Missions," 243; McMichael, "Francis and the Encounter with the Sultan," 132–33; and Short, "The *Rule* and the Life," 55.

THE MENDICANTS

eighty-three-year-old monk was stoned to death by his Muslim listeners. In short, though Raymund Lull emulated Francis' vision for martyrdom, he clearly departed from the friar's core value of peaceful engagement.[54]

Diplomatic Missions

While Christians and Muslims were continuing to fight the Crusades, the Mongol Empire had conquered much of China and Central Asia and was even beginning to make inroads into Europe. A number of Christians, including mendicant monks, were killed during Mongol attacks in Eastern Europe. As a result, Pope Innocent IV sent the Italian Franciscan monk John de Piano di Carpini (ca. 1180–1252) and his Polish colleague Benedict on an official mission to the Mongol khan in 1246 that was both political and evangelistic in nature.[55]

The friars travelled across the rugged terrain of Central Asia and arrived at the court of the khan where they were welcomed in peace and shown hospitality. The men delivered letters from the pope that expressed concern over the Mongol's violence, called for peace, and also announced the Christian message to the khan. Though hospitable, the khan rejected the pope's call for peace and for Christian baptism. While the mission was not very fruitful spiritually, Carpini took careful notes and conducted his own ethnographic survey of the Mongols, which helped the mendicant missionaries who came after him. Also, the friar made the surprising discovery of Church of the East believers living and worshipping freely among the Mongols.[56]

In 1247, in response to the Mongol leader's initiative toward King Louis of France, the king sent the Dominican Andre de Longjumeau (d. 1270) as his emissary and preacher to the khan. Though the khan continued to show no interest in the gospel, Longjumeau discovered more eastern Christians, which increased the pope's concern for them and desire to minister to them. As a result, in 1253, the Franciscan William of Rubruck (1220–ca. 1293) was sent to continue the mission, ministering to diaspora Christians and slaves, and attempting to no avail to communicate the gospel

54. Peers, *Ramon Lull*; also Zwemer, *Raymund Lull*.

55. Jackson, "Franciscans as Papal and Royal Envoys," 224–25; also Lawrence, *The Friars*, 206–7.

56. Jackson, "Franciscans as Papal and Royal Envoys," 226; also Lawrence, *The Friars*, 208–8.

to the khan. Like Carpini, Rubruck engaged in ethnographic and linguistic studies in order to better understand the Mongol culture.[57]

Finally, in 1289 Pope Nicolas IV sent the Franciscan John of Montecorvino (1247–1328) all the way to China to reach out to the khan. By this time, the Mongol leader had actually converted to Buddhism; however, he allowed Montecorvino much freedom to preach the gospel among his people. The friar reported baptizing some six thousand Mongols and started a church, making his mission the most fruitful work in the thirteenth century among this Asian people.[58]

Church-Centered Mission

The friars' love and respect for the church was a final characteristic of mendicant missions. As discussed, Francis' initial call to the ascetic life and ministry included rebuilding the physical church at San Damiano, which also symbolized his work to call the universal church to repentance and renewal. Francis' love for the church was also evident through his words in his *Testament*: "We adore You, Lord Jesus Christ, in all your churches throughout the world."[59] He also seemed to highly revere the clergy because of their important role in overseeing the sacraments in worship.[60]

Francis and the Friars Minor looked to the church and its authority for their very existence as an order. As shown, in 1209, Francis reached out to the pope and sought approval for the new order and their way of life. He also looked to Bishop Guido I and Cardinal Hugolino (who later became Pope Gregory IX) for guidance in developing the monastic rule for the Friars Minor. The Fourth Lateran Council of 1215 seemed to give encouragement and shape to the Franciscan order and a number of the theological resolutions of the council were included in Francis' *Earlier Rule*. Once recognized by the church, the Franciscans continually submitted to the church's leadership. Francis' rules were explicit in acknowledging this authority and he regularly deferred to church leadership on important decisions regarding the order.[61]

---

57. Lawrence, *The Friars*, 175, 209–14; also Jackson, "Franciscans as Papal and Royal Envoys," 228–36; and Daniel, "Franciscan Missions," 246, 253–54.

58. Lawrence, *The Friars*, 214–17; also Daniel, "Franciscan Missions," 253–54.

59. Francis, *Testament*, 5, cited in Armstrong and Brady, *Francis and Clare*, 154.

60. Francis, *Earlier Rule* prologue; 2; also Francis, *Admonitions*, 26.

61. Francis, *Earlier Rule*, 19–20; 23.7; Francis, *Rule* 1.2; 2.2; 9; also Short, "The Rule

Francis was also convinced that all preaching should be done in light of the church. That is, the Friars' preaching should conform to the church's doctrine and all evangelistic preaching should be done with the aim and expectation that new believers would become a part of the existing church. Francis allowed himself to be ordained as a deacon in the church, which gave great legitimacy to the friars, and Bishop Guido gave him the opportunity to preach in the churches around Assisi.[62]

Similarly, Dominic and the Friar Preachers were initially given a platform to preach by the bishop of Toulouse, and it seems that the church valued their role both as preachers to the Cathars and those who could train church leaders in dealing with heresy. As discussed, the Fourth Lateran Council also brought the order into alignment with the church and it seemed to be a catalyst for Dominican global mission efforts.

Summary

Responding to the changing economic and social climate of Europe, the Franciscan and Dominican mendicant orders resisted these changes and embraced lives of voluntary poverty, begging, wandering, and preaching. Initially focused on Europe, their vision and ministry extended from North Africa to East Asia where they encountered Muslims, Mongols, and other non-believers. As wandering preachers, they had the ability to relate to all manner of men—educated intellectuals, the poor, urban and village dwellers, and, at times, kings and other political leaders. The Franciscan and Dominican orders inspired other smaller orders of friars to spring up in the thirteenth century prompting an even greater legacy of missionary monasticism.[63] Of course, the Franciscans, Dominicans, and other mendicant orders continue to this day.

---

and the Life," 52–61; Robson, "Writings of St. Francis," 42–43; Cusato, "Francis and the Franciscan Movement," 21, 28.

62. Francis, *Earlier Rule,* 17.1; also Robson, "Writings of St. Francis," 45.
63. Lawrence, *The Friars,* 89–101; also Andrews, *The Other Friars.*

CHAPTER 13

The Jesuits

ROLAND JOFFÉ'S 1986 AWARD-WINNING film *The Mission* was a fictional account of a group of Catholic missionaries striving to evangelize the Guarani, an indigenous people living in the Iguassu Falls region of present day Paraguay. Led by Father Gabriel, the missionaries navigated the jungle and risked their lives to make contact with the Guarani and eventually establish a reduction or mission community among them. However, the greatest opposition that they encountered was with the expanding Spanish and Portuguese empires that were maneuvering to take control of South America. While the missionaries wanted to make Christians of the Guarani, the Portuguese wanted to enslave them. Although fictional, the film succeeds in capturing the difficulties, competing interests, and confusion associated with Christian mission efforts in the age of empire. Further, the film introduces on a popular level the work of the most significant Roman Catholic missionary movement in the world during the sixteenth to eighteenth centuries—the Society of Jesus or the Jesuits.

As shown, in the first fifteen centuries the words "mission" or "missions" were not used to describe what is commonly known as mission today. Instead, as Bosch has noted, terms such as "propagation of the faith, preaching of the gospel," and "apostolic proclamation" among others were use.[1] While the Jesuits were innovative cross-cultural evangelists beginning in the sixteenth century, they were also some of the first to call their work "mission." Luke Clossey notes that while Jesuit missionary work included engaging heretics (Catholic or Protestant) and even ministering to those within the existing church, "by around 1580 Jesuit sources used

1. Bosch, *Transforming Mission*, 228.

'mission' to mean a place where one preaches the gospel."[2] As the Jesuit narrative unfolded, these preaching places included Europe, the Americas, and Asia.

In this chapter, beginning with a brief survey of the thought and work of Jesuit founder Iñigo or Ignatius of Loyola (1491–1556),[3] we will discuss the emergence of the Jesuits as a monastic missionary order. In describing and evaluating early Jesuit mission efforts, our discussion will be limited to the sixteenth and seventeenth centuries and will focus on the work of three innovative Jesuit missionary monks—Francis Xavier (1506–1552) in India and Japan; Matteo Ricci (1552–1610) in China; and Roberto de Nobili (1577–1656) in India.

Ignatius of Loyola and the Origin of the Jesuits

Ethnically Basque, Ignatius of Loyola grew up in northern Spain. At the age of fifteen, he was taken into the Spanish royal court. Though not a professional soldier, he sometimes took part in military campaigns, and in 1521, during a battle against the French, a cannonball crushed his leg. During the long period of recovery in which he was largely confined to bed, Ignatius passed the time reading. At some point, he was introduced to some Christian devotional literature including Ludolph of Saxony's *Life of Christ* and Jacob of Voraigne's *The Golden Legend*, a compendium of saints' lives. While reading these devotional works, Ignatius was ultimately converted to faith in Christ. As he read the saints' lives, he was particularly moved by the testimonies of Francis of Assisi and Dominic and yearned to emulate their mendicant lifestyle.[4]

Upon his recovery, Ignatius travelled to Manresa near Barcelona where he was given a place to stay in a Dominican monastery and spent nearly a year in prayer and meditation. At this time he began work on his famous *Spiritual Exercises*—a manual on his thoughts and approach to the ascetic life that developed as he wrote down his reflections on imitating Christ and the lives of saints. In 1524, Ignatius made a pilgrimage to the

2. Clossey, *Salvation and Globalization*, 14. Cf. Paul Kollman, "At the Origins of Mission and Missiology," 425–58.

3. Born Iñigo, he took the name Ignatius upon beginning his studies in Paris in 1528.

4. Peters, *Story of Monasticism*, 216; also Ganss, *Ignatius of Loyola*, 14–26; and Hollis, *History of the Jesuits*, 7.

Holy Land to walk in the steps of Christ but also to evangelize Muslims living in the region. Convinced that he needed more academic study in order to minister, Ignatius followed the example of the Dominicans and Franciscans and entered the University of Alcalá in Spain in 1526. Not a natural scholar, Ignatius first studied Latin in order to read the academic works of his day before turning his focus to philosophy. After two years of study at Alcalá, Ignatius moved to Paris in 1528 where he spent seven years studying theology.[5] Entering the French university at the age of thirty-seven, Ignatius mused that he "studied with children."[6]

At Paris, six friends, including Francis Xavier, joined Ignatius in a community centered on Christian living according to his *Spiritual Exercises*. In a solemn worship service in 1534, they covenanted to live together as a society and to offer their services to the pope. In 1540, the Society of Jesus was officially recognized as a monastic order through a papal bull. On one hand they were continuing the mendicant tradition of voluntary poverty and begging and were also characterized by imitating Christ, obedience, and spiritual care for believers and non-believers. On the other, they were distinct because of their allegiance to the pope.[7] In their *Constitutions*, Ignatius wrote that the "Society also makes an explicit vow to the sovereign pontiff as the present or future vicar of Christ our Lord. This is a vow to go anywhere his Holiness will order, whether among the faithful or the infidels."[8] In this sense, they were more than just a monastic order but a type of spiritual, military troop ready to go wherever the pope chose to send them—including to the ends of the earth as missionaries and to resistant peoples such as Muslims. In an early mission statement, the group stated that they saw themselves as "a community founded chiefly to strive for the progress of souls in Christian life and doctrine, and for the propagation of the faith by means of the ministry of the word, the Spiritual Exercises, and works of charity, and specifically by the instruction of children and unlettered persons in Christianity."[9] Later, in his *Constitutions of the Society of Jesus*, Ignatius added this more concise statement: "The end of this Society

---

5. Ignatius, *Autobiography*, 8, 23; also Peters, *Story of Monasticism*, 216; and Hollis, *History of the Jesuits*, 9, 14,

6. Ignatius, *Autobiography*, 73 (unless otherwise noted, all English translations of Ignatius' works are from Ganss, *Ignatius of Loyola*).

7. Ganss, *Ignatius of Loyola*, 36–37, 217–18; also Hollis, *History of the Jesuits*, 14–17; Clossey, *Salvation and Globalization*, 21–22, 29; and O'Malley, *The Jesuits*, 2–4.

8. Ignatius, *Constitutions* I.1.5 (Ganss, 284).

9. Ganss, *Ignatius of Loyola*, 45.

is to devote itself with God's grace not only to salvation and perfection of the members' own souls, but also with that same grace to labor strenuously in giving aid toward the salvation and perfection of the souls of their neighbors."[10] In 1541, Ignatius was elected superior general or leader of the Society of Jesus. By the time of his death in 1556, the order included over a thousand members and new communities had been started in Portugal, Spain, Italy, Sicily, France, and Germany as well as in Brazil and India. By 1615, the Society included over thirteen thousand members globally.[11]

Ignatius is not remembered for being a scholarly theologian, however, he did produce a number of influential works that shaped the theology and direction of the Society. His greatest work was, of course, his *Spiritual Exercises*, which he began in 1522, revised continually until 1541, and then published in 1548. Describing this practical manual for spiritual living, Ignatius wrote: "By the term Spiritual Exercises we mean every method of examination of conscience, meditation, contemplation, vocal or mental prayer, and other spiritual activities . . . any means of preparing or disposing our soul to ride itself of all its disordered affections and then, after their removal, of seeking and finding God's will in the order of our life for the salvation of our soul."[12] Divided into weeks, the major themes in the *Spiritual Exercises* were purifying the soul, imitating Christ, experiencing union with Christ, and contemplating the love of God. They became the basis for the Jesuit ministry of retreat and shaped the structures of Jesuit houses around the world.[13]

The content of Ignatius' *Constitutions of the Society of Jesus* was essentially the values of the *Spiritual Exercises* applied to the organization of the community. A living document that Ignatius acknowledged should develop over time, the principles in the *Constitutions* were innovative because they offered clear steps for a new member entering and progressing within the community. Ignatius' other major works included his *Autobiography*, which covered his spiritual journey from the time of his injury in 1521 until he arrived in Rome in 1538. He also wrote over seven thousand letters in which his counsel rehearsed many of the same themes found in his *Spiritual Exercises* and *Constitutions*.[14]

10. Ignatius, *Constitutions* I.1.1 (Ganss, *Ignatius of Loyola*, 283–84).
11. Ganss, *Ignatius of Loyola*, 46; also O'Malley, *The Jesuits*, 33–42.
12. Ignatius, *Spiritual Exercises*, Introduction.1 (Ganss, *Ignatius of Loyola*, 121).
13. Ganss, *Ignatius of Loyola*, 50–54, 57–58, 117–19; also O'Malley, *The Jesuits*, 9–10.
14. Ganss, *Ignatius of Loyola*, 55–57, 277; also O'Malley, *The Jesuits*, 11.

As we evaluate Ignatius' theology, the primary theme resounding through his writings and letters was God's glory. In his *Spiritual Exercises*, he wrote: "Human beings are created to praise, reverence, and serve God our Lord."[15] For Ignatius, bringing glory to God was naturally integrated with serving him and serving others. Ignatius' writings also emphasized salvation history, a narrative that included creation, redemption, and the glorification of human beings. Finally, a thoroughly Trinitarian theology comes through in his works as he emphasized the personalities and work of the Father, Son, and Holy Spirit.[16]

Though Ignatius spent the year after his conversion in ascetic withdrawal, Ganns notes, "he was not to remain a solitary pilgrim imitating the saints in prayer and penance, but to labor with Christ for the salvation of others."[17] His monastic vision bore fruit not only in expanding communities of like-minded monks but also in outward service to others and to engagement in Christian mission. For Ignatius, Jesus was the primary model for mission and he regarded Christ as "the inspiring King sent by his Father on a mission to conquer the world, in order to win all humankind to faith and salvation; and calling for cooperators who would volunteer for this enterprise."[18] Ganss adds that, over time, "Ignatius' thought . . . was . . . becoming apostolic, with the whole world as its scope."[19]

Jesuit Missions

Driven by the vision to "labor strenuously in giving aid toward the salvation and perfection of the souls of their neighbors" and to "go anywhere his Holiness [the pope] will order, whether among the faithful or the infidels," the Jesuits quickly became engaged in global mission efforts in the sixteenth century.[20] As the Jesuit leader, Jeronimo Nadal (1507–1580), put it, "the world is our house."[21] While Ignatius himself served primarily in the Society's base of operations in Rome, he was responsible for deploying

---

15. Ignatius, *Spiritual Exercises,* First Week 23 (Ganss, *Ignatius of Loyola*, 130).
16. Ganss, *Ignatius of Loyola*, 60, 229–70.
17. Ibid., 31.
18. Ibid., 32–33.
19. Ibid.
20. Ignatius, *Constitutions* I.1.1, 5 (Ganss, *Ignatius of Loyola*, 283–84).
21. O'Malley, *The* Jesuits, ix.

many Jesuits in cross-cultural and global mission during his lifetime.[22] Let us now consider three representative examples of Jesuit mission work in the sixteenth and seventeenth centuries.

Francis Xavier

Francis Xavier is arguably the most famous Roman Catholic missionary in church history. Ethnically Basque like Ignatius and born in the Kingdom of Navarre (northern Spain), Xavier was among the original group of Jesuits that gathered around Ignatius in Paris. Xavier arrived in Goa, India in 1542 as a representative of the Portuguese king and as a papal envoy. His task was to minister to Portuguese expatriates in India but to minister to Indian peoples as well.[23]

Xavier's Indian ministry began when he encountered the Paravas—a group of Tamil-speaking pearl fishers who had been baptized several years prior by some Franciscan missionaries who subsequently abandoned the work. Apparently, the Paravas had converted to Christianity in exchange for military protection from the Portuguese against their Muslim neighbors. So, Xavier's ministry was focused on discipling this people who had received little teaching after their conversion. Xavier learned only basic Tamil and was able to oversee a rough translation of the liturgy in the local language. He also started a church and organized the believing Paravas into sixteen villages—strict communities centered on spiritual formation. Xavier particularly focused his ministry on children and in one month alone, he baptized some ten thousand Paravas children. Given this successful ministry, the Portuguese king sent twelve more Jesuits to join Xavier. While the international laborers increased among the Paravas, Xavier failed to set apart any indigenous church leaders. In 1546, Xavier travelled to Malacca (Indonesia) where he served for two years before returning to Goa.[24]

In 1549, Xavier, along with two fellow Jesuits and Yajiro—a Japanese man that they had met in India—travelled to Japan to begin ministry there. Following in the footsteps of other missionary monks, Xavier made his first connections in Japanese society with local leaders (*daimyos*). Having gained their favor, he was provided an interpreter and given the freedom

22. Ibid., 3.
23. Hollis, *History of the Jesuits*, 36–37.
24. Ganss, *Ignatius of Loyola*, 47; also Neill, *History of Christian Missions*, 127–31; Hollis, *History of the Jesuits*, 35–37; and O'Malley, *The Jesuits*, 44.

to preach the gospel throughout the country. Struggling in general with the language, Xavier encountered difficulty communicating some key biblical ideas in Japanese; therefore, he chose to transliterate them directly from Portuguese. Though connecting through language did not come naturally, Xavier greatly admired the virtues and ethics present within local Japanese culture and he managed to discover relevant bridges on which to communicate the gospel. Describing this shift in Xavier's thinking that would influence Jesuit and Roman Catholic missiology, Stephen Neill writes:

> In earlier years, he had been inclined to accept uncritically the doctrine of the *tabula rasa*—the view that in non-Christian life and systems there is nothing on which the missionary can build, and that everything must simply be leveled to the ground before anything Christian can be built up[;] . . . now that he was confronted by a civilization with so many elements of nobility in it, he saw that while the gospel must transform and refine and recreate, it need not necessarily reject as worthless everything that has come before.[25]

After serving for two years, Xavier reported that around a hundred Japanese had been baptized. Following a bout with poor health, Xavier died in 1552 while attempting to begin work in another mission field—China. In the generation following Xavier's death, there was a significant response to the gospel in Japan as Jesuits and other missionaries baptized around three hundred thousand new believers.[26]

Matteo Ricci

Though Xavier failed to reach China, another Jesuit colleague, the Italian Matteo Ricci was able to access the country and innovate mission strategies there. Beginning in 1579, the Jesuit superior and official papal visitor, Alessandro Valigno (1539–1606), visited Macao, a Portuguese island off the mainland of China where western missionaries could live and serve. Many church leaders at the time believed that Macao was as close as any missionary would ever get to China; however, Valigno adamantly rejected this conclusion. Instead, he appointed Ricci and two other Jesuits to go to Macao, study Chinese, and wait for the right opportunity to enter China.

---

25. Neill, *History of Christian Missions*, 133.

26. Hollis, *History of the Jesuits*, 37–39, 42; also Neill, *History of Christian Missions*, 131–38; and Brockey, *Journey to the East*, 246.

The men also received training in building clocks and designing maps—professional skills that would prove to be very interesting to the Chinese. In 1583, Ricci received permission to enter the provincial capital Zhaoqing. Later, in 1600, he moved to Peking (Beijing) where he resided for ten years until his death.

Indeed, Ricci gained favor in the Chinese capital by presenting gifts of clocks, paintings, models of western architecture, and maps. He also adopted Chinese dress and focused his ministry on intellectuals and the upper classes. Ricci was also innovative and controversial for how he contextualized the Christian message in China. For instance, he borrowed the Chinese term *Tianzhu* ("Lord of heaven") as his functional equivalent for the God of the Christian Scriptures. Also, just as Aquinas had used Aristotelian categories for doing theology, Ricci made connections between Confucian ideas and the Scriptures. He also considered the Chinese practice of honoring departed ancestors as acceptable and compatible with the Christian faith. At the time of Ricci's death in 1610, the Chinese church had about two thousand members, including some members of the royal family and some leading scholars. Though changing imperial favor and even persecution against the church in 1616 and 1622 presented challenges, Ricci's greatest legacy was in the indigenous Chinese clergy that he set apart to lead the church.

Ricci's methods set the standard for Jesuit mission practices in China; however, they were also met with resistance from other missionaries, including the Dominicans and Franciscans. In 1704, nearly a century after Ricci's death, Pope Clement XI denounced the Jesuit contextualization strategy in China and sent a messenger, Charles Thomas Maillard de Tournon, to China and other parts of Asia ordering missionaries to cease with such approaches. While many missionaries on the field labored unsuccessfully to have this decision repealed, the Chinese emperor reacted even more strongly and decreed that only those missionaries who shared Ricci's philosophy of ministry could remain in China. Yet, the Roman Catholic Church remained resolute in its decision, which stifled mission work in China until the twentieth century.[27]

---

27. Neill, *History of Christian Missions*, 139–41, 164–65; also Hollis, *History of the Jesuits*, 60–68; and O'Malley, *The Jesuits*, 51, 64–68.

Roberto de Nobili

To complete our brief survey, we return to India to consider the work of another Italian Jesuit, Roberto de Nobili, who spent forty-two years ministering among the Tamil-speaking Madurai people. When de Nobili arrived in India in 1605, another Jesuit priest named Fernandez was already laboring there. After baptizing the Madurai, Fernandez essentially trained them to be culturally Portuguese Christians. Certainly influenced by Ricci in China, de Nobili was convinced that to reach Indians with the gospel, missionaries must also become Indian. Eliminating everything that could possibly offend the Madurai (such as eating meat or wearing leather shoes), de Nobili dressed as an Indian holy man, and mastered the classical Tamil, Telugu, and Sanskrit languages as well as the literature of the Brahmins.

In an effort to distance himself from Portuguese Catholic Christianity, de Nobili deliberately cut himself off from the existing church and chose to live in a simple hut. He engaged Hindu intellectuals by holding public discussions on the nature of God and creation. Believing that only the idolatrous elements of a culture should be discarded, de Nobili labored to keep the rest of Indian culture intact. This included working within the caste system. When new believers from different castes were baptized, he chose to establish separate churches. By 1623, de Nobili reported that around a hundred Indians had been baptized.

Similar to Ricci's experience in China, some Catholic leaders accused de Nobili of accommodating Hinduism, not truly preaching the gospel, and also dividing the church. Though Fernandez complained about him and other church leaders reprimanded him, de Nobili was ultimately exonerated by Pope Gregory XV in 1623. Ironically, despite distancing himself from the established Portuguese church, de Nobili was still accused by some Indians of being a *Parangi* (Portuguese Catholic).[28] His response to these charges was quite interesting, revealing his common ground posture toward the Indians and a fascinating use of spiritual vocabulary. He wrote:

> I am not a *Parangi*. . . . I came from Rome, where my family hold the same rank as respectable Rajas (princes) hold in this country. . . . The law which I preach is the law of the true God, which from ancient times was by his command proclaimed in these countries by *sannyyasis* (holy men) and saints. Whoever says that is the law

---

28. Neill, *History of Christian Missions*, 156–60; also Hollis, *History of the Jesuits*, 54–58.

of the *Parangis*, fit only for low castes, commits a very great sin, for the true God is not the God of one race but the God of all.[29]

Approaches to Mission

The examples of Ignatius, Xavier, Ricci, and de Nobili reveal much diversity in Jesuit mission practices in the first one hundred years of the Society, a trend that would only continue as the movement spread into different parts of the world. In this brief discussion, let us consider seven elements that characterized Jesuit approaches to mission in this initial period.

First, similar to a number of the missionary monks studied in this book, the Jesuits also had a high regard for the church and established their order within the existing church structures. As shown, one of their core values as a Society was a deep loyalty to the pope and a willingness to serve wherever the church leader sent them. Jesuit missionaries were sent out by the church, and their ministry also resulted in new churches. In India, Francis Xavier started a church and translated liturgical materials to facilitate worship. Though de Nobili distanced himself from the existing Roman Catholic Church in India, he did not reject the idea of a Christian community; rather, he objected to a Portuguese form of it being imposed on Indian peoples. Even though he worked among different castes, he was still engaged in the work of church planting. Finally, despite the conflict that de Nobili and Ricci experienced with Rome over their missionary methods, they continued to respect the universal church and labored to start new churches as a viable expression of the body of Christ.

Second, as the Society was birthed in an academic, university environment, the Jesuits continued to value education as a part of their missionary strategy and training. By 1710, they had started some 612 colleges around the world educating lay people in various disciplines of study. O'Malley notes that for the Jesuits "their vocation as missionaries provided them with opportunities for creating knowledge in geography, cartography, anthropology, and botany that were extraordinary."[30] With Scripture as their foundation, the Jesuits integrated a Christian worldview throughout the diverse curricula of study with the end goal of sending "capable and zealous leaders into the social order in numbers large enough to leaven it effectively

---

29. Cited in Neill, *History of Christian Missions*, 158.
30. O'Malley, *The Jesuits*, 31.

for good."[31] Certainly Matteo Ricci's training in mathematics at the Jesuit school in Rome helped prepare him to make meaningful connections with Chinese intellectuals.

The Jesuits not only started schools to disciple and educate people on their fields of mission, they also began theological seminaries to train other missionaries. In addition to courses in Scripture and theology, some schools taught Arabic and Turkish so that missionaries would be equipped linguistically for these mission fields.[32]

Third, like other missionary monks encountered in this study, the Jesuits were accustomed to making contact with political leaders before beginning mission work. In Francis Xavier's case, he was sent to India by the Portuguese king, which naturally led to connections with Indian leaders. Later, upon arriving in Japan, he reached out to the *daimyo* or local leader. O'Malley notes that the "*daimyo*, fascinated and delighted with the gifts [brought by Xavier], gave Xavier permission to preach and also put an unused Buddhist temple at his disposal."[33]

In another instance in India, the Mogul leader Akbar took the initiative and invited Christian missionaries to his court. Around 1580, the Italian Jesuit Rudolph Aquaviva met with Akbar and held public discussions on spiritual matters. Although Akbar never embraced the gospel and ended up adopting his own form of Islam, the Jesuit missionaries still demonstrated skill at engaging leaders of his stature.[34]

Brockey notes that in China, Matteo Ricci's "idea was to seek out the highest level of political patronage possible by appealing directly to the emperor."[35] He certainly found favor among leaders, especially as he presented his gifts of advanced technology. Later Jesuits made similar contact with Emperor Kangxi, the longest reigning emperor in Chinese history (1661–1722). Kangxi had studied with the Jesuits during his youth and was attracted to their intellectual capabilities. In 1692, the emperor expressed his favor by issuing an edit of toleration for all Christians in China.[36]

---

31. Ganss, *Ignatius of Loyola*, 280.

32. Ignatius, *Constitutions* II.1.2 (Ganss, *Ignatius of Loyola*, 299); also Ganss, *Ignatius of Loyola*, 49, 279–80; and O'Malley, *The Jesuits*, ix–x, 12

33. O'Malley, *The Jesuits*, 49; cf. Brockey, *Journey to the East*, 42.

34. O'Malley, *The Jesuits*, 44–45; also Neill, *History of Christian Missions*, 129–31.

35. Brockey, *Journey to the East*, 42.

36. O'Malley, *The Jesuits*, 57.

Fourth, preaching was central to Jesuit mission work and O'Malley argues that it held "pride of place" among the Society's ministries.[37] Interestingly, Ignatius' proclamation ministry was initially carried out in small and highly personal contexts. In his *Autobiography*, he wrote: "we do not preach ... but we do speak familiarly with some people about the things of God; for example, after dinner with some people who invite us."[38] Ignatius departed from his earlier monastic ideals of silence and cultivated "the art of conversation," which certainly helped his ability to evangelize nonbelievers.[39] Over time, Jesuit preaching strategies were broadened and some members of the Society preached in churches and on street corners, while others participated in itinerant preaching tours through villages. Finally, some Jesuits gave public lectures on books of the Bible and other spiritual topics.[40]

A fifth area that the Jesuits emphasized on a number of fields was children's ministry. As shown, from the outset of the formation of the Society, the brothers were committed to "the propagation of the faith by means of the ministry of the word, ... specifically by the instruction of children and unlettered persons in Christianity."[41] O'Malley writes that "from the beginning [the Jesuits] engaged in various forms of catechesis with both children and adults, and they devised imaginative ways to make the lessons attractive, such as setting them to verse or to popular tunes."[42] As shown, Xavier's primary focus among the Paravas people was to evangelize, catechize, and baptize the children. The early success of Jesuit work in Brazil in 1549 was directly tied to catechism classes started for children in Bahia.[43]

Sixth, once the Jesuits had evangelized a people, they often organized them into discipleship communities characterized by strict spiritual disciplines such as the ones overseen by Xavier in India. The Jesuits worked from the assumption that new believers could not grow spiritually in their communities of origin and that this extraction strategy was necessary. In the Brazilian context, the Jesuits initiated *aldeias* or fixed communities in which new believers "could be weaned from superstition, drunkenness, and

---

37. Ibid., 18.
38. Ignatius, *Autobiography* 65 (Ganss, *Ignatius of Loyola*, 96).
39. O'Malley, *The Jesuits*, 8.
40. Ibid., 18.
41. Ganss, *Ignatius of Loyola*, 45.
42. Ibid., 18.
43. Ganss, *Ignatius of Loyola*, 48–49; also O'Malley, *The Jesuits*, 22.

cannibalism and be instructed in the Christian faith."[44] In other parts of the Americas, the Spanish Jesuits started similar communities known as *reducciones* (reductions) that became so self-sufficient that they functioned like small towns. This was the Jesuit strategy among the Guarani people.[45]

A final element of Jesuit missions was contextualizing the gospel and Christianity. In order to connect with his Japanese hosts, Xavier traded in his mendicant beggar attire for clothes that gave him more respect and acceptance in Japan. Alessandro Valigno, the influential Jesuit envoy, was also convinced of this approach and he urged other missionaries in Asia to follow suit. As noted, as Xavier admired much of the Japanese worldview, he made connections from Japanese ideas to the gospel in his preaching and teaching. Similarly, under Valigno's influence, the Jesuits constructed church buildings that resembled the architecture of Buddhist temples. Also, as they pioneered new schools in Japan, the study of Japanese art became a valued part of the curriculum.[46]

Also due to Valigno's influence, Matteo Ricci connected with Chinese intellectuals through math, science, and technology. Later, the German Jesuit, Johann Adam Schall von Bell (1592–1666) and his Swiss colleague Terrenz Screck (1576–1630)—both trained astronomers—continued similar relationships with Chinese thinkers. Upon entering the country, they brought a gift of seven thousand science books for their hosts. Ricci was, of course, innovative and controversial for the way he described God using the Chinese language, how he incorporated a Confucian framework in his preaching and theology, and for allowing the Chinese to continue to honor their ancestors.[47]

In adopting local dress and diet, learning the language and literature of the Brahmins, and separating himself from western forms of Christianity, de Nobili also valued contextualizing Christianity in India. Though de Nobilis' approach was not without controversy, he and the other Jesuits demonstrated that "the Christian religion was not of its essence an especially European religion and they did right to show the Indians that it could discard its European trappings."[48]

---

44. O'Malley, *The Jesuits*, 46.
45. Ibid., 47–48, 57.
46. Hollis, *History of the Jesuits*, 57; also O'Malley, *The Jesuits*, 48–50.
47. O'Malley, *The Jesuits*, 51–53.
48. Hollis, *History of the Jesuits*, 57.

Summary

Founded in 1534 as a small group of likeminded brothers following Ignatius' *Spiritual Exercises,* the Society of Jesus was driven by a large vision and quickly became the most significant missionary force in Roman Catholic history. Committed to spirituality, community, education, preaching, and contextualization, the Jesuits were both innovative and controversial. Ultimately, it was controversy that caught up with them in 1773 when the Society was officially shut down through a decree from Pope Clement XIV. For some time, priests and church leaders had been bothered by the Jesuits' controversial methods, perceived arrogance, increasing involvement in political affairs, and the increasing wealth they were accumulating through the *reducciones* and other communities. At the time of their suppression, some three thousand Jesuit missionaries were ordered to abandon their fields of service. Though some left the order and remained in their places of ministry in a rogue status, the suppression of the Jesuits greatly diminished Catholic global mission work in the late eighteenth century. The ruling was not permanent, however, as Pope Pius VII restored the order in 1814 and the Society of Jesus continues to operate around the world to the present day.[49]

---

49. O'Malley, *The Jesuits,* 75–81.

EPILOGUE

Toward a Monastic Theology of Mission

FROM THE CHILLY ISLAND of Iona, to the urban centers of Cappadocia, to the court of the caliph in Egypt, and to the imperial capital of China, we have journeyed with monks and monastic orders who led the way in global mission from the fourth to the seventeenth centuries. We have narrated their faith stories, evaluated their practices, and considered their thoughts about mission. While these accounts reflect much diversity and development in mission thought and practice, what are some of the prevailing themes from missionary monks? Are there elements of a monastic theology of mission?

Monastic Theology of Mission Themes

From our study, several prominent themes emerge as key points of monastic theology of mission. First, in the monks and monastic movements that we have studied, their monastic spirituality naturally resulted in Christian mission. In the case of Basil, his monastic rule was undergirded by love of God and love of neighbor. For the Celtic monks, the spiritual discipline of pilgrimage put them in the vicinity of pagans who needed to hear the gospel and so mission was a natural outcome. In Ignatius's thinking, bringing glory to God was integrally related to serving others. In short, for many of the missionary monks that we have studied, the lines between the contemplative life (prayer and study) and the active life (service and mission) became forever blurred. Further, for many missionary monks, their monastic labor—that which facilitated prayer—became cross-cultural mission work.

Second, many of the monks in our study demonstrated a theology of suffering. As monasticism emerged as a protest to Christianity's worldly success in the fourth century, monks became the new martyrs. In many respects, the monastic disciplines of prayer, fasting, keeping vigil, and living in austere and simple conditions were self-imposed forms of hardship and suffering. The fortitude developed in the practice of these spiritual disciples made the monks resilient and capable of persevering in difficult situations. This was certainly true of Martin in Gaul, Patrick in Ireland, Augustine of Canterbury and his monks travelling between Italy and England, Boniface in Frisia, Askar in Scandinavia, Francis in Egypt, and the mendicants travelling across the Central Asia steppe to meet the Mongol khan. While some monks like Francis of Assisi yearned for martyrdom, others like Boniface and Raymund Lull literally achieved it.

Third, the monks that we have met preached the gospel in word and in deed. Through catechesis, baptism, and church planting, the monks proclaimed the death, burial, and resurrection of Christ and an unwavering belief in a Trinitarian God. This ministry of proclamation was naturally integrated with attention to human needs—education, medicine, agriculture, and poverty. As shown, some monks such as Basil, Patrick, Anskar, and Cyril and Methodius also confronted the social injustice of slavery through the course of their ministries. Finally, as the monks we have studied pushed out into the world and founded new monasteries—communities of prayer, study, and service—their way of life together became "cities on a hill" and an attractive, transformative witness to local peoples. In short, they ministered in word, deed, and by example.

Fourth, many of the monks that we have met successfully engaged and even shaped culture. For example, Cyril and Methodius (Russian, Slavic), Raymund Lull (Arabic), Robert de Nobili (Tamil, Telugu, Sanskrit) and the Church of the East monks (Chinese) worked very hard to master the local languages. John de Piano di Carpini and William of Rubruck were early ethnographers who endeavored to understand Mongol culture. In addition to understanding culture, some monks were quite involved in shaping culture from a Christian worldview. Through using local art forms and cultural texts, the Celtic monks helped the gospel to find a home among the Pictish peoples. Of course, Cyril and Methodius' work of developing the Slavonic alphabet and Scriptures forever shaped Orthodox Christianity in Russia and Eastern Europe as well as Slavic culture in general. Finally, a number of monasteries, particularly Dominican and Jesuit houses, became centers of learning that integrated the study of Scripture and theology with other academic disciplines.

Finally, a prevailing theme of missionary monasticism was a commitment to the church. Many of the monks that we have met were also ordained bishops. Some bishops of Rome, most notably Gregory the Great, were also quite involved with sending monks into cross-cultural mission. As discussed, the Franciscans and Dominicans were deeply loyal to the church and a key Jesuit core value was their allegiance to the pope. Finally, a clear outcome of the work of many missionary monks was the establishment of new churches that, of course, related to the universal church. Though missionary monks were a distinct group within church and mission history, they never operated independently from the established church.

Missionary monasticism was characterized by a spirituality that led to mission, a willingness to suffer and persevere, preaching the gospel in word and deed, engaging and shaping culture; and a love for the church. These were qualities that enabled the monks to be innovative and effective in mission for over a thousand years of ministry. They are also principles that missionaries today should continue to value.

Bibliography

Adam von Bremen. *History of the Archbishops of Hamburg-Bremen*. Translated by Francis Joseph Tschan. New York: Columbia University Press, 1959.
Adomnan. *Life of Columba*. Translated by Larry Sharpe. London: Penguin, 1995.
Alcuin. *Life of Willibrord*. Translated by C. H. Talbot. *Medieval Sourcebook*. Online: http://sourcebooks.fordham.edu/basis/Alcuin-willbrord.asp.
Andrews, Frances. *The Other Friars: Carmelite, Augustinian, Sack and Pied Friars in the Middle Ages*. Martlesham, UK: Boydell, 2006.
Armstrong, Regis J., and Ignatius C. Brady, eds. and trans. *Francis and Clare: The Complete Works*. New York: Paulist, 1982.
Atiya, Aziz S. *History of Eastern Christianity*. Piscataway, NJ: Gorgias, 2010.
Ayres, Lewis. "The Cappadocians." In *Augustine through the Ages: An Encyclopedia*, edited by Allan D. Fitzgerald, 121–24. Grand Rapids: Eerdmans, 2009.
Barnett, Mike C., "The Missing Key to the Future of Evangelical Mission." In *MissionShift: Global Issues in the Third Millenium*, edited by David J. Hesselgrave and Ed Stetzer, 223–32. Nashville, TN: B. & H. Academic, 2010.
Basil of Caesarea. *Letters, Volume 1 (1–185)*. Fathers of the Church 13. Translated by Agnes Clare Way. Washington, DC: Catholic University Press, 1951.
———. *Letters, Volume 2 (186–368)*. Fathers of the Church 28. Translated by Agnes Clare Way. Washington, DC: Catholic University Press, 1955.
———. *Long Rules, Short Rules, Morals*. In *Saint Basil's Ascetical Works*. Fathers of the Church 5. Translated by M. Monica Wagner. Washington, DC: Catholic University Press, 1962.
———. *On the Holy Spirit*. Translated by David Anderson. Crestwood, NY: St. Vladimir's Seminary Press, 1980.
Baum, Wilhelm, and Dietmar W. Winkler. *The Church of the East: A Concise History*. London: Routledge, 2000.
Bede. *Ecclesiastical History of the English People*. Edited by Judith McClure and Roger Collins. Oxford: Oxford University Press, 2009.
Blastic, Michael W. "Francis and His Hagiographic Tradition." In *The Cambridge Companion to Saint Francis of Assisi*, edited by Michael J. P. Robson, 68–83. Cambridge: Cambridge University Press, 2012.

BIBLIOGRAPHY

Blocher, Jacques A., and Blandenier, Jacques. *The Evangelization of the World: A History of Christian Missions*. Pasadena, CA: William Carey Library, 2012.

Boniface. *Letters*. Translated by C. H. Talbot. *Medieval Sourcebook*. Online: http://sourcebooks.fordham.edu/basis/boniface-letters.asp.

Bosch, David. *Transforming Mission: Paradigm Shifts in Theology of Mission*. Maryknoll, NY: Orbis, 1991.

Brockey, Liam Matthew. *Journey to the East: The Jesuit Mission to China, 1579–1724*. Cambridge: Harvard University Press, 2007.

Cabaniss, Allen. "Motives for Conversion in the Mission of Anskar," *The Lutheran Quarterly* 5 (1953) 378–85.

Cardoza-Orlandi, Carlos F., and Justo Gonzalez. *To All Nations from All Nations: A History of the Christian Missionary Movement*. Nashville, TN: Abingdon, 2013.

Clossey, Luke. *Salvation and Globalization in Early Jesuit Missions*. Cambridge: Cambridge University Press, 2008.

Cooper, Henry R. Jr. "The Translation of the Bible into the Slavonic Languages: Biblical Citations in the *Lives of Cyril and Methodius* and the First Slavic Bible Translation." *Slavica Tergestina* 5 (1997) 51–61.

Cragg, Kenneth. *The Arab Christian: A History in the Middle East*. Louisville, KY: John Knox, 1991.

Cummins, W. A. *The Age of the Picts*. Gloucester, UK: Sutton, 1995.

Cusato, Michael F. "Francis and the Franciscan Movement (1181/2–1226)." In *The Cambridge Companion to Saint Francis of Assisi*, edited by Michael J. P. Robson, 17–33. Cambridge: Cambridge University Press, 2012.

Daley, Brian E. "Building a New City: The Cappadocian Fathers and the Rhetoric of Philanthrophy." *Journal of Early Christian Studies* 7.3 (1999) 431–61.

Daniel, E. Randolph. "Franciscan Missions." In *The Cambridge Companion to Saint Francis of Assisi*, edited by Michael J. P. Robson, 240–57. Cambridge: Cambridge University Press, 2012.

Decret, François. *Early Christianity in North Africa*. Translated by Edward L. Smither. Eugene, OR: Cascade, 2009.

Delehaye, Hippolyte. *Legends of the Saints: An Introduction to Hagiography*. Translated by V. M. Crawford. *Medieval Sourcebook*. Online: http://www.fordham.edu/halsall/basis/delehaye-legends.asp.

Demacopoulos, George E. *Gregory the Great: Ascetic, Pastor, and First Man of Rome*. Notre Dame, IN: University of Notre Dame Press, 2015.

Dinan, Andrew. "Manual Labor in the Life and Thought of St. Basil the Great." *Logos: A Journal of Catholic Thought and Culture* 12.4 (2009) 133–57.

Duichev, Ivan, ed. *Kiril and Methodius: Founders of Slavonic Writing. A Collection of Sources and Critical Studies*. New York: Columbia University Press, 1985.

Dunn, Marilyn. *The Emergence of Monasticism: From the Desert Fathers to the Middle Ages*. Oxford: Blackwell, 2003.

Dvornik, Francis. *Byzantine Missions among the Slavs: SS. Constantine-Cyril and Methodius*. New Brunswick, NJ: Rutgers University Press, 1970.

———. "The Significance of the Missions of Cyril and Methodius." *Slavic Review* 23.2 (1964) 195–211.

———. *The Slavs: Their Early History and Civilization*. Boston: American Academy of Arts and Sciences, 1956.

Every, George. *Understanding Eastern Christianity*. Rome: SCM, 1980.

BIBLIOGRAPHY

Freeman, Philip. *St. Patrick of Ireland: A Biography*. New York: Simon and Schuster, 2005.
Frend, W. H. C. *The Rise of Christianity*. Philadelphia: Fortress, 1984.
Ganss, George E., ed. *Ignatius of Loyola: Spiritual Exercises and Selected Works*. New York: Paulist, 1991.
Godet-Calogeras, Jean François. "Francis and Clare and the Emergence of the Second Order." In *The Cambridge Companion to Saint Francis of Assisi*, edited by Michael J. P. Robson, 115–26. Cambridge: Cambridge University Press, 2012.
Goehring, James E. "Monasticism." In *Encyclopedia of Early Christianity*, edited by Everett Ferguson, 769–75. London: Routledge, 1999.
Green, Michael. *Evangelism in the Early Church*. Rev. ed. Grand Rapids: Eerdmans, 2003.
Gregory of Nazianus. *Oration 43*. In *Nicene and Post-Nicene Fathers* 2.7, Christian Classics Ethereal Library. Online: http://www.ccel.org/ccel/schaff/npnf207.iii.xxvi.html
Gregory of Tours. *History of the Franks*. Medieval Sourcebook. Online: http://www.fordham.edu/halsall/basis/gregory-hist.asp.
Harakas, Stanley S. "Caesarea in Cappadocia." In *Encyclopedia of Early Christianity*, edited by Everett Ferguson, 201–2. London: Routledge, 1999.
Harmless, William. *Desert Christians: An Introduction to the Literature of Early Monasticism*. Oxford: Oxford University Press, 2004.
———. "Monasticism." In *The Oxford Handbook of Early Christian Studies*, edited by Susan Ashbrook Harvey and David G. Hunter, 493–517. Oxford: Oxford University Press, 2008.
Harnack, Adolph von. *The Mission and Expansion of Christianity in the First Three Centuries*. Christian Classics Ethereal Library. Online: http://www.ccel.org/ccel/harnack/mission.html.
Henderson, George, and Isabel Henderson. *The Art of the Picts: Sculpture and Metal Work in Early Medieval Scotland*. New York: Thames & Hudson, 2004.
Hildebrand, Stephen M. *Basil of Caesarea*. Grand Rapids: Baker Academic, 2014.
Hollis, Christopher. *The History of the Jesuits*. London: Weidenfeld and Nicolson, 1968.
Holman, Susan R. *The Hungry Are Dying: Beggars and Bishops in Roman Cappadocia*. New York: Oxford University Press, 2001.
———. "The Hungry Body: Famine, Poverty, and Identity in Basil's Hom. 8." *Journal of Early Christian Studies* 7.3 (1999) 337–63.
Ihssen, Brenda Llewellyn. "Basil and Gregory's Sermons on Usury: Credit Where Credit Is Due." *Journal of Early Christian Studies* 16.3 (2008) 403–30.
Jackson, Peter. "Franciscans as Papal and Royal Envoys to the Tatars (1245–1255)." In *The Cambridge Companion to Saint Francis of Assisi*, edited by Michael J. P. Robson, 224–39. Cambridge: Cambridge University Press, 2012.
Jenkins, Phillip. *The Lost History of Christianity: The Thousand-Year Golden Age of the Church in the Middle East, Africa, and Asia—and How It Died*. New York: HarperOne, 2009.
Jonas. *The Life of St. Columban*. Edited by Dana C. Munro. Medieval Sourcebook. Online: http://legacy.fordham.edu/halsall/basis/columban.asp.
Kelly, J. N. D. *Early Christian Doctrines*. Reprint. Peabody, MA: Hendricksen, 2003.
Kollman, Paul. "At the Origins of Mission and Missiology: A Study in the Dynamics of Religious Language." *Journal of the American Academy of Religion* 79.2 (2011) 425–58.
Laboa, Juan María. *The Historical Atlas of Eastern and Western Christian Monasticism*. Collegeville, MN: Liturgical, 2003.

Larkin, William J. "Mission." In *Evangelical Dictionary of Biblical Theology*, edited by Walter A. Elwell, 534. Grand Rapids: Baker, 1996.

Larkin, William J., and Joel F. Williams, eds. *Mission in the New Testament: An Evangelical Approach*. Maryknoll, NY: Orbis, 1998.

Latourette, Kenneth Scott. *History of the Expansion of Christianity: The First Five Centuries*. Reprint. Grand Rapids: Zondervan, 1966.

Lawrence, C. H. *The Friars: The Impact of the Early Mendicant Movement on Western Society*. London: Longman, 1994.

Lieu, Samuel N. C., and Ken Parry. "Deep into Asia." In *Early Christianity in Contexts: An Exploration across Cultures and Continents*, edited by William Tabbernee, 143–80. Grand Rapids: Baker Academic, 2014.

MacMullen, Ramsay. *Christianity & Paganism from the Fourth to Eighth Centuries*. New Haven: Yale University Press, 1997.

Markus, Robert A. "The Chronology of the Gregorian Mission to England: Bede's Narrative and Gregory's Correspondence." *Journal of Ecclesiastical History* 14 (1963) 16–30.

———. "Gregory the Great and a Papal Missionary Strategy." In *The Mission of the Church and the Propagation of the Faith*, edited by G. J. Cumming, 29–38. Cambridge: Cambridge University Press, 1970.

———. *Gregory the Great and his World*. Cambridge: Cambridge University Press, 1997.

Mayr-Harting, Henry. *The Coming of Christianity to Anglo-Saxon England*. State College, PA: Penn State University Press, 2001.

McDaniel, Ferris L. "Mission in the Old Testament." In *Mission in the New Testament: An Evangelical Approach*, edited by William J. Larkin and Joel F. Williams, 11–20. Maryknoll, NY: Orbis, 1998.

McGuire, Brian Patrick. *Friendship and Community: The Monastic Experience 350–1250*. Cistercian Studies 95. Kalamazoo, MI: Cistercian, 1988.

McHugh, Michael P. "Augustine of Canterbury (d. before 610)." In *Encyclopedia of Early Christianity*, edited by Everett Ferguson, 154–55. London: Routledge, 1999.

———. "Cappadocia." In *Encyclopedia of Early Christianity*, edited by Everett Ferguson, 213–15. London: Routledge, 1999.

———. "Martin of Tours (ca. 316–397)." In *Encyclopedia of Early Christianity*, edited by Everett Ferguson, 724. London: Routledge, 1999.

McMichael, Steven J., "Francis and the Encounter with the Sultan (1219)." In *The Cambridge Companion to Saint Francis of Assisi*, edited by Michael J. P. Robson, 127–42. Cambridge: Cambridge University Press, 2012.

McNeill, John T. *The Celtic Churches: A History A.D. 200–1200*. Chicago: University of Chicago Press, 1974.

Meehan, Bernard. *The Book of Kells: An Illustrated Introduction to the Manuscript in Trinity College Dublin*. London: Thames & Hudson, 1995.

Moffett, Samuel H. *A History of Christianity in Asia, Volume I: Beginnings to 1500*. Maryknoll, NY: Orbis, 1998.

Moorman, John. *A History of the Franciscan Order: From its Origins to the Year 1517*. Oxford: Clarenden, 1968.

Moreau, A. Scott, Gary R. Corwin, and Gary B. McGee. *Introducing World Missions: A Biblical, Historical, and Practical Survey*. Grand Rapids: Baker Academic, 2004.

BIBLIOGRAPHY

Muers, Rachel. "Adoptionism: Is Jesus Christ the Son of God by Nature or by Adoption?" In *Heresies and How to Avoid Them: Why it Matters What Christians Believe*, edited by Ben Quash and Michael Ward, 50–58, Peabody, MA: Hendricksen, 2007.

Neill, Stephen. *A History of Christian Missions*. London: Penguin, 1990.

———. *Salvation Tomorrow*. Cambridge: Lutterworth, 1976.

Nelson Janet L. "The Frankish Empire." In *The Oxford Illustrated History of the Vikings*, edited by Peter Sawyer, 19–47. Oxford: Oxford University Press, 1997.

Nibbs, Eric. *Ansgar, Rimbert and the Forged Foundations of Hamburg-Bremen*. Farnham, UK: Ashgate, 2011.

Noll, Mark A. *Turning Points: Decisive Moments in the History of Christianity*. Grand Rapids: Baker Academic, 2012.

O'Loughlin, Thomas. *Discovering Saint Patrick*. Mahwah, NJ: Paulist, 2005.

———. *St. Patrick: The Man and His Works*. London: SPCK, 1999.

O'Malley, John W. *The Jesuits: A History from Ignatius to the Present*. Lanham, MD: Rowan & Littlefield, 2014.

Obolensky, Dimitri. *Byzantium and the Slavs*. Crestwood, NY: St. Vladimir's Seminary Press, 1994.

Okholm, Dennis. *Monks Habits for Everyday People: Benedictine Spirituality for Protestants*. Grand Rapids: Brazos, 2007.

Olsen, Ted. *Christianity and the Celts*. Downers Grove, IL: IVP, 2003.

Ott, Craig, Steven J. Strauss, and Timothy C. Tennent. *Encountering Theology of Mission: Biblical Foundations, Historical Developments, and Contemporary Issues*. Grand Rapids: Baker Academic, 2010.

Patitsas, Timothy, "St. Basil's Philanthropic Program and Modern Microlending Strategies for Economic Self-Actualization." In *Wealth and Poverty in Early Church and Society*, edited by Susan R. Holman, 267–86. Grand Rapids: Baker Academic, 2008.

Peers, E. Allison. *Ramon Lull: A Biography*. London: SPCK, 1929.

Peters, Greg. *The Story of Monasticism: Retrieving an Ancient Tradition for Contemporary Spirituality*. Grand Rapids: Baker Academic, 2015.

Ramsay, William R. *The Historical Geography of Asia Minor*. New York: Cooper Square, 1972.

Ramsey, Boniface. *Beginning to Read the Fathers*. Mahwah, NJ: Paulist, 1985.

Rimbert. *Life of Askar, the Apostle of the North, 801–865*. Translated by C. H. Robinson. *Medieval Sourcebook*. Online: http://legacy.fordham.edu/halsall/basis/anskar.asp.

Ritchie, Anna. *Iona Abbey and Nunnery*. Edinburgh: Historic Scotland, 2001.

Robert, Dana. *Christian Mission: How Christianity Became a World Religion*. Oxford: Wiley-Blackwell, 2009.

Robson, Michael J. P. *The Franciscans in the Middle Ages*. Martlesham, UK: Boydell, 2009.

———. "Introduction." In *The Cambridge Companion to Saint Francis of Assisi*, edited by Michael J. P. Robson, 1–14. Cambridge: Cambridge University Press, 2012.

———, ed. *The Cambridge Companion to Saint Francis of Assisi*. Cambridge: Cambridge University Press, 2012.

———. "The Writings of Francis." In *The Cambridge Companion to Saint Francis of Assisi*, edited by Michael J. P. Robson, 34–49. Cambridge: Cambridge University Press, 2012.

Rousseau, Philip. *Basil of Caesarea*. Berkley, CA: University of California Press, 1998.

Rudolph of Fulda. *Life of Leoba*. Translated by C. H. Talbot. *Medieval Sourcebook*. Online: http://legacy.fordham.edu/halsall/basis/leoba.asp.

Sanneh, Lamin. *Translating the Message: The Missionary Impact on Culture*. Maryknoll, NY: Orbis, 2009.

Sawyer, Peter H. *Kings and Vikings: Scandinavia and Europe AD 700–1100*. New York: Barnes & Noble, 1994.

———, ed. *The Oxford Illustrated History of the Vikings*. Oxford: Oxford University Press, 1997.

Schnabel, Eckhard. *Early Christian Mission: Paul and the Early Church*. Downers Grove, IL: IVP, 2004.

Şenocak, Neslihan. "Voluntary Simplicity: The Attitude of Francis towards Learning in the Early Biographies." In *The Cambridge Companion to Saint Francis of Assisi*, edited by Michael J. P. Robson, 84–100. Cambridge: Cambridge University Press, 2012.

Severus, Sulpicius. *Dialogues*. Translated by Alexander Roberts. *Nicene Post Nicene Fathers* 2.11. Online: http://www.ccel.org/ccel/schaff/npnf211.ii.iv.html.

———. *Life of St. Martin*. Translated by Alexander Roberts. *Nicene Post Nicene Fathers* 2.11. Online: http://www.ccel.org/ccel/schaff/npnf211.ii.ii.html.

———. *Vita Sancti Martini Episcopi et Confessoris*. Online: http://www.thelatinlibrary.com/sulpiciusseverusmartin.html.

Short, William J. "The *Rule* and the Life of the Friars Minor." In *The Cambridge Companion to Saint Francis of Assisi*, edited by Michael J. P. Robson, 50–67. Cambridge: Cambridge University Press, 2012.

Sinkewicz, Robert E. *Evagrius of Pontus: The Greek Ascetic Corpus*. Oxford: Oxford University Press, 2003.

Smith, Carl B. "Post-Bauer Scholarship on Gnosticism(s): The Current State of Our 'Knowledge.'" In *Orthodoxy and Heresy in Early Christian Contexts: Reconsidering the Bauer Thesis*, edited by Paul A. Hartog, 60–88. Eugene, OR: Pickwick, 2015.

Smither, Edward L. *Augustine as Mentor: A Model for Preparing Spiritual Leaders*. Nashville, TN: B. & H. Academic, 2008.

———. "Augustine, Missionary to Heretics? An Appraisal of Augustine's Missional Engagement with the Donatists." In *A Uniquely African Controversy: Studies on Donatist Christianity*, edited by A. Dupont, M. A. Gaumer, and M. Lamberigts, 269–88. Late Antique History and Religion 9. Leuven: Peeters, 2015.

———. "Did the Rise of Constantine Mean the End of Christian Mission?" In *Rethinking Constantine: History, Theology, and Legacy*, edited by Edward L. Smither, 130–45. Eugene, OR: Pickwick, 2014.

———. "Lessons from a Tentmaking Ascetic in the Egyptian Desert: The Case of Evagrius of Pontus." *Missiology: An International Review* 39.4 (2011) 485–96.

———. *Mission in the Early Church: Themes and Reflections*. Eugene, OR: Cascade, 2014.

———. "'To Emulate and Imitate': Possidius' *Life of Augustine* as a Fifth-Century Discipleship Tool." *Southwestern Journal of Theology* 50.2 (2008) 146–68.

Snyder, Graydon F., and William Tabbernee. "The Western Provinces and Beyond." In *Early Christianity in Contexts: An Exploration Across Cultures and Continents*, edited by William Tabbernee, 433–75. Grand Rapids: Baker Academic, 2014.

Sørensen, Preben Meulengracht. "Religions Old and New." In *The Oxford Illustrated History of the Vikings*, edited by Peter Sawyer, 19–47. Oxford: Oxford University Press, 1997.

Sozomen. *Ecclesiastical History*. In *Nicene and Post-Nicene Fathers* 2.2. Christian Classics Ethereal Library. Online: http://www.ccel.org/ccel/schaff/npnf202.iii.xi.xxxiv.html.

BIBLIOGRAPHY

Stancliffe, Clare. *St. Martin and His Hagiographer: History and Miracle in Sulpicius Severus.* Oxford: Clarenden, 1983.

Stark, Rodney. *The Rise of Christianity: A Sociologist Reconsiders History.* Princeton: Princeton University Press, 1997.

Sterk, Andrea. *Renouncing the World Yet Leading the Church: The Monk-Bishop in Late Antiquity.* Cambridge: Harvard University Press, 2004.

Stewart, John. *Nestorian Missionary Enterprise: The Story of a Church on Fire.* Edinburgh: T. & T. Clark, 1928.

Sunquist, Scott. *Understanding Christian Mission: Participation in Suffering and Glory.* Grand Rapids: Baker Academic, 2013.

Sunquist, Scott, and Dale T. Irvin. *History of the World Christian Movement Volume 1: Earliest Christianity to 1453.* Maryknoll, NY: Orbis, 2001.

Sweet, John. "Docetism: Is Jesus Christ Really Human or Did He Just Appear to Be So?" In *Heresies and How to Avoid Them: Why It Matters What Christians Believe*, edited by Ben Quash and Michael Ward, 24–31. Peabody, MA: Hendricksen, 2007.

Tachioas, Anthony-Emil N. *Cyril and Methodius of Thessalonica: The Acculturation of the Slavs.* Crestwood, NY: St. Vladimir's Seminary Press, 2001.

Talbot, C. H., ed. *The Anglo-Saxon Missionaries in Germany.* New York: Sheed and Ward, 1954.

———. "St. Boniface and the German Mission." In *The Mission of the Church and the Propagation of the Faith*, edited by G. J. Cumming, 45–57. Cambridge: Cambridge University Press, 1970.

Tucker, Ruth A. *From Jerusalem to Irian Jaya: A Biographical History of Christian Mission.* Grand Rapids: Zondervan, 2004.

Tugwell, Simon, ed. *Early Dominicans: Selected Writings.* New York: Paulist, 1982.

Tyler, Damian. "Reluctant Kings and Christian Conversion in Seventh-Century England." *History* 92 (2007) 144–61.

Van Dam, Raymond. *Saints and their Miracles in Late Antique Gaul.* Princeton: Princeton University Press, 1993.

Vlasto, A. P. *The Entry of the Slavs into Christendom: An Introduction to the Medieval History of the Slavs.* Cambridge: Cambridge University Press, 1970.

Ward, Kevin. "Africa." In *A World History of Christianity*, edited by Adrian Hastings, 194–96. Grand Rapids: Eerdmans, 1999.

Wilken, Robert L. *The First Thousand Years: A Global History of Christianity.* New Haven: Yale University Press, 2012.

Willibald. *Life of Boniface.* Translated by C. H. Talbot. *Medieval Sourcebook.* Online: http://legacy.fordham.edu/halsall/basis/willibald-boniface.asp.

Wilson-Hargrove, Jonathan. *The New Monasticism: What It Has to Say to Today's Church.* Grand Rapids: Brazos, 2008.

Winroth, Anders. *The Conversion of Scandinavia: Vikings, Merchants, and Missionaries in the Remaking of Northern Europe.* New Haven: Yale University Press, 2012.

Wood, Ian. "The Mission of Augustine of Canterbury to the English." *Speculum* 69.1 (1994) 1–17.

Zinn, Grover. "Gregory I the Great (ca. 590–604)." In *Encyclopedia of Early Christianity*, edited by Everett Ferguson, 488–90. London: Routledge, 1999.

Zwemer, Samuel M. *Raymund Lull: First Missionary to the Muslims.* New York: Funk and Wagnalls, 1902.

Index

Adomnan, 68–69, 72
Aiden, 64, 68, 73–76
Alcuin, 93–97
Alopen, 138, 143, 145
Ammoun, 19–20
Anchorites, anchoritic, 17–21
Anskar, 107–118, 132, 181
Antony, 17–18, 22
Arian, Arianism, 9, 28, 30, 35–36, 43, 46, 48, 78–79
Armenia, 7, 12, 25, 29, 39, 119, 123, 129, 139, 141,
Asia Minor, 7, 10, 20, 25, 27–30, 35, 39, 41, 120, 122,
Athanasius, 17–18, 30
Augustine of Canterbury, 22, 24, 82–92, 102, 104–5, 116, 181
Augustine of Hippo, 9, 12, 16, 21, 28, 153

Baptism, 9, 13, 25, 59–60, 72, 95, 114, 153, 163, 181
Basil of Caesarea, 16, 18–22, 24–25, 27–42, 44, 83, 122, 132, 159, 180–81
Basileas, 32, 37–41
Bede, 65–69, 73–76, 82, 85–97
Benedict of Nursia, 2, 14, 16, 19, 22–24, 83, 163
Benedictines, 108, 151, 158
Bertha, Queen, 84, 88
Book of Kells, 71–73
Boniface, 93–106, 110, 112, 125, 181

Bremen, 108–9, 112–14, 116–17
British Isles, Britain, 7, 52–53, 55, 63, 65, 67, 69–70, 92, 103,
Brute, King, 65, 67–68, 73

Cappadocia, 16, 25, 27–33, 35, 41, 120, 139, 180
Catechesis, 13, 59–60, 66, 101, 177, 181
Celts, 1–2, 21–22, 25, 52–58, 63–81, 87, 91, 93–94, 98, 106, 180–81
China, 7, 138–39, 142–47, 163–64, 167, 172–74, 176, 180
Church of the East, 2, 7, 138–47, 163, 181
Coenobites, 17–22, 40, 122, 141, 150, 154
Columba, 1, 11, 21, 64–73, 75, 78
Columban, 21–22, 64, 76–80, 108, 117
Constantine, Emperor, 7, 11, 15, 27, 30, 36, 46, 84, 88, 140
Council of Nicaea
Cyril (Constantine), 119–37, 181

Denmark, Danish, 95, 107–8, 110, 112–14, 116–17, 153, 155
Dominic de Guzman, 155–56, 165, 167
Dominicans, 26, 148–49, 153–60, 163, 167–68, 173, 181–82

Edessa, 7, 139–41
Egypt, 15–21, 23–24, 66, 78, 83, 129, 141, 152–53, 161, 180–81

191

INDEX

England, English, 14, 22, 24, 51, 74–76, 82, 84–88, 92–93, 96, 98, 101, 103, 105–7, 155, 181
Ethelbert, King, 84, 86–88, 90, 92
Evagrius of Pontus, 18, 20–21

Francis of Assisi, 26, 149–65, 167, 181
Francis Xavier, 167–68, 171–72, 175–78
Franciscans, 149–52, 154, 157–60, 163–65, 168, 173, 182
Franks, 78–79, 86, 92, 94–95, 100–101, 105–9, 112, 116, 127–28, 135
Frisia, Frisians, 93–98, 100–103, 105, 110, 181

Gregory of Nazianzus, 28, 30, 32–33, 36–39, 120
Gregory Thaumaturgus, 11, 27, 30, 33
Gregory the Great I, 20, 23–24, 82–93, 102, 105, 116, 141, 182

Hamburg, 108, 112–13, 115–17
Hilary of Poitiers, 43, 46, 49

Ignatius of Loyola, 167–71, 175–77, 179–80.
India, 4, 7, 139, 141, 145, 167, 169, 171, 174–78
Irenaeus, 10, 52, 77
Islam, Muslims, 8, 12, 26, 121–24, 133, 142, 145, 147, 149, 151–53, 155, 160–63, 165, 168, 171, 176

Japan, 167, 171–72, 176, 178
Jesuits, Society of Jesus, 166–79
Jews, Judaism, 8, 15, 123–24, 129, 133, 143, 149
John Cassian, 20–22, 78
Justin Martyr, 10–12

Khazara, Khazars, 123–25, 127, 129, 132–33, 135–36

Leoba, 103–4

Macrina, 18, 27, 39

Martin of Tours, 10, 28, 42–50, 62, 66, 77, 79, 86, 115, 181
Matteo Ricci, 167, 172–76, 178
Methodius, 119–37, 181
Michael III, Emperor, 123–27, 135–36
Miracles, 50, 75, 89–90, 92, 96–97, 156
Mongols, 163–65, 181

Nicene Creed, 9, 30, 46, 59–60, 122
North Africa, 7, 21, 162, 165

Origen, 9–11, 16
Oswald of Northumbria, 73–76

Pachomius, 17–23
Pagans, 8, 23, 25–26, 30, 43, 46–50, 52–53, 55–57, 67–70, 74, 79–81, 83–85, 88–92, 94, 96, 98–102, 104–7, 109–11, 113–14, 117, 123, 125–26, 136, 149, 180
Patrick of Ireland, 11, 51–64, 66–67, 76, 114, 116, 181
Pepin of Herstal, 94–96, 100–101
Peregrinus, peregrini (pilgrims), 25, 54, 58, 64–65, 76–77, 79–81, 93, 98, 105–6
Persia, Persian, 7–8, 29, 126, 129, 138–47
Picts; Pictish people, 1, 51, 65–73, 76, 181
Power encounters, 47–49, 68–69, 75, 80, 89, 96–97, 102

Ratislav of Moravia, 125–28, 131–33, 135
Raymund Lull, 26, 162–63, 181
Roberto de Nobili, 167, 174–75, 178, 181
Roman Empire, 7–8, 10, 26, 30, 46, 51, 53, 84, 120, 126
Russia, 7, 119, 123–24, 126, 132–34, 181

Semi-hermitic monasticism, 44, 50, 66, 78, 81, 83
Shapur II, Shah, 140–41
Shenoute, 20, 23
Silk Road, 139, 142, 144–45, 147
Slavs, Slavic, Slavonic, 112, 119–20, 123, 125–37, 181
Sweden, 107–8, 111–17, 155

INDEX

Syria, 7, 16, 20–21, 29, 39, 66, 83, 129, 138–43, 153

Trilingualist controversy, 128–31, 135

Vikings, 107, 109–10, 113–16, 118

Willibrord, 93–101, 103–6.

www.ingramcontent.com/pod-product-compliance
Lightning Source LLC
Chambersburg PA
CBHW031428150426
43191CB00006B/450